TEXTBOO

Law of The European Union

CONSULTANT EDITOR: LORD TEMPLEMAN
EDITOR: ROBERT M MACLEAN
LLB (Hons), Dip LP, LLM, PhD,
Solicitor, CMS Cameron McKenna, Brussels

OLD BAILEY PRESS

OLD BAILEY PRESS
200 Greyhound Road, London W14 9RY

First published 1997
Second edition 1999
Reprinted 2000

© The HLT Group Ltd 1999

ISBN 1 85836 311 X

British Library Cataloguing-in-Publication.
A CIP Catalogue record for this book is available from the British Library.

Acknowledgement

The publishers and author would like to thank the Incorporated Council of Law Reporting for England and Wales for kind permission to reproduce extracts from the Weekly Law Reports, and Butterworths for their kind permission to reproduce extracts from the All England Law Reports.

Printed and bound in Great Britain

Contents

Law of the European Convention on Human Rights

Recent Cases

Preface

Old Bailey Press textbooks are written specifically for students. Whatever their course they will find our books clear and concise, providing comprehensive and up-to-date coverage. Written by specialists in their fields, our textbooks are reviewed and updated on a regular basis. Companion Casebooks, Revision WorkBooks and Statutes are also published.

This *Law of the European Union* textbook is designed for use by undergraduates who have European law/European Community law within their syllabus. It will be equally useful for all CPE/LLDip students who must study European Union/European Community law as one of their 'core' subjects.

Both the European Union/European Community sections of the textbook and those dealing with European Human Rights law have required considerable updating in light of the recent developments taking place in both these areas of law.

In the field of European Union/European Community law, the Amsterdam Treaty came into effect on 1 May 1999. This Treaty made a number of changes to the institutional and operational structure of the European Union, although these adjustments were not as radical as those that took place under the Treaty on European Union. Nevertheless, in order to maintain accuracy, these adjustments have been incorporated into the text where appropriate.

Moreover, the Treaty of Amsterdam re-numbered almost all of the articles of the EC Treaty. This re-numbering has also been followed in the text since this is the proper method of referring to each provision now that these changes have come into effect. We have avoided cross-referencing to previous article numbers simply because of the confusion that this methodology creates.

Equally, significant developments have taken place in other areas of EU/EC law, including monetary union (with the creation of the single currency), competition law and the internal market. All important developments have been reported where appropriate. Important cases before the ECJ and CFI have also been included.

As regards European human rights law, the 11th Protocol has now entered into force. This has completely restructured the institutional structure created by the European Convention on Human Rights. Equally, the UK's Human Rights Act 1998, giving effect to many of the provisions of the Convention, has been approved by Parliament. Both these developments required a complete rewriting of the sections of this textbook dealing with European human rights law.

This textbook takes into account the developments in European Union/European human rights law as at 14 July 1999.

Table of Cases

Table of Treaty Articles, Statutes and Other Materials

Law of the European Union

1

The Evolution of the European Union

1.1 Historical background

1.2 The structure of the European Community

1.3 Geographical expansion and vertical integration

1.4 The legal nature of the European Community

1.5 The special nature and qualities of European Community law

1.6 Transformation from a European Community into a European Union

1.1 Historical background

The period immediately following the Second World War witnessed a host of projects designed to stimulate integration among European states, including the negotiation of the European Convention on Human Rights and Fundamental Freedoms 1950 and plans to promote political, economic and military co-operation. The majority of these projects failed to reach fruition with the notable exception of the Treaty of Paris, signed in 1952, which established the European Coal and Steel Community (ECSC). Six states participated in this organisation – Belgium, France, Germany, Italy, Luxembourg and the Netherlands – which was designed to place under joint control the production of coal and steel. These commodities are essential components in the production of arms and munitions and, by depriving France and Germany of their independence in the production of these commodities, it was widely believed that future conflict between these two countries would be prevented.

The purpose of the ECSC Treaty was to create a common market for coal and steel. A common market is an area where goods and commodities flow free from the interventions of national governments. Not only was such co-operation designed to increase economic efficiency in coal and steel production, but the process also encouraged economic integration which, it was hoped, would result in closer integration in other areas.

The success of the ECSC stimulated interest in a more comprehensive form of economic integration. Two further agreements were signed in Rome in 1957, namely the European Economic Community (EEC) Treaty and the European Atomic Energy (Euratom) Treaty. The EEC Treaty, as it was then known, was a

3

comprehensive economic integration agreement between the original six Member States designed to create a common market for areas of economic activity other than those covered by the ECSC Treaty and the Euratom Treaty. The Euratom Treaty, on the other hand, was an agreement with the more limited purpose of creating a specialised market for atomic energy.

Collectively, these three agreements formed the constitution of the organisation known as the European Community which was the forerunner of the European Union. Since 1993, the European Community has become an integral part of this even more comprehensive European organisation which spans not only economic activities but also political, social, monetary and cultural affairs. Nevertheless, the European Community continues to exist under the superstructure of the European Union.

1.2 The structure of the European Community

The European Community in fact consisted of three separate Communities (the European Coal and Steel Community, the European Economic Community and Euratom), although, since 1967, the organisation functioned through common institutions. Of these, the most important is the Community created by the EEC Treaty (which, since the Treaty on European Union, is to be referred to as the European Community (EC) Treaty).

The ECSC Treaty is the only one of these three agreements which is expressed to have a limited duration and is due to expire in 2001. Already the European Commission is exploring the best means of bringing the activities regulated by that agreement within the scope of the EC Treaty.

The EC Treaty originally created a common market among the founding Member States. This structure had four main features:

1. Liberalisation of the factors of production inside the territory of the Community. Four key fundamental freedoms were introduced to facilitate this goal, namely the free movement of goods, labour, services and capital.
2. Progressive approximation of the key economic policies which underpin trade liberalisation by harmonising national legislation relating to certain economic activities and introducing common Community policies in sectors such as agriculture, transport and competition.
3. The erection of a Common Customs Tariff (CCT) to regulate and administer customs duties and related charges for goods imported into the Community from non-Member States.
4. The formulation of a Common Commercial Policy (CCP) for the conduct of trading relationships between the Community and the rest of the international trading system.

The practical effect of creating this structure, from an intra-Community perspective, was the consolidation of the individual markets and economies of the Member States into one single enlarged internal market. From an international perspective, one single international entity was formed among these states to conduct economic and commercial relationships with third countries.

Authority to administer the development and evolution of the organisation was delegated by the Member States to centralised Community agencies such as the Council of Ministers, the European Commission and, to a lesser extent, the European Court of Justice. This devolution of sovereign powers to a centralised institutional structure allowed these agencies to function independently from the influence of one or more Member States. The formation of the European Community therefore involved the transfer of a considerable degree of national sovereignty in order to create a supranational body capable of regulating its own affairs.

The legislative authority of the European Community extends to measures necessary to pursue the activities identified in Article 3 of the EC Treaty. Originally, this provision vested the European Community institutions with power to pursue, inter alia, the following activities:

1. the elimination, as between Member States, of customs duties and of quantitative restrictions on the import and export of goods, and of all other measures having equivalent effect;
2. the establishment of a common customs tariff and a common commercial policy towards third countries;
3. the abolition, as between Member States, of obstacles to the free movement of persons, services and capital;
4. the adoption of a common agricultural policy;
5. the adoption of a common transport policy;
6. the creation of a Community competition policy;
7. the approximation of the laws of the Member States to the extent required for the proper functioning of the common market;
8. the association of overseas countries and territories in order to increase trade and promote economic development.

Authority to pursue these activities was, and still remains, vital to secure the four necessary features of the common market as set out earlier above.

The original activities which the European Community was authorised to pursue were largely economic in nature and neither political or social. However, since 1987, the list of activities which fall within the competence of the European Community has been radically expanded by amendments on three occasions: (i) the Single European Act 1986; (ii) the Treaty on European Union 1992; and (iii) the Amsterdam Treaty 1997.

1.3 Geographical expansion and vertical integration

Of course, the European Community has not remained in a static form since the EC Treaty was signed in 1957. The changes occurring to the organisation may be grouped into two general categories. On the one hand, there has been geographical expansion through the accession of new Member States. On the other hand, there has been vertical integration insofar as its constitution has been amended, on several occasions, to increase its competence in areas not originally contemplated.

Geographical expansion

In 1957, only six European states constituted the European Community, these being Belgium, France, the Federal Republic of Germany, Italy, Luxembourg and the Netherlands.

The Community was enlarged in 1973 by the accession of Denmark, Ireland and the United Kingdom to the three Community Treaties. Norway did not join after its population voted against membership in a referendum held on the matter. Greece was admitted in 1981; Spain and Portugal became members in 1986. East Germany, having been reunited with the Federal Republic of Germany to become simply Germany, was de facto assumed within the Community in 1990.

Since 1 January 1995, the membership of the Community has been increased to 15 Member States following the accession of Austria, Finland and Sweden.

The European Community entered negotiations on membership in April 1998 with six other countries: Cyprus, the Czech Republic, Estonia, Hungary, Poland and Slovenia. It has also formally opened the accession process with five other countries that have applied to join, namely: Bulgaria, Latvia, Lithuania, Romania and Slovakia. Additionally, the Community has approved a number of accession partnership agreements to assist the applicant countries from central and eastern Europe to prepare for membership. These agreements set out the economic and political priorities to be achieved before formal accession can be completed.

Vertical integration

The EC Treaty has been amended on a number of occasions since its negotiation but the three most fundamental constitutional amendments have been made by the Single European Act 1986, the Treaty on European Union 1992 and the Treaty of Amsterdam 1997.

In retrospect, the most radical overhaul took place when the Treaty of European Union came into effect. The Treaty of Amsterdam 1997 made a number of further changes to the EC Treaty but these are relatively minor compared to the transformation brought about by the Treaty on European Union. One important change which was made by the Amsterdam Treaty 1997 was the re-numbering of almost all of the articles of the EC Treaty. This re-numbering has been followed in this edition of the textbook.

Single European Act

The Single European Act 1986 can be seen in retrospect as a positive movement towards the transformation of the European Community into a true European Union. Its provisions reflect the desire on the part of the Member States to secure three primary objectives.

The first objective was to formalise true political co-operation among the Member States as a first step towards political union. The second was to introduce new policy objectives into the EC Treaty in an attempt to expand the competencies of the organisation. The third and final objective was to modify the institutional and decision-making processes to enhance the status of the European Parliament while at the same time reducing, to a limited extent, the powers of individual Member States to block Community measures.

Since the Treaty on European Union came into effect, most of the changes brought by the Single European Act have become of historical significance, the most notable exception being the single internal market programme.

Treaty on European Union

The Treaty on European Union 1992 (TEU), also known as the Maastricht Agreement, fundamentally altered the constitutional structure of the European Community by making that organisation an integral part of the European Union. The TEU, in effect, absorbed the pre-existing European Community, which remained primarily economic in structure, into the constitution of the European Union.

Amsterdam Treaty

The Treaty of Amsterdam 1997 continued the process of transforming the European Community into a European Union. This was achieved by refining the modalities of decision-making within the European Union and, in particular, by extending the participation of the European Parliament in the legislative process. Where relevant, these changes are identified in the appropriate sections of the textbook. The Treaty was given effect in UK law by the European Communities (Amendment) Act 1998.

1.4 The legal nature of the European Community

Even since its conception, the European Community has been recognised as having a unique nature which has resulted in it being characterised as a 'supranational organisation'. The European Union will undoubtedly be given a similar characterisation. A supranational organisation is one which has transcended the form of a mere international organisation, as that term is used in public international law, but which has not yet attained the level of integration among its participants to achieve the quality of statehood.

Analysis of the consequences of the unique legal nature of the European Community is best tackled by considering its character from two viewpoints: first, the relations between the Community and the Member States, and secondly, the relations of the Community with non-Member States.

The relations between the Community and the Member States

The European Community was inaugurated by the setting up of permanent institutions which have been vested with legislative, executive and judicial powers. These powers have been transferred from the Member States in order to allow these institutions to exercise authority in areas of Community competence. Since the legal existence of the Community is based on the transfer of sovereign powers in certain areas two immediate consequences arise.

First, the Community can only exercise those powers which are expressly or impliedly conferred on it by the constitutional treaties. This competence is only derived or attributed. A wide interpretation may be placed on these competencies where they are used in relation to an authority granted to achieve a Community objective. The Community cannot on its own authority assume any additional powers or bring new areas within the ambit of its competence.

The ambit may, however, be widened by the Member States acting through their own representatives meeting in the Council of Ministers as, for example, when the Council of Ministers increased the number of representatives in the European Parliament in February 1993; see Council Decision 93/81/Euratom, ECSC, EC. Alternatively, additional competencies may be brought about by a formal revision of the constitutional treaties which was the case with the Single European Act and the Treaty on European Union. Any action taken by the Community institutions which fall outside this field of competence will lack legal foundation and will be deemed void ab initio.

Second, the transfer of power to the Community has resulted in a corresponding limitation of the sovereign rights of each of the Member States. A unilateral national measure incompatible with the terms of a constitutional treaty will not be given effect. Further, the Member States are under a positive obligation to ensure that they take all appropriate measures to ensure compliance with their treaty obligations and must abstain from any measure which would jeopardise the attainment of Community objectives; see, for example, *EC Commission* v *Greece (Re Electronic Cash Registers)* Case C–137/91 [1992] 3 CMLR 117.

The practical effect of this obligation is that Member States are precluded from legislating in certain areas and from entering into international agreements which conflict with their obligations at the Community level. These restrictions are simply the natural corollary of the benefits derived from membership of the organisation. In those areas which are not within Community competence, Member States do, however, continue to retain their organic legislative powers: see *Donckerwolke* v *Procureur de la République* Case 41/76 [1976] ECR 1921.

The relations of the Community with non-Member States

The European Community, and now the European Union, acts as a legal person in its external relations. Its legal personality in international law is derived from customary international law which ascribes such personality to certain international organisations: see *ILO Convention Case* Opinion 2/91 [1993] 3 CMLR 800. This competence is also expressly stated in the Community Treaties themselves. For example, Article 6 ECSC Treaty and Article 281 EC Treaty state that 'the Community shall have legal personality'.

The Community has the power and capacity to enter into international agreements and this authority is considered in more detail in Chapter 13.

1.5 The special nature and qualities of European Community law

It should not be surprising that, because European Community law is a unique species of law, it also has a special nature and special qualities. This special character is derived from the fact that the Community legal system is a supranational, uniform and unitary legal order, albeit within a limited field of application: *Van Gend en Loos* v *Netherlands* Case 26/62 [1963] ECR 1. Its provisions belong neither to the realm of public international law nor of municipal law. European Community law and the national laws of each Member State constitute two distinct legal orders which are separate yet, at the same time, related. The former is based on the constitutional treaties of the organisation while the others are based on national constitutions.

Following from the logic of this separation, Community institutions therefore have no jurisdiction to interpret, apply, enforce, repeal or annul legislative or administrative acts of a Member State nor to pronounce on their validity under national law: see, for example, *Schumacher* v *Hauptzollamt Frankfurt am Main-Ost* Case C–215/87 [1990] 2 CMLR 465. The Community institutions can only require Member States, within the framework of Community proceedings, to adjust any national provisions that have been found contrary to Community law.

Conversely, while national organs have to interpret, apply and enforce Community law, they have, in principle, no jurisdiction to test the validity of Community provisions or their compatibility with national law, even constitutional law, and so cannot declare invalid or annul Community measures or suspend their application or enforcement. The validity of Community measures can only be judged by the European Court in light of Community law: see *Firma Foto-Frost* v *Hauptzollamt Lübeck-Ost* Case 314/85 [1988] 3 CMLR 57. Any other course would effectively undermine the legal and constitutional basis on which the Community operates.

The European Court has made a number of important pronouncements on the nature of Community law. In one of its early landmark cases, it observed that:

'[By] creating a Community of unlimited duration, having its own institutions, its own personality and its own capacity in law, apart from having international standing and, more particularly, real powers resulting from a limitation of competence or a transfer of powers from the States to the Community, the Member States, albeit within limited spheres, have restricted their sovereign rights and created a body of law applicable both to their nationals and to themselves. The integration into the laws of each Member State of provisions which derive from the Community, and more generally the terms and the spirit of the treaty, make it impossible for the states to accord precedence to a unilateral and subsequent measure over a legal system accepted by them on a basis of reciprocity': *Costa v ENEL* Case 6/64 [1964] 3 CMLR 425; [1964] ECR 585.

From this judgment, two of the most fundamental principles of Community law can be gleaned: the principle of the supremacy of Community law over national law and the concept of the direct effect of Community legislation. The principle of supremacy means that Community law, whether in the form of Treaty provisions, regulations or directives, prevails over prior and subsequent inconsistent provisions of national law. The concept of direct effect, on the other hand, allows private individuals to rely on certain Community rights and duties.

The subjects of Community law include not only the Member States and the Community institutions but also the nationals of the Member States. Individuals and other legal persons are entitled to rely on Community law to enforce rights and to defend themselves against illegally imposed restrictions or obligations. Further, these rights can be relied on in national courts and tribunals as well as in the Community court structure.

Community law also defines the substantive powers, rights and obligations of its subjects and has created a wide range of sanctions, remedies and procedures for the vindication of these rights and duties. Many of these rights are embodied in the EC Treaty itself, including the right of free movement of workers, the right to equal pay for equal work and the right not to be subjected to discrimination on the grounds of nationality. Other rights have been created by the European Court of Justice through its role as the guardian of Community law, such as the direct effect of Community treaty provisions and directives: see *Amministrazione delle Finanze dello Stato v Simmenthal SpA* Case 106/77 [1978] ECR 629.

1.6 Transformation from a European Community into a European Union

The European Community as a step towards a European Union

The EC Treaty is centred around recognition that economic integration is the catalyst to progressive political, social, cultural, financial and monetary cohesion among the Member States. The ultimate goal of this process has always been the creation of a European Union among the Member States founded on an amended EC Treaty which will continue to act as the primary vehicle for closer integration.

The Treaty on European Union took the process of integration much further; integration is no longer merely economic but also political, social and cultural. By recognising that coherence in all these areas must be achieved, the TEU marks the transition from a European Community based on primarily economic principles and concepts to a new order designed to increase political harmony among the populations of the 15 Member States.

The TEU itself recognises that the European Union is a 'new stage in the process of European integration' initially started by the EC Treaty. In order to advance this process of integration, a concept of citizenship of the Union has been introduced, as have mechanisms to increase economic, monetary and fiscal co-operation among the Member States.

The relationship between the law of the European Union and European Community law

The Treaty on European Union amended the original three Community Treaties in order to bring forward the goals of closer European political, social, cultural, economic and monetary union. It also added two completely new areas of competence exercised by the new organisation, namely the establishment of a common foreign policy and security policy as well as institutionalised co-operation in the fields of justice and home affairs.

However, before proceeding to consider the constitutional structure of the European Union, three main points must be noted.

First, notwithstanding the addition of these completely new areas of competence, the heart of the Union remains the EC Treaty, as amended. Therefore, in practical terms, the substantive law of the European Union has not radically changed from that of the European Community. The four freedoms contained in the EC Treaty, for example, continue to play a crucial role in the functioning of the European Union, as does the body of competition policy developed by the European Community.

Secondly, while new powers have been conferred on the European Union which were not exercised by its predecessor, the institutional framework of the organisation continues in broadly the same shape. The European Council, the Council of Ministers, the European Commission and the European Parliament all have new powers and responsibilities, but their composition and functions remain generally the same. Similarly, the authority of the European Court of Justice and the Court of First Instance to perform the function of judicial review over the acts of the organisation remain as extensive as ever. Only recognition of the Court of Auditors as a fully-fledged institution differentiates the institutional structure of the European Union from that of the European Community, although the Council and the

Commission are now also assisted by a Committee of Regions which acts in an advisory capacity.

Finally, the sources of law, fundamental principles of law and the principles of interpretation for the law of the European Union will continue to apply in much the same fashion as before. While the evolution of new fundamental principles such as subsidiarity has occurred, the fundamental principles embodied in the EC Treaty will continue to apply with as much vigour. Similarly, those principles developed by the European Court in its jurisprudence will not suddenly disappear or disapply; they may be modified and new principles developed, but only with the passage of time shall we see how these changes will occur.

The changes made by the Treaty of Amsterdam

The Treaty of Amsterdam was signed on 2 October 1997 by the 15 Member States of the European Union and came into effect on 1 May 1999, after ratification by all 15 Member States. Despite the extensive public discussions surrounding its approval, the aims and objectives of the Amsterdam Treaty are far more limited than its predecessor, the Treaty on European Union. Indeed, most of the provisions of the Amsterdam Treaty concern adjustments to the original EC Treaty and the TEU rather than any radical transformation of the institutional structure and competencies of the European Union.

In general terms, the four main aims of the Treaty of Amsterdam are to:

1. define with greater precision the scope of the Common Foreign and Security Policy and Co-operation in Justice and Home Affairs;
2. adjust earlier provisions of both the EC Treaty and the TEU to improve their operation;
3. expand the participation of the European Parliament in the institutional decision-making process;
4. introduce a limited number of new policy areas and to strengthen certain existing ones.

The Amsterdam Treaty amends both the TEU and the EC Treaty but continues to maintain a separation between those competencies and powers established under Pillars 2 and 3 of the Treaty on European Union, on the one hand, and those enshrined in the EC Treaty itself (Pillar 1), on the other.

2

The Constitutional Pillars of the European Union

2.1 Introduction

2.2 The constitutional pillars of the European Union

2.3 The political, economic and monetary aspects of the European Union

2.4 The addition of new policy objectives to the EC Treaty

2.5 Establishment of a common foreign policy and security policy

2.6 Co-operation in the fields of justice and home affairs

2.1 Introduction

In accordance with the requirement that all existing Member States of the European Community ratify its terms, the Treaty on European Union (TEU) entered force on 1 November 1993. The European Community has, however, not in fact ceased to exist but has been subsumed within the European Union. References to the European Community are correct when used to refer to the operations of the European Union in exercise of the authority contained in the reconstituted EC Treaty which forms one of the three cornerstones of the European Union. In reality, the amended EC Treaty is by far the most significant of these three cornerstones.

From the point of view of terminology, the term 'European Union', on the other hand, must be used when referring to the new organisation functioning within its total competencies.

The constitutional structure of the European Union is no work of legal simplicity or beauty. The Treaty on European Union, which is the main constitutional instrument of the organisation, builds on the structure put in place by the three original Community Treaties and in particular the EC Treaty. The broad terms of that treaty are retained, but substantially amended by changes to convert that structure into one of the three pillars of the new constitutional order. The other two pillars are the provisions dealing with foreign policy and security, on the one hand, and those concerning justice and home affairs on the other hand.

The Amsterdam Treaty 1997 did not fundamentally disturb this constitutional structure. It merely added additional functions and powers and distributed these among the organs of the organisation in a way that enhanced the position of the European Parliament, particularly in the legislative process. The three pillars of the constitution therefore remain unaltered.

2.2 The constitutional pillars of the European Union

The starting point in understanding the constitution of the European Union is to consider the seven main chapters of the Treaty on European Union which are as follows:

Title I: Common provisions – these are the provisions dealing with the general operation of the European Union;

Title II: Provisions amending the EC Treaty (**Pillar 1**);

Title III: Provisions amending the ECSC Treaty;

Title IV: Provisions amending the Euratom Treaty;

Title V: Provisions on the Establishment of the Common Foreign Policy and Security Policy (**Pillar 2**);

Title VI: Provisions on Co-operation in the Fields of Justice and Home Affairs (**Pillar 3**);

Title VII: Final Provisions.

In the most simple terms, Titles II, V and VI define the organic competencies of the European Union while the remaining titles contain provisions intended to ensure that the powers conferred on the organisation under the three separate pillars function in an integrated fashion within a unified constitutional framework.

Pillar 1: The European Community

The main substantive changes brought to the EC Treaty were as follows:

1. The creation of the concept of citizenship of the European Union.
2. The adoption of the principle of subsidiarity.
3. Redefinition of the institutional and organisational structure of the decision-making processes within the organisation.
4. The introduction of new provisions to regulate economic policy co-operation.
5. The introduction of new competencies in the field of monetary policy co-operation.
6. The addition of new areas of competence to supplement the activities previously pursued by the European Community.

Pillar 2: Common Foreign Policy and Security Policy

A separate Title of the Treaty created new competencies in the field of foreign policy but in fact co-operation in this field had been taking place informally for at least a decade previous to the TEU. The Single European Act first placed co-operation on foreign policy matters on a formal basis, but discussions on this subject took place largely outside the institutional framework on which the Community operated at that time.

Quite clearly, political co-operation in this form will become increasingly important, but the principles on which the common foreign policy is to be structured required further clarification which has occurred with the coming into force of the Treaty of Amsterdam.

Pillar 3: Justice and Home Affairs

Co-operation on justice and home affairs falls inside Title VI of the Treaty and is handled within a separate institutional framework.

To a large extent, this new competence has also been erected on past co-operation which occurred as a corollary of the original operations of the European Community. Nevertheless, the formal assumption of these competencies by the European Union will strengthen the effectiveness of action in these fields.

Notably, existing Community legal instruments and measures may be used to implement policy decisions in this field.

2.3 The political, economic and monetary aspects of the European Union

The creation of the concept of European citizenship and the powers in the area of economic and monetary co-operation have been achieved by amendments made directly to the EC Treaty.

The political dimension – citizenship of the European Union

Article 17 of the EC Treaty, as inserted by the TEU, establishes the concept of citizenship of the European Union which extends to every person bearing the nationality of one of the Member States. Although the concept is essentially a political device to consolidate European solidarity, there are some tangible legal rights and duties which will eventually flow to private individuals. A slight modification was made to the original terms of Article 17 by an amendment introduced by the Amsterdam Treaty which clarifies the principle that citizenship of the Union is complementary to national citizenship and does not replace individual national citizenships.

Article 18 confers on every citizen of the European Union the right to move and reside freely within the territory of any Member State, subject to the limitations and conditions laid down in the EC Treaty and by measures which will be adopted to give effect to this right.

The right of citizenship of the Union is potentially far greater than the corresponding freedom of movement of workers or the freedom of establishment both of which, we shall see later, are tied to economic activity. European citizenship will most likely eventually supersede the right of the free movement of workers which was one of the four fundamental freedoms embodied in the EC Treaty.

An even more significant political right is the right of private individuals to stand as candidates and to vote in the Member State in which they reside regardless of their nationality: Article 19. Proposals were formulated by the Commission to give effect to these rights and two directives were adopted by the Council of Ministers. Council Directive 93/109/EC (1993) lays down the arrangements for allowing citizens of the European Union the right to vote and stand as candidates in elections for the European Parliament in the Member State in which they are residing. Similarly, Council Directive 94/80/EC (1994) creates rights to participate in municipal elections for citizens residing in Member States other than their own.

Finally, under Article 20, every citizen of the Union is entitled to diplomatic protection in states outside the European Union from the authorities of any Member State in the event that his or her own state does not maintain diplomatic representatives in that state. The Member States themselves are instructed to establish the necessary rules among themselves to secure this protection which will also entail discussions with third countries.

Economic policy co-ordination

The Treaty on European Union inserted new provisions into the EC Treaty structure to create a far more comprehensive framework for co-operation on matters of economic policy than those operating when the organisation existed as the European Community.

The development of economic policy within the European Union is to be based on encouraging open market economics with free competition and a favouring of an efficient allocation of resources but always subject to the achievement of the principles set out in Article 4 of the EC Treaty. The overall objective of this policy is to ensure the convergence of performance among the economic policies of Member States.

The principles prescribed in the EC Treaty for the purpose of achieving the necessary degree of convergence are however only stated in broad terms. The following are the few express requirements stated in sufficient detail to be legally binding:

1. Member States shall avoid excessive government deficits: Article 104(1).
2. Member States are required to maintain budgetary disciplines and the

Commission is empowered to monitor the development of the budgetary situation and the stock of government debt in the Member States on the basis of two criteria: (i) whether the ratio of the planned or actual government deficit to gross domestic product exceeds a specific reference value; and (ii) whether the ratio of government debt to gross domestic product exceeds a specific value: Article 104(1).
3. Overdraft facilities or any other type of credit facilities with the European Central Bank (ECB), or with the central banks of the Member States, in favour of central, regional or local governments or public bodies are prohibited: Article 101(1).

The Commission is empowered to submit proposals based on these principles to the Council of Ministers in order to regulate the conduct of economic policies within both Member States and the European Union. The Council of Ministers is required, in turn, to approve broad guidelines on the basis of these recommendations which are then to be submitted to the European Council for discussion. The conclusions of these discussions are to be returned to the Council of Ministers to facilitate the adoption of definitive guidelines: Article 99(2) EC Treaty.

Responsibility for monitoring progress on the economic performance of each Member State is given to the Council of Ministers which will act on the basis of periodic reports submitted to it by the Commission. It is therefore the Council of Ministers which will ultimately ensure compliance with these guidelines by the Member States. If the Council decides that the economic policies of a specific Member State are not consistent with the broad guidelines adopted for the convergence of economic performance and it may direct 'necessary recomm-endations' to the Member State to correct any misalignment of policy. These censures may be made public.

There are two particular exceptions contained in Article 100 to the requirement to adhere to the economic policy guidelines set out by the Council of Ministers:

1. The Council may decide to adopt appropriate measures 'if severe difficulties arise in the supply of products'. It is likely that this power is intended to apply to shortages of particular products at the European level rather than at national level since the EC Treaty is intended to facilitate the free movement of goods.
2. The Council may authorise, under certain conditions, financial assistance to a Member State which is 'in difficulties or is seriously threatened with severe difficulties caused by exceptional circumstances beyond its control'. This provision clearly envisages economic difficulties other than those caused by natural disasters which is later cited as an illustration of such circumstances.

Monetary policy co-ordination

The Treaty on European Union formally sanctioned a the three-stage programme towards economic and monetary union which had been informally pursued by the Member States prior to its negotiation. The first stage was increased co-operation among the Member States within the framework of the European Monetary System (EMS). Achievement of the necessary degree of co-operation involved membership of the EMS and adherence to the Exchange Rate Mechanism (ERM) by all Member States.

The second stage for achieving economic and monetary union began on 1 January 1994. This was the establishment of a European Monetary Institute (EMI), a body consisting of a President and the governors of all the national central banks of the Member States. The statute of the EMI is laid out in a protocol annexed to the EC Treaty.

The inaugural session of the EMI was held on 11 January 1994, in Frankfurt, the seat of this institution. The main functions pursued by the EMI were as follows:

1. to strengthen co-operation between national central banks.
2. to strengthen co-ordination of the monetary policies of the Member States with the aim of ensuring price stability.
3. to monitor the functioning of the European Monetary System.
4. to hold consultations concerning issues falling within the competence of the national central banks and affecting the stability of financial institutions and markets.

The third stage involved the creation of a central banking system for the whole of the European Union and the adoption of a single currency. Both of these final objectives were achieved on 1 January 1999, with the establishment of the European System of Central Banks and the introduction of the single currency, the Euro.

European central banking system
Article 8 of the EC Treaty authorised the establishment of a European System of Central Banks (referred to as the ESCB) and a European Central Bank (referred to as the ECB). Both institutions came into existence on 1 January 1999. Neither of these institutions should be confused with the European Bank for Reconstruction and Development (the EBRD) which is a separate non-European Union institution set up in 1991 for the purposes of investing in the reconstruction of Eastern Europe.

The functions and powers of the ESCB and the ECB are regulated by a separate protocol attached to the EC Treaty. However, neither of these bodies is formally recognised as a fully fledged European Union institution within the meaning ascribed by Article 7 of the EC Treaty.

Adoption of the single European currency
Eleven Member States fulfilled the criteria required for inclusion, and agreed to participate, in the single European currency programme which commenced on 1 January 1999. These countries were Austria, Belgium, Finland, France, Germany, Ireland, Italy, Luxembourg, The Netherlands, Spain and Portugal, and collectively they constitute the 'Eurozone'. Three Member States declined to participate, namely the United Kingdom, Sweden and Denmark, while Greece failed to meet the

necessary requirements set down in Article 121 of the EC Treaty. As a result, these currencies remain outside the Eurozone.

The eligibility of the 11 Member States to participate was confirmed earlier in May 1998 by a Council Decision taken by common accord of the governments of the Member States adopting the single currency, following consultation with the European Parliament and the European Monetary Institute. Having decided which Member States would adopt the single currency, the Council formally adopted Council Regulation 974/98 on its introduction. This regulation, and Council Regulation 975/98, set up the legal framework for the use of the new currency.

Council Regulation 974/98 confirms that the single European currency is called the 'Euro'. Under the regulation, with effect from 1 January 1999, the Euro has been substituted for the currency of each of the participating Member States at fixed conversion rates. The actual conversion rates were not in fact definitively fixed until Council Regulation 2866/98 was adopted by the Council on 31 December 1998.

The regulation also sets out measures which each participating Member State may take during the transitional period, notably to redenominate in the Euro unit any outstanding debt issued by the Member State's central government in its national currency unit, and to enable the change of the unit of account of their operating procedures from the national currency unit to the Euro.

On 1 January 2002 the ECB and the Central Banks of the participating Member States will put into circulation bank notes denominated in Euro and from this date the Euro notes and coins are legal tender. As from the same date participating Member States will issue coins denominated in Euro or in cents. Bank notes and coins in the national currency will remain legal tender within their territorial limits up until six months after the end of the transitional period at the latest; this period may be shortened by national law.

2.4 The addition of new policy objectives to the EC Treaty

The Single European Act introduced a number of important new policy objectives into the EC Treaty in 1987 and both the Treaty on European Union and the Treaty of Amsterdam develop these areas of competence and, at the same time, add a number of other completely new policy objectives. For example, the internal market programme started by the SEA remains largely untouched by the Treaty on European Union. However, the changes made by the SEA to the EC Treaty for the purposes of regulating monetary capacity, social policy, economic and social cohesion, research and technical development and environmental protection are virtually all superseded by amendments which widen the powers of the European Union in these fields.

The Treaty on European Union and the Amsterdam Treaty also amended Article 3 of the EC Treaty by adding a significant number of new activities which fall within the competence of the organisation. The original structure of the European

Community as a common market is however preserved insofar as the four primary features are maintained: see Article 4(1) and (2) EC Treaty.

Broadly the expanded areas of competence can be grouped into three categories: (a) the development of new common policies; (b) the formulation of an industrial policy; and (c) the pursuit of social and cultural policy. Attempts have also been made to erect a legal structure to protect human rights and fundamental freedoms, although these attempts are far short of the wholesale incorporation of the European Convention of Human Rights into the structure of the organisation. Nevertheless, these efforts merit consideration at this point. Equally, the Amsterdam Treaty authorised smaller groups of Member States to engage in closer co-operation among themselves as long as this co-operation remains consistent with the overall objectives of the European Community.

The development of new common policies

The amendments to Article 3 of the EC Treaty required the formulation of additional common policies in the following fields: (a) encouragement for the establishment and development of trans-European transportation networks; (b) environmental protection policy; (c) consumer protection policy; and (d) a policy for the attainment of a higher level of health protection. In addition, the Treaty of Amsterdam inserted a further primary policy objective into Article 3, namely the promotion of co-ordination between employment policies among the Member States and the development of a co-ordinated strategy for employment issues.

The formulation of an industrial policy

Although a Community industrial policy was in place before the ratification of the TEU, this was incoherent and fragmented. The TEU consolidated industrial policy by making this policy a primary area of European Union responsibility.

The industrial policy is intended to achieve three goals: (a) to strengthen the competitiveness of European Union industries vis-à-vis third country producers; (b) to promote research and technological development; and (c) to introduce measures in the spheres of energy, civil protection and tourism.

The pursuit of a social and cultural policy

This is a miscellaneous classification involving the following objectives: (a) the strengthening of economic and social cohesion; (b) the formulation of a policy in the sphere of development co-operation; and (c) a contribution to education and training of quality and to the flowering of the cultures of the Member States.

Protection of human rights and fundamental freedoms

The Treaty does not expressly include measures to ensure the protection of human rights and fundamental freedoms. This omission is not rectified by the oblique references to the protection of human rights in Title I, Article 6 of the Treaty itself or the jurisprudence of the European Court of Justice.

In *Re the Accession of the Community to the European Human Rights Convention* (Opinion 2/94) [1996] 2 CMLR 265, the Council of Ministers requested an opinion from the European Court to confirm whether or not the Community, as it now stands, could accede to the European Convention on Human Rights. In the event of an affirmative answer, the Council intended to open discussions with the relevant parties to allow the Community to join the system. An adverse ruling would require the Member States to amend the EC Treaty as a pre-condition for membership.

The Court ruled that, as the EC Treaty presently stands, there was no legal basis to allow accession on the European Community as a whole, to the European Convention. Such a putative act would amount to a usurpation of the constitutional system maintained in the Community. The only possible avenue to allow the Community to join would be to amend the EC Treaty itself. Although it was widely anticipated that the Treaty of Amsterdam would make this amendment, in fact the Treaty, in its final version, did not.

Closer co-ordination among groups of Member States

Article 11 of the EC Treaty, inserted by the Treaty of Amsterdam, authorises groups of Member States to establish closer co-operation between themselves using the institutions, procedures and mechanisms contained in the EC Treaty. This type of co-operation is permitted as long as proposed measures or actions:

1. do not concern areas which fall within the exclusive competence of the Community;
2. do not affect Community policies, actions or programmes;
3. do not concern the citizenship of the Union or discriminate between nationals of Member States;
4. remain within the limits of the powers conferred upon the Community by the EC Treaty;
5. do not constitute a discrimination or a restriction of trade between Member States and do not distort the conditions of competition between these states.

This mechanism will allow the more progressive EU Member States to pursue closer economic, social and political integration without the need to continue to persuade less progressive countries to participate in such programmes. The ability of such groups to do so is, however, circumscribed by the above-mentioned conditions.

2.5 Establishment of a common foreign policy and security policy

Title V of the European Union Treaty specifies fundamental objectives on which the European Union will base its common foreign policy and security policy. These include the safeguarding of common values, fundamental interests and the independence of the Union, as well as the promotion of democracy, the rule of law and the protection of human rights and fundamental freedoms: Article 11 TEU.

Member States are obliged to support the Union's foreign and security policy 'actively and unreservedly in a spirit of loyalty and mutual solidarity'. They are required to refrain from any action contrary to the interests of the Union or which is likely to impair its effectiveness as a cohesive force in international relations.

Common foreign policy

The European Union pursues a common foreign policy by establishing procedures for systematic co-operation between the Member States in the conduct of policy and by gradually implementing decisions on joint action in those areas in which the Member States have important interests in common: Article 12 TEU. Three separate kinds of joint actions are contemplated: (a) the definition of principles and general guidelines for the common foreign policy; (b) the adoption of joint actions; and (c) the adoption of common positions.

Defining principles and general guidelines

The European Council is authorised under Article 13 of the TEU to define the principles and general guidelines for the common foreign policy. In addition, the European Council can also decide on common strategies to be implemented by the European Union in areas of foreign policy where the Member States have important interests in common.

These principles and general guidelines will be the basis for decisions taken within the Council of Ministers that will define and implement the common foreign policy. The Council of Ministers is also authorised to recommend common strategies to the European Council. The Council of Ministers will implement common strategies by means of the adoption of both joint actions and common positions.

The adoption of joint actions

As mentioned above, the Council of Ministers is authorised to adopt joint actions by Article 14 of the TEU. Joint actions are instruments which commit the Member States to the common positions. Member States must therefore act in a manner consistent with joint actions when engaging in foreign policy matters.

Joint actions address specific situations where operational action at a European Union level is necessary. Each of these measures must define their objectives, their scope and the means to the European Union for their implementation as well as the conditions required for giving effect to them.

Examples of joint actions taken by the Council of Ministers include: Council Decision 97/817/CFSP on the eradication of anti-personnel landmines, Council Decision 98/301/CFSP on action in support of the government of Montenegro, Council Decision 98/375/CFSP on the appointment of a special EU envoy to Yugoslavia and Council Decision 97/288/CFSP on the promotion of transparency in nuclear-related export controls.

The adoption of common positions

Common positions differ from joint actions in that common positions require the Member States to adopt a united front to the international community, whereas joint actions involve a proactive element. In other words, joint actions entail the participation of the Member States to implement a specific policy objective while common positions are effectively statements of general common foreign policy.

By virtue of Article 15 of the TEU, common positions define the approach that will be taken by the European Union towards a particular international matter. Member States are obliged to ensure that their individual national policies are consistent with these instruments. Hence, common positions are more akin to statements of international policy: see, for example, Council Decision 97/356/CFSP concerning conflict prevention and resolution in Africa; Council Decision 98/606/CFSP concerning the promotion of non-proliferation and confidence-building in the south Asian region; and Council Decision 98/633/CFSP on stability and good-neighbourliness in south-east Europe.

Common security policy

The common security policy is essentially an attempt to build a common European defence policy using the vehicle of the Western European Union (WEU): Article 17 TEU. The Council of Ministers is instructed to consult with the institutions of the WEU on the adoption of the necessary practical arrangements for the implementation of such a policy.

The WEU was created in 1954 but has been largely dormant from its inauguration. Nevertheless, this organisation is identified as the 'defence component' of the European Union.

At the same time, the obligation to formulate a common defence policy is expressly stated not to compromise to duties of certain Member states, including the United Kingdom, under the North Atlantic Treaty Organisation (NATO).

2.6 Co-operation in the fields of justice and home affairs

The fields which are expressly included within the ambit of this policy include: (a) asylum policy; (b) control of external frontiers; (c) immigration policy; (d) drug enforcement and drug addiction; (e) international fraud; (f) co-operation between civil and criminal courts; (g) customs co-operation; and (h) co-operation among the police forces of the Member States: Article 29 TEU.

In these fields, Member States shall consult with one another within the Council of Ministers with a view to co-ordinating their actions. Co-ordination is to be facilitated by collaboration between the relevant departments of the administrations of the Member States.

The Council of Ministers may adopt joint positions, joint action and international conventions where these are required to contribute to the pursuit of objectives in these fields. The procedure for the adoption of these measures is specified in Article 31 TEU.

3

The Institutions of the European Union

3.1 Introduction

Despite the constitutional changes brought by the Treaty on European Union and the Treaty of Amsterdam, the functions of the institutions remain largely defined by the terms of the EC Treaty. Of course, the Council and the Commission had their respective powers enlarged by the assumption of competencies in the fields of foreign and security policy on the one hand and justice and home affairs on the other hand. These new competencies have already been discussed in detail in Chapter 2. Henceforth, we shall be concerned exclusively with the operation of the institutions of the European Union under the EC Treaty.

For the purpose of this chapter, and the remaining chapters of the Textbook for that matter, unless otherwise expressly stated, all references to the constitution of the organisation will be to the EC Treaty, as amended, and the operation of the European Community as a component part of the European Union. This is because of the present prevailing influence of the EC Treaty in the operations of the European Union.

Article 7 of the EC Treaty provides that the tasks entrusted to the Community will be carried out by the following institutions: a European Parliament, a Council, a

Commission, a Court of Justice and a Court of Auditors. The institutions are to act within the powers conferred on them by the Treaty and subsequent Treaties and Acts. The Council and the Commission are assisted by an Economic and Social Committee and a Committee of the Regions acting in an advisory capacity.

The European Council is not specifically identified in Article 7 of the Treaty as a Community institution, because it is more a mechanism for inter-governmental co-operation rather than a purely Community institution. Its existence and functions, originally recognised in the Single European Act, are now dealt with by Article 4 of the Treaty on European Union.

Similarly, the Court of First Instance is technically attached to the Court of Justice and is not a separate Community institution, yet its function and role within the Community legal order require that it be treated as such at this point in order to render a proper and accurate description of the Community institutional framework.

3.2 The European Council

Article 4 of the Treaty on European Union states:

> 'The European Council shall provide the Union with the necessary impetus for its development and shall define the general political guidelines thereof. The European Council shall bring together the Heads of State or of Government of the Member States and the President of the Commission. They shall be assisted by the Ministers for Foreign Affairs of the Member States and by a Member of the Commission ... The European Council shall submit to the European Parliament a report after each of its meetings and a yearly written report on the progress achieved by the Union.'

There was no provision in the original EC Treaty for such a periodic meeting, but the dictates of closer economic and political integration required the co-ordination and harmonisation of common positions in the fields of foreign and economic policy. After a meeting in Paris in 1974, a decision was made to arrange such meetings ('Summits') regularly three times each year to discuss issues generally affecting European and international concerns.

The European Council meets under the chairmanship of the Head of State or of Government of the Member State which holds the Presidency of the Council. The position of chairman is important because this gives an opportunity for individual Member States to influence the agenda for discussion and, indirectly, the direction of the Community. Thus, when the German, French or Dutch governments hold the presidency the agenda usually deals with matters of accelerating European integration, while the presidency of the British or the Danish government usually involves reversing or slowing down the process of integration.

Both the European Commission and the European Parliament are closely involved with the formulation of policy at this level. The views of the European Parliament are continuously sought, and the body is regularly informed about current political issues.

European Council discussions range across a whole host of matters of both European and international concern. For example, the final conference held during the UK Presidency in the second half of 1992, the Edinburgh Summit, proved to be particularly successful and agreement was reached on the expansion of the representatives in the European Parliament, the conclusion of the single European market and the promotion of the principle of subsidiarity. The Danish and Belgian Presidencies held in the first and second halves of 1993 respectively, focused on encouraging greater transparency in EC affairs, enlargement of the membership of the Community and economic assistance for central and eastern Europe.

In recent years, much of the work efforts of the Presidencies has been focused on economic and monetary union. This was the case for the Italian Presidency which lasted for the first six months of 1996 and during which much of the preparatory work for the Inter-Governmental Conference (IGC) was achieved. The pursuit of national Italian interests was not, however, neglected. In particular, the Italian Presidency placed high on its agenda the pacification and reconstruction of the former Yugoslavia, the Middle East peace process and strengthening co-operation and dialogue with Russia and the other countries of the former USSR.

In the first half of 1999 the Federal Republic of Germany took over the Presidency of the European Union. The start of the German Presidency coincided with the launch of the Euro. The principal political tasks taken up by the German Presidency were:

1. to improve the framework conditions for higher levels of employment;
2 to adopt a policy of integration of the energy markets;
3. the pursuit of a successful conclusion to the Agenda 2000 issue;
4. to improve the framework conditions for industry, particularly small and medium-sized enterprises;
5. the liberalisation in the telecommunications sector and further liberalisation of the postal sector;
6. to create an effective transport policy; and
7. the development and consolidation of existing relations with third countries and international organisations.

The respective agendas of these countries illustrate the ability of individual Member States to influence the internal and external policies of the EU during their tenure of the Presidencies and to pursue goals close to their national interests during such times.

3.3 The Council of Ministers

Articles 202–210 EC Treaty

Composition

The Council consists of a representative of each Member State at ministerial level, authorised to commit the government of that Member State: Article 203. Unlike that of the Commission the membership of the Council will vary from time to time, depending on the nature of the meeting. If the meeting is to discuss general matters, the Foreign Ministers of the Member States will attend; if it is to consider a specialist matter, like agricultural policy, it will be attended by the appropriate minister of the Member State.

Functions

To ensure that the objectives set out in the EC Treaty are attained, the Council is required, in accordance with the provisions of the Treaty, to:

1. ensure co-ordination of the general economic policies of the Member States;
2. take decisions;
3. confer on the Commission powers for the implementation of the rules which the Council lays down. The Council may impose certain requirements in respect of the exercise of these powers. The Council may also reserve the right, in specific cases, to exercise directly implementing powers itself.

A committee consisting of the Permanent Representatives of the Member States is responsible for preparing the work of the Council and for carrying out the tasks assigned to it by the Council. The Council is assisted by a General Secretariat, under the direction of a Secretary-General who is appointed by the Council acting unanimously: Article 207.

Conduct of meetings

The presidency of the Council rotates among the Member States, according to six-year cycles, each holding the office for six months: Article 203. The President presides over the meetings, which can take place anywhere within the Community but will usually be in Brussels. The Council meets when convened by its President on his initiative or at the request of one of its members or of the Commission: Article 204.

Article 205(1) states:

> 'Save as otherwise provided in this Treaty, the Council shall act by a majority of its members.'

In practice the Council will rarely act by a simple majority. Unanimity used to be the rule until it was found that Community business was hopelessly slow. The Council began to act more frequently by means of a qualified majority defined by Article 205(2) of the Treaty.

After the amendments made to Article 205(2) of the EC Treaty by the Treaty of Accession for Austria, Finland and Sweden, the votes of the Member States are weighted in the following manner:

Germany, France, Italy and the United Kingdom – 10 votes each;
Spain – 8 votes;
Belgium, Greece, the Netherlands and Portugal – 5 votes;
Austria and Sweden – 4 votes;
Denmark, Ireland and Finland – 3 votes;
Luxembourg – 2 votes, making a total of 87 votes.

For the adoption of measures by a qualified majority, there must be at least 62 votes in favour where the EC Treaty requires such acts to be adopted on a proposal from the Commission, and 62 votes in favour, cast by at least ten members in all other cases. This formula is an attempt to ensure that the larger states cannot coerce the smaller members.

The use of majority voting in the Council became more common after the passing of the Single European Act which extended majority voting to a substantial range of matters. Similarly, the Treaty on European Union continued this process and enlarged the number of areas subject to majority voting.

After the accession of the new Member States in January 1995, a blocking minority became 26 votes. This number of votes allows a coalition of Member States to prevent the adoption of measures which require a qualified majority.

Unanimity is usually required in matters of great importance, such as the admission of a new Member State to the Community (Article 49 TEU) and matters concerning the approximation of laws (Article 94 EC Treaty). In addition, the appointment of the President of the European Commission requires unanimity among Member States, a requirement which allowed the United Kingdom to veto the Franco-German sponsored nomination for the President in June 1994. Abstentions by members present in person or represented do not prevent the adoption by the Council of acts which require unanimity: Article 205(3) EC Treaty.

Luxembourg Accords

If the vital interest of a Member State is threatened, an understanding exists within the Community whereby a Member State may effectively veto a measure to which it objects. This convention, known as the Luxembourg Accords, provides that wherever important interests are at stake, discussion should be continued until a unanimous decision is reached.

Legislative competence

The Council of Ministers is the primary legislative body within the Community and embodies the collective interests of the Member States. While the power to legislate is limited by the fact that the Commission is authorised to submit proposals to the Council for approval, and the Commission retains the authority to decide the contents and nature of these proposals, at the end of the day it is the Council that adopts the overwhelming majority of Community legislation.

The composition of the Council clearly indicates that the Community is not an autonomous institution which enacts legislation separate from the Member States. It is the Member States, through their representatives on the Council, which pass European legislation. Although individual Member States may often be out-voted when particular measures are passed on a majority vote, it is the Member States acting together which decide the substantive content of European law.

In order to enact a measure, the Council must ensure that the procedural requirements for passing the measure have been complied with and also that its authority to enact the measure is derived from the terms of the Community Treaties. In other words, the Council, if it acts ultra vires, may find the European Court striking down its measures on the basis of a complaint from either another Community institution or a Member State. Individuals also have standing to bring actions for judicial review of the Council's actions.

The most common ground of complaint from Member States against measures adopted in the Council is when a measure is approved on the basis of an article requiring a qualified majority as opposed to another provision needing a stricter voting requirement such as unanimity. If a Member State believes that a measure is being adopted in the incorrect legal basis an application for annulment to the European Court of Justice is the proper procedure.

For example, in *United Kingdom* v *EC Council (Re Hormones)* Case 68/86 [1988] 2 CMLR 453, the United Kingdom government challenged the legal basis on which the Council adopted a directive prohibiting the use of certain types of hormones. The critical point was that the measure was adopted under Article 37 – which required a qualified majority. But the United Kingdom claimed that the legitimate legal authority was Article 94 requiring unanimity. In fact the Court held that the proper legal basis was Article 37, although the measure was eventually declared void on technical procedural grounds.

Again, in *United Kingdom* v *EC Commission (Re Working Hours Directive)* Case C–84/94 [1996] 3 CMLR 671, the United Kingdom challenged the Working Hours Directive on the grounds that it should have been adopted under either Article 94 or 308, both of which required unanimity, as opposed to Article 138 which concerns the adoption of social policy measures including health and safety. The ECJ held that the Council had not adopted the directive on an incorrect legal basis as far as the measures were designed to limit the maximum permissible hours that employees were required to work and the various other work-related measures. These were issues which fell inside the scope of the health and safety of workers and the

Council was free to regulate such matters under Article 138. This also allowed the Council to act by a majority vote.

The European Commission is also a relatively frequent visitor to the European Court to challenge measures adopted by the Council when the Council opts to alter the contents or legal basis of a proposal from the Commission. In *EC Commission v EC Council (Re Generalised Tariff Preferences)* Case 45/86 [1987] ECR 1493, just such a dispute arose in relation to two Council regulations concerning tariff preferences for developing countries. The Council adopted the measure on the authority of Article 308 which specified unanimity, while the Commission believed that the Council had authority to adopt the measures under Article 133, a provision requiring merely a qualified majority. In the event, the European Court sustained the arguments of the Commission and declared the measures void on the ground that they had been adopted on the incorrect legal basis: see also *EC Commission v EC Council (Re Harmonised Commodity Descriptions)* Case 123/88 [1990] 1 CMLR 457.

It is also open to private parties to challenge the legal basis for the adoption of measures either under Article 230 or the preliminary reference procedure of Article 234 of the EC Treaty. An example of the latter procedure being used occurred in *Eurotunnel SA and Others* v *SeaFrance* Case C–408/95 [1998] 2 CMLR 293.

Eurotunnel brought proceedings in the French courts against SeaFrance, claiming that SeaFrance was cross-subsidising its ferry fares with revenues from the sale of goods free of tax and excise duty. SeaFrance had been authorised to provide duty free sales on the basis of authorisations given by the French government. Eurotunnel alleged that these authorisations gave SeaFrance an unfair competitive advantage. As part of its case, Eurotunnel claimed that the two Council directives authorising exemptions from excise tax had been unlawfully adopted by the Council because, when the Council adopted these measures, it had departed from the terms of the Commission's original proposal to such an extent that the final text could not be said to have been adopted on the basis of the Commission's proposal.

The Court held that the Council had power to amend the proposal from the Commission provided that the voting requirements on which the measure was based had been fulfilled. Hence, the Council had not exceeded its powers to make amendments to the proposal and, consequently, the regulations in question could not be annulled on this ground. See Chapter 16, section 16.1, for further details.

Power to conclude international agreements

Article 300 stipulates that where the Treaty provides for the conclusion of agreements between the Community and one or more States or international organisations, the Commission makes recommendations to the Council, which in turn authorises the Commission to open the necessary negotiations. The Commission conducts these negotiations in consultation with special committees appointed by the Council to assist it in this task and within the framework of such directives as the Council may issue to them.

Subject to the powers vested in the Commission in this field, the agreements are concluded by the Council, acting by a qualified majority on a proposal from the Commission. However, the Council acts unanimously when the agreement covers a field for which unanimity is required for the adoption of internal rules, and for the agreements referred to in Article 310 (agreements establishing an association involving reciprocal rights and obligations, common action and special procedures).

The Council normally concludes agreements after consulting the European Parliament, but agreements referred to in Article 310, other agreements establishing a specific institutional framework by organising co-operation procedures, agreements having important budgetary implications for the Community and agreements entailing amendment of an act adopted under the procedure referred to in Article 251 can be concluded only after the assent of the European Parliament has been obtained.

The Council, the Commission or a Member State may obtain the opinion of the Court of Justice as to whether an agreement envisaged is compatible with the provisions of the Treaty. Where the opinion of the Court of Justice is adverse, the agreement may enter into force only in accordance with Article 48 of the Treaty on European Union.

Public access to the Council's deliberations and documents

The Treaty on European Union contained, as an appendix, a declaration on the rights of public access to information from Community institutions. The objectives of this declaration were given effect by Council Decision 93/731/EC on public access to Council documents. Article 1 of that decision states that the public shall have access to measures adopted by the Council unless the release of such documents would undermine the protection of:

1. the public interest;
2. individual privacy;
3. commercial and industrial secrecy;
4. the Community's financial interests; or
5. confidentiality requested by natural or legal persons providing information on the contents of that document.

The right of interested private individuals to obtain access to the Council's deliberations and documents under this measure was tested in the Court of First Instance in *Carvel & Guardian Newspapers Ltd* v *EC Council* Case T–194/94 [1995] ECR II–2765. The European Affairs Editor of *The Guardian* made a request for the documents, reports, minutes and the voting record of the Social Affairs and Justice Council meetings held in October and November 1993, and the Agricultural Council meeting in January 1994. The Council's Secretariat refused this request on the grounds that the documents directly referred to the deliberations of the Council and therefore could not be disclosed. The Court held that the Council failed to properly balance the interests involved before refusing access to these documents. The correspondence between the parties indicated that the Council automatically refused to meet the applicant's request. Such a response could not be considered a proper appraisal of the merits of a request as required by the terms of the Council's decision.

3.4 The European Commission

Articles 211–219 EC Treaty

Composition

After the accession of Austria, Finland and Sweden, the Commission consists of 20 members, selected on the grounds of their general competence and whose independence is beyond doubt. The number of members of the Commission may only be altered by the Council, acting unanimously. Only nationals of Member States may be members of the Commission. The Commission must include at least one national of each of the states, but may not include more than two members having the nationality of the same state. The members of the Commission act in the general interest of the Community, completely independent in the performance of their duties: Article 213. At present there are two members of the Commission from France, Germany, Italy, Spain and the United Kingdom and one each from Austria, Belgium, Denmark, Finland, Greece, Ireland, Luxembourg, the Netherlands, Sweden and Portugal.

In the performance of their duties, the Commissioners must neither seek nor take instructions from any government or from any other body. They must refrain from any action incompatible with their duties. Each Member State undertakes to respect this principle and not to seek to influence the members of the Commission in the performance of their tasks.

The Commissioners may not, during their terms of office, engage in any other occupation, whether gainful or not. When entering upon their duties they are required to give a solemn undertaking that, both during and after their terms of office, they will respect the obligations arising therefrom and in particular their duty to behave with integrity and discretion as regards the acceptance, after they have ceased to hold office, of certain appointments or benefits. In the event of any breach of these obligations, the Court of Justice may, on application by the Council or the Commission, rule that the member concerned be, according to the circumstances, either compulsorily retired, in accordance with Article 216, or deprived of his rights to a pension or benefits instead. The first time such action was taken was in July 1999 when proceedings were initiated against former Commissioner Bangemann for accepting a position in a Spanish telecommunications company which had been regulated by his Commission department!

Appointment

By virtue of Article 214 of the EC Treaty, the members of the Commission are appointed for a period of five years. Their term of office is renewable. The governments of the Member States nominate by common accord the person whom they intend to appoint as President of the Commission. This nomination has to be approved by the European Parliament. The governments of the Member States, by common accord with the nominee for President, then nominate the other persons whom they intend to appoint as members of the Commission.

The President and the other members of the Commission are subject as a body to a vote of approval by the European Parliament. After approval by the European Parliament, the President and the other members of the Commission are officially appointed by common accord of the governments of the Member States. These new rules introduced by the Amsterdam Treaty applied for the first time after the Santer Commission resigned in March 1999. The appointment of Mr Prodi as President of the Commission was made on basis of this new procedure.

Apart from normal replacement, or death, the duties of a Commissioner end when he or she resigns or is compulsorily retired. The vacancy thus caused is filled for the remainder of the member's term of office by a new member appointed by common accord of the governments of the Member States. The Council may, acting unanimously, decide that such a vacancy need not be filled. In the event of resignation, compulsory retirement or death, the President is replaced for the remainder of his term of office. The procedure laid down in Article 214 is applicable for the replacement of the President. Save in the case of compulsory retirement under Article 216 (see below), members of the Commission remain in office until they have been replaced.

The Commission may appoint one or two Vice-Presidents from among its members: Article 217.

Functions

The functions and powers of the Commission are set out in Article 211 of the EC Treaty. These may be classified as follows:

1. to ensure respect for the rights and obligations imposed on Member States and Community institutions by both the Community Treaties and measures made under the authority of these agreements;
2. to formulate, participate in and initiate policy decisions authorised under the Community Treaties;
3. to promote the interests of the Community both internally and externally; and
4. to exercise the powers delegated to it by the Council for the implementation and administration of Community policy.

The European Commission is therefore intended to embody the interests of the

Community and has the final responsibility of ensuring that the interests of the Community are protected.

Powers of supervision

Briefly, the function of the Commission is to ensure that the rules and principles of the Community are respected and that the rules are applied correctly. If a Member State wants a waiver or derogation from the rules then the Commission will decide the matter.

The Commission is the 'watchdog of the treaties' and as such has powers of detection: see Articles 88(3) and 134, where a duty to keep the Commission informed concerning certain matters is imposed on Member States.

The Commission also enjoys powers of investigation. Article 284 empowers the Commission to gather information and carry out checks which are necessary for the performance of the tasks entrusted to it, subject, of course, to the provisions of the treaty. Sometimes Member States or individuals will bring matters to the attention of the Commission by way of complaint, or Parliament will submit a written question: Article 197. The Commission, after investigation, can impose fines on individuals and companies against which an appeal may be made to the European Court of Justice. The Commission has powers under Articles 226 and 228 to ensure that the Member States comply with their obligations.

There are three distinct stages to the Article 226 procedure: the informal stage, the reasoned opinion stage and the Court of Justice stage; see section 4.3 below.

Powers to formulate policy

In order to carry out its task, the Commission (and others) may, in accordance with the provisions of the Treaty, propose regulations and directives, take decisions, make recommendations or deliver opinions: Article 249. The Commission is often referred to as the initiator of policy and the procedure for doing so is considered in section 3.5, below.

Powers to promote the interests of the Community

The Commission is instructed to protect the interests of the Community both internally and externally. The Commission has established a network of representative offices in each of the Member States to co-ordinate the disbursement of information and to liaise on Community matters with national governmental representatives.

Missions are also dispatched by the Commission to the capitals of major partners. These delegations are organised under the auspices of the Commission and are intended to safeguard Community interests in those countries.

In addition, the Commission also participates in a number of international organisations and conferences concerning matters which fall within the scope of the Community's competence. For example, the Commission has representatives at both the WTO and the OECD, and in the past has participated in international negotiations such as those leading to the UN Convention on the Law of the Sea 1982.

Exercise of delegated powers

The EC Treaty authorises the delegation of responsibility for decision-making from the Council to the Commission in a number of Articles such as, for example, Article 83. These delegated powers are of both an executive and a legislative nature.

The purpose of delegating authority is to prevent the day-to-day administration of Community policy from stifling the work of the Council of Ministers. Thus, authority to investigate matters and to administer policy is frequently conferred on the Commission. The two most obvious areas in which the Commission acts under delegated authority are the fields of competition and anti-dumping.

In the discharge of its duty under Community competition policy, the Commission has authority, in certain circumstances, to investigate complaints, to impose fines on companies considered to have infringed the competition rules, and to require Member States to take appropriate action against unlawful state aid.

Its powers under the anti-dumping basic regulations are quite similar. The Commission is empowered to impose duties on foreign companies found to have been dumping, to investigate allegations, to hold discussions and conferences and to conduct reviews. Although the final measures are adopted by the Council, the Commission has considerable competence in the area of anti-dumping, mostly obtained by delegation.

Procedure

In accordance with Article 218, the Council and the Commission consult each other and settle by common accord their methods of co-operation. The Commission adopts its rules of procedure so as to ensure that both it and its departments operate in accordance with the provisions of this Treaty.

The Commission acts by a majority of its members. A meeting of the Commission is valid only if the number of members laid down in its rules of procedure is present: Article 219.

The Commission is required to publish annually, not later than one month before the opening of the session of the European Parliament, a general report on the activities of the Community: Article 212.

To assist its work the Commission has an administrative staff of about 14,000 officials divided among 23 directorates-general About 20 per cent of the Commission's personnel are engaged on linguistic work as the Community uses eleven official languages.

3.5 The European Parliament

Articles 189–201 EC Treaty

Composition

The European Parliament sits in plenary session in Strasbourg and consists of a total of 626 Members of the European Parliament (MEPs). The distribution of seats, as modified by the Treaty of Accession for Austria, Finland and Sweden, is as follows:

99 representatives – Germany;
87 representatives – France, Italy and the United Kingdom;
64 representatives – Spain;
31 representatives – Netherlands;
25 representatives – Belgium, Greece and Portugal;
22 representatives – Sweden;
21 representatives – Austria;
16 representatives – Denmark and Finland;
15 representatives – Ireland;
 6 representatives – Luxembourg.

The distribution of seats in the United Kingdom is regulated by the European Parliamentary Elections Act 1978, as amended by the European Parliamentary Elections Act 1993 (c.41, 1993). Constituencies are drawn up by the Boundary Commissioners and at present 72 seats are allocated to England, eight to Scotland, four to Wales, and three to Northern Ireland. Members of the European Parliament are seated according to their political affiliations and views and not their nationalities.

The majority of parties in the European Parliament are coalitions between national parties. In June 1999, the European Peoples Party (EPP) was the largest single party, followed by Socialist Party (PES), and then the Liberal Democratic and Reformist Group (ELDR).

The MEPs have three main tasks – to advise the Council about the Commission's proposals for Community-wide laws, to consider the Community budget, and to exert some control over the Council and Commission by means of questions about aspects of the Community's business, and otherwise. A number of other tasks were added by the Treaty on European Union and these are now considered together with the original tasks.

The role of Parliament: the supervisory function

Article 189 states that the Parliament shall exercise the advisory and supervisory powers conferred on it by the Treaty. To give substance to these powers, Article 201 has given to the Parliament a powerful weapon in that members may, by a two-thirds majority, compel the Commission to resign as a body. This motion of censure is circumscribed by certain procedural requirements. To date, it has only been effectively invoked on one occasion In January 1999 the European Socialist Party in the European Parliament tabled a motion to compel the Commission under the Presidency of Jacques Santer to resign. This motion was defeated since the necessary two-thirds majority was not obtained. However, a commission of inquiry was established to investigate allegations of maladministration by the Commission which resulted in an adverse report criticising a number of individual Commissioners. As a result, all the Commissioners resigned their positions since liability for maladministration involved collective responsibility of all members.

Three further provisions, inserted by the Treaty on European Union, should also be noted. First, it is acknowledged that political parties at European level are important as a factor for integration within the Union as they contribute to forming a European awareness and to expressing the political will of the citizens of the Union: Article 191. Second, as provided in the Treaty, the European Parliament must participate in the process leading up to the adoption of Community acts by exercising its powers under the procedures laid down in Articles 251 and 252 and by giving its assent or delivering advisory opinions. It may, acting by a majority of its members, request the Commission to submit any appropriate proposal on matters on which it considers that a Community act is required for the purpose of implementing the Treaty: Article 192.

Third, in the course of its duties, the European Parliament may, at the request of a quarter of its members, set up a temporary Committee of Inquiry to investigate alleged contraventions or maladministration in the implementation of European law, except where the alleged facts are being examined before a court and while the case is still subject to legal proceedings. Indeed, this was the procedure that was involved which ultimately led to the resignation of the Santer Commission.

Annual general report

Under the terms of Article 212 of the EC Treaty, as amended, the Commission must publish annually, not later than one month before the opening session of the Parliament, a general report on the activities of the Communities. The Parliament must discuss this report in open session. Since 1970, the Commission's President has also presented to the Parliament an annual programme of the future activity of the Communities. The report is generally presented at the beginning of each year. This enables the Parliament to scrutinise and comment on the framing of Community policies at an early stage and indeed challenge the proposals.

Petition procedure

Article 194 of the EC Treaty entitles any citizen of the Union, and any natural or legal person residing or having his or her registered office in a Member State, to petition the European Parliament on matters which fall within the Community's fields of activity and which affect him, her or it directly.

Now, under the Treaty on European Union, the European Parliament has appointed an Ombudsman empowered to receive complaints from any citizen of the Union or any natural or legal person residing or having his or her registered office in a Member State. The jurisdiction of the Ombudsman extends to maladministration on the part of all Community institutions or bodies except the European Court and the Court of First Instance.

Once a complaint has been received by the Ombudsman, he or she refers the matter to the institution concerned which has three months to submit its views on the matter. The Ombudsman then forwards a report on the complaint to the institution concerned, and the European Parliament and the person who lodged the complaint is informed of the outcome of the inquiries. The Ombudsman must submit an annual report to the Parliament on the outcome of his inquiries.

However, there still remains the problem of effective remedies for legitimate complaints. The Ombudsman is merely empowered to report the matter to the Parliament, and there is no indication in the EC Treaty as to the powers available to rectify legitimate grievances.

Questions

MEPs enjoy the right to be informed about the progress of the Commission's work. They may exercise this right by means of parliamentary questions. Article 197(3), rules 58–62 of Parliament's rules of procedure, determines that the Commission must reply to questions put to it by the Parliament or its members. The questions must be replied to within a specified time. Questions may be for a written answer, or for an oral answer with or without debate. The answers are published in the Official Journal. Written answers are the norm because the pressure on the Parliament's time necessitates a limit to oral question time. The advantage of the oral question is that a related supplementary question may be asked. Questions may also be asked of the Council or of the Foreign Ministers meeting in European political co-operation.

The legislative function

The legislative competence of the European Parliament has progressed through three distinct phases. The first phase can be described as the original legislative role of the Parliament when its role was primarily consultative. The second phase was brought about by the amendments made by the Single European Act which introduced the so-called 'co-operation procedure'. The third phase is the revised legislative role brought about by the Treaty on European Union.

The European Parliament's traditional role was to comment on proposals put forward by the Commission before the Council made its decision on the final text of the legislation. The Parliament had the right to be consulted on certain subjects. Failure to consult the Parliament in these areas resulted in the adoption of any putative measure being declared null and void.

However, in practice, the Commission regularly sought the opinion of the Parliament on proposed legislation even though technically it was not required to do so. Proposals were submitted to the Parliament and discussed in the relevant parliamentary committees. These committees prepared reports on the proposed measures which were debated by the full Parliament prior to being returned to the Commission.

The second stage in the development of the Parliament's legislative competence was brought about by the Single European Act. The SEA established the co-operation procedure which ensured that, on certain subjects, both the Council and the Commission were required to consider the amendments to legislation proposed by the Parliament. However, even in this process the Parliament's proposals were not binding and could be superseded by a unanimous vote of the Council.

The effect of the co-operation procedure was effectively to introduce a second parliamentary reading for legislative proposals on measures requiring approval through the co-operation process. The first reading was required when the Commission submitted its draft proposals for consideration, and the second stage reading was required when the Council passed the measure to the Parliament after it had arrived at a common position.

The third stage in the evolution of this function was established by the changes made by the Treaty on European Union which introduced the 'co-decision procedure'.

The new system is complicated, but essentially Articles 250–252 introduces a new comprehensive legislative process modelled on the co-operation procedure. The essential difference is that this procedure applies to a considerable range of legislative proposals although not all. Its application is far more extensive than the co-operation procedure which was previously the European Parliament's main influence in the legislative procedure.

Now the Commission is required to submit a significant amount of legislative proposals to both the European Parliament and the Council. The Council, acting by qualified majority, after obtaining the opinion of the Parliament, adopts a common position on the proposal. This common position is then communicated to the Parliament.

The Parliament can approve the common position, in which case the Council may adopt the measure. If no decision is taken by the Parliament within three months of the transmission of a proposal, again the Council can adopt the measure.

If the Parliament suggests amendments to the common position, then, depending on whether the relevant legislative process is that of Article 251 or 252, either the matter is referred to a Conciliation Committee where both organs explain their views or the matter is returned to the Council for reconsideration. Ultimately, if no agreement is reached between the organs, the Council may only adopt a measure by a unanimous vote.

The most significant amendment made by the Treaty of Amsterdam to the existing legislative process is that the co-decision procedure will be extended to a further 23 subject-matters. The co-decision procedure itself is also refined. Specifically, the third reading in Parliament has been abolished. In such cases, if the Council and the European Parliament do not reach a compromise in the Conciliation Committee, there is simply no agreement and the proposed measure falls. As a result of this change the two institutions are now obliged to produce some result or allow proposals to fall: Article 251 EC Treaty, as amended.

The budget

Initially the European Community was financed by contributions from the exchequers of the Member States. It was always intended that these contributions should be replaced by the Community's own resources. It was not until 1970 that a decision was taken to establish an 'own resource' system, now Council Decision of 31 October 1994 on the Communities' System of Own Resources. A Financial Provisions Treaty of 1975 was agreed and came into force in 1977.

The Treaty originally gave the Parliament increased powers over the budget and created the Court of Auditors. The Parliament now has the final say on all 'non-compulsory' expenditure – administrative and operational expenditure (Social Fund, research, etc) – approximately 30 per cent of the budget. Regarding the rest of the budget (ie, expenditure (mainly agricultural) which is the inevitable consequence of Community legislation), provided that they do not increase total expenditure the Parliament can propose modifications which are then deemed to be accepted unless the Council rejects them by a qualified majority. Finally, the Parliament can reject the budget as a whole. Article 272(8) provides that 'the European Parliament acting by a majority of its members and two-thirds of the votes cast, may if there are important reasons reject the draft budget and ask for a new draft to be submitted to it'.

It is the Parliament's President who has the task of declaring that the budget has been adopted once all the procedures have been followed.

The Treaty on European Union made significant changes to the budgetary provisions. Article 268 now stipulates that all items of revenue and expenditure of the Community, including those relating to the European Social Fund, are to be included in estimates to be drawn up for each financial year and shown in the budget. Administrative expenditure occasioned for the institutions by the provisions of the Treaty on European Union relating to common foreign and security policy and to co-operation in the fields of justice and home affairs must be charged to the budget. The operational expenditure occasioned by the implementation of these provisions may, under the conditions referred to therein, be charged to the budget. The revenue and expenditure shown in the budget have to be in balance.

Article 270 provides that, with a view to maintaining budgetary discipline, the Commission must not make any proposal for a Community act, or alter its proposals, or adopt any implementing measure which is likely to have appreciable implications for the budget, without providing the assurance that the proposal or that measure is capable of being financed within the limit of the Community's own resources arising under provisions laid down by the Council pursuant to Article 269.

Committees

According to rule 109 of the Rules of Procedure, the Parliament may set up standing and temporary committees. The powers of standing committees are defined in the rules, while those of temporary committees are defined when they are set up. There are now over 20 standing committees, including Foreign Affairs and Security, Legal Affairs and Citizens' Rights, Budgets, Environment, Public Health and Consumer Protection, Women's Rights and Institutional Affairs. From time to time the Parliament will set up a temporary committee to deal with matters that fall outside the ambit of the permanent committees.

The reports of the committees serve as the basis for most debates in the Parliament. Any member may table a motion for a resolution on a matter within the range of Community activities. That motion will then be referred to the appropriate committee. A similar procedure is followed when the Council asks for an opinion on a matter. A report will then be prepared, and each committee will appoint one of its members to be responsible for a particular report. That person is known as the rapporteur, and he or she will lead the debate when the matter comes before Parliament.

Powers of the Parliament to compel judicial review of the acts of other institutions

The power of the European Parliament to challenge the validity of acts of other Community institutions and Member States was not explicitly stated in the EC Treaty along with those of the Council of Ministers and the European Commission. The European Parliament brought a series of such actions in repeated attempts to have its right to bring them recognised. Its right to bring actions for failure to act under Article 232 was eventually recognised in *European Parliament* v *EC Council (Re Common Transport Policy)* Case 13/83 [1985] ECR 1513 where the Court held that the term 'institutions of the Community' included the European Parliament.

The European Parliament was finally successful in an application for judicial review of a measure adopted under the EC Treaty by the Council in *European Parliament* v *EC Council (Re Students' Rights)* Case C–295/90 [1992] 3 CMLR 281. In this judgment, the contention that the Parliament had standing to bring actions to protect its interests was accepted by the Court so long as two conditions were fulfilled. First, the proceedings must be brought for the explicit purpose of safeguarding the prerogatives of the Parliament. Second, the action must be founded only on submissions alleging infringements of these rights.

Articles 230 and 232 were both replaced by the Treaty on European Union. Article 230 now provides, inter alia, that the Court of Justice shall review the legality of acts adopted jointly by the European Parliament and the Council, of acts of the Council, of the Commission and of the European Central Bank, other than recommendations and opinions, and of acts of the European Parliament intended to produce legal effects vis-à-vis third parties. For this purpose the Court has jurisdiction in actions brought by a Member State, the Council or the Commission on grounds of lack of competence, infringement of an essential procedural requirement, infringement of the Treaty or of any rule of law relating to its application, or misuse of powers. The Court has jurisdiction, under the same conditions, in actions brought by the European Parliament and by the European Central Bank for the purpose of protecting their prerogatives.

In its present form, Article 232 stipulates, inter alia, that should the European Parliament, the Council or the Commission, in infringement of the Treaty, fail to act, the Member States and the other institutions of the Community may bring an action before the Court of Justice to have the infringement established. The Court of Justice has jurisdiction, under the same conditions, in actions or proceedings brought by the European Central Bank in the areas falling within the latter's field of competence and in actions or proceedings brought against the latter.

3.6 The European Court of Justice

Articles 220–248 EC Treaty

Composition

The Court of Justice, which sits in Luxembourg, now has 15 judges who are assisted by eight advocate-generals although, as a transitional compromise until 6 October 2000, an additional advocate-general has been appointed. They are appointed for six years by the Member States, and are eligible for re-appointment. Like the Commissioners, their independence is assured by the EC Treaty provisions.

It is the duty of the advocates-general, 'acting with complete impartiality and independence, to make, in open court, reasoned submissions on cases brought before the Court of Justice'. Their activities are of great importance, especially because their impartial submissions regarding facts as well as legal argument can form a valuable basis for the decision to be taken by the Court in the first and last instance.

The appointment of the judges and the advocates-general is by mutual agreement (Article 222) among the governments of the Member States. They are chosen from 'persons whose independence is beyond doubt and who possess the qualifications required for appointment to the highest judicial offices in their respective countries, or who are jurisconsults of recognised competence': Article 223. Provisions relating to the taking of the oath, privileges and immunities, incompatible secondary functions and deprivation of office are intended to ensure the independence of both judges and advocates-general.

Every three years there is a partial replacement of the judges (eight and seven alternatively) as well as advocates-general (four on each occasion). The judges elect the President of the Court of Justice from among their number for a term of three years, although he or she may be re-elected.

The Court of Justice sits in plenary session, although it may form chambers each consisting of three or five judges, either to undertake certain preparatory inquiries or to adjudicate on particular categories of cases in accordance with rules laid down for these purposes. Nevertheless the Court of Justice sits in plenary session when a Member State or a Community institution that is a party to the proceedings so requests.

Should the Court of Justice so request, the Council may, acting unanimously, increase the number of judges and make necessary adjustments to the second and third paragraphs of Article 221 (sittings) and to the second of Article 223 (partial replacement of judges).

Duties and powers

The Court of Justice ensures the observance of law in the interpretation and application of the treaties and their implementing rules: Articles 31 ECSC, 220 EC Treaty and 136 Euratom. To this end, a number of powers have been conferred on the Court. These are mainly intended to enable the Court to judge the acts and omissions of the institutions and the Member States in accordance with Community law, and to ensure uniformity of interpretation of Community law in its application by municipal courts. The conditions under and the manner in which the Court is required to exercise the powers, which form part of this core of its jurisdiction, will be discussed later.

Jurisdiction and procedure

The task of the Court of Justice is, in general, to ensure that in the interpretation and application of the Community Treaties, and of the rules laid down for their implementation, the law is observed. This implies that the Court has as its duty, on the one hand, to control the legality of the conduct of the institutions as well as the conformity with Community law of that of the Member States and, on the other hand, to safeguard the rights and legitimate interests of all those subject to Community jurisdiction – the Community itself, the Member States, and private individuals.

In order to enable the Court of Justice to carry out its tasks, the Treaties have conferred upon it a precisely delimited jurisdiction. The exercise of that jurisdiction is governed by the simultaneous operation of three fundamental principles – separation of powers, exclusiveness of powers and express conferment of powers – which pervade all its aspects and basically determine the nature and scope of the various forms of actions.

By Article 46 of the TEU the jurisdiction of the European Court covers the interpretation and application of the EC Treaty, the ECSC Treaty and the Euratom Treaty. As a consequence of the coming into force of the Amsterdam Treaty, the Court also has limited jurisdiction to give rulings on the validity and interpretation of decisions, on the interpretation of conventions, and on the validity and interpretation of measures implementing conventions adopted in the area of co-operation in justice and home affairs.

Advisory opinions

Both the Council of Ministers and the European Commission are authorised to submit legal questions to the European Court for advisory opinions. This power has been used most often by the European Commission to limit the competence of the Council to act, or alternatively to reinforce its own constitutional position: see *EC Commission* v *EC Council (Re ERTA)* Case 22/70 [1971] ECR 263.

One of the most significant cases was *Re the Draft Treaty on a European Economic Area (No 1)* Opinion 1/91 [1992] 1 CMLR 245. This case centred around the question of whether a treaty between the European Community and the European Free Trade Association (EFTA) was compatible with European Union law. The agreement in question sought to create a territorial area consisting of the Member States of both organisations in which the four Community freedoms – free movement of goods, persons, services and capital – as well as Community competition law would apply.

The European Court ruled parts of the treaty as being contrary to the EC Treaty. The agreement undermined the rule of law in the Community and in particular the jurisdiction of the European Court to settle disputes arising in connection with the interpretation of the EC Treaty. The concept of 'homogeneity' was developed by the court to explain that the agreement would prevent the application of subsequent European law to the whole territory covered by the treaty.

The treaty establishing the European Economic Area (EEA) was subsequently amended before it was adopted in March 1992. The European Court was again asked for an advisory opinion on the text, which was approved in *Re The Draft Treaty on a European Economic Area (No 2)* Opinion 1/92 [1992] 3 CMLR 217.

Rules of procedure of the European Court

The ordinary procedure before the Court of Justice consists of two main parts, written and oral. Where necessary, preparatory inquiries may take place between the two parts.

Generally speaking, the written stage, which is not open to the public, is by far the more important part of the procedure. It consists of the communication by the Registrar to the parties, and to the institutions whose measures are in dispute, of the various pleadings, such as applications, defences and statements of case, as well as all papers and documents submitted with them.

Within a month of service by the Registrar of the application on the defendant, a defence must be lodged; failure to do so may lead to the Court giving judgment in default. The remaining parts of this written procedure are also subject to strict time limits.

The written procedure ends with the Judge Rapporteur's preliminary report as to whether a preliminary inquiry is necessary. When the Court orders such an inquiry, it may undertake it itself, or may assign it to a chamber which may then exercise the powers vested in the Court. Where the Court decides to open the oral procedure without an inquiry, the President of the Court is required to fix the opening date.

Preparatory inquiries

The purpose of these inquiries is to determine issues of fact where the Court finds this necessary in order to enable it to give judgment. The measures that may be adopted include the personal appearance of the parties, request for information, and production of documents and experts' reports.

Oral procedure

The oral procedure consists of the reading of the reports presented by the Judge Rapporteur and the hearing by the Court of agents, advisers and lawyers and of the opinion of the Advocate-General, as well as the hearing of witnesses and experts. On the whole, the hearing is normally brief as the main arguments of the parties are already set out in the written pleadings.

Upon the conclusion of the oral procedure the Court goes on to the deliberation of the case. These deliberations are secret. The opinion reached by the majority of the judges after final discussion determines the decision of the Court. A single judgment is always given, and no separate or dissenting opinions are published.

The judgment consists of three main parts: a summary of the facts and of the conclusions, submissions and arguments of the parties, the grounds for the decision, and the operative part including the decision as to costs.

Costs

In all contentious proceedings before it, the Court of Justice must adjudicate upon costs even if the parties have made no submissions in this respect. As a matter of practice the judgment or order of the Court merely states who is to bear the costs, without quantifying them. Generally speaking, there are three main rules as to how costs are to be disposed of between the parties:

1. The unsuccessful party is ordered to pay the costs, but only if they have been asked for in the successful party's submissions. Where a successful party has made no formal submissions on this matter, he must bear his own costs. Where neither party has made any submission on costs, each must be ordered to bear his own costs.
2. Where each party succeeds on some and fails on other heads, the Court may apportion the costs.
3. The Court may order even a successful party to pay costs which it considers that party to have unreasonably or vexatiously caused the opposite party to incur.

Interim measures

Under Article 243 of the EC Treaty the Court of Justice may in any cases before it prescribe interim measures. An application for such a measure may only be made by a party in a case before the court. Such a measure will only be granted if a prima facie case is made out for it and it is necessary to avoid serious and irreparable damage: see *NTN Toyo* v *EC Council* Case 121/77R [1977] ECR 1721; and *Ford AG and Ford of Europe* v *EC Commission* Cases 225 and 229/82 [1982] ECR 3091.

3.7 The Court of First Instance

Article 225

The Single European Act added what became Article 225 to the EC Treaty and authorised the Council to enact legislation to create a Court of First Instance. A Court of First Instance was duly established by Council Decision 88/591 (1988) as an integral part of the European Court of Justice and its powers and jurisdiction are derived from those of the original Court. The creation of the new Court did not, therefore, alter the jurisdictional relationship between the European Court system on the one hand and the individual national courts and tribunals of the Member States on the other hand.

Article 225 was replaced when the Treaty on European Union came into effect. Paragraph 1 provides that the Court of First Instance has jurisdiction to hear and determine at first instance certain classes of action or proceedings defined in accordance with the conditions specified in Paragraph 2. These actions or proceedings are subject to a right of appeal to the Court of Justice on point of law only.

The Court of First Instance is composed of 15 judges appointed for terms of six years. These judges are not assisted by advocates-general although they can themselves be called upon to perform the task of advocate-general. The members of the Court themselves are chosen from persons whose independence is beyond doubt and who possess the ability required for appointment to judicial office.

Duties and powers

The original jurisdiction of the Court of First Instance was strictly circumscribed by Council Decision 88/591 (1988). Three classes of action fell, and continue to fall, within the jurisdiction of the Court:

1. Actions or proceedings brought by the staff of the Community institutions against their employers.
2. Actions for annulment and actions for failure to act brought against the Commission by natural or legal persons and concerning the application of Articles 50 and 57–66 of the ECSC Treaty. Such actions relate to decisions issued by the Commission concerning levies, production controls, pricing practices, agreements and concentrations.
3. Actions for annulment or actions for failure to act brought by natural or legal persons against a Community institution and relating to the implementation and execution of Community competition policy.

In addition to these original grounds of jurisdiction, two additional grounds were added in 1993 to allow the CFI to review all actions brought by natural or legal persons under both Articles 230 and 232: Council Decision 93/350 (1993) and Council Decision 94/149 (1994).

Where these actions are accompanied by claims for damages, the Court of First Instance has jurisdiction to hear the related claim.

The Court of First Instance cannot hear cases brought by either Member States or Community institutions. Nor can the Court answer questions submitted by national courts by way of a preliminary reference under Article 234 EC Treaty. Such questions are reserved to the European Court.

Appeal to the European Court of Justice

An unsuccessful plaintiff can appeal a decision of the Court of First Instance (CFI) to the European Court on any one of three grounds:

1. Lack of competence on the part of the Court of First Instance, such as the Court ruling on a matter which exceeded its jurisdiction.
2. A breach of an essential procedural requirement which has an adverse effect on the interests of the appellant.
3. An infringement of Community law by the Court of First Instance, such as an error in the interpretation or application of the principles of Community law.

A substantial number of appeals have now been heard by the European Court of Justice under the appeal procedure, the majority of which concern decisions of the CFI on competition matters: see, for example, *Publishers Association* v *EC Commission* Case C–360/92P [1995] ECR I–23. The Court of Justice, in particular, has assiduously stood by the principle that it will refuse to consider appeals alleging errors of fact as opposed to errors of law: see *Hilti AG v EC Commission (No 2)* Case C–53/92P [1994] 4 CMLR 614.

Appeals must be brought within a period of two months from the publication of the decision of the Court. Articles 49 to 54 of the Statute of the European Court, together with Articles 110 to 123 of the Rules of Procedure of the European Court, have been inserted to regulate the matter of appeal between the two courts.

An appeal does not suspend the decision of the Court of First Instance, unless an order to that effect is made by the Court of Justice. However, a decision by the Court of First Instance annulling a Community regulation does not take effect before the expiry of the two-month period allowed for the lodging of the appeal.

3.8 The Court of Auditors

The Court of Auditors was created by the Financial Provisions Treaty of 1975, and it took over the responsibilities of the EC and Euratom Audit Board and the ECSC Auditor. It audits the accounts of the Community and of Community bodies, examines whether revenue and expenditure have been properly and lawfully received and incurred, checks that financial management has been sound and reports back to the Community institutions.

The provisions of the Treaty on European Union relating to the constitution and work of the Court of Auditors are to be found in Articles 246–248. The Court of Auditors carries out the audit: Article 246. It consists of twelve members who are chosen from among persons who belong or have belonged in their respective countries to external audit bodies or who are especially qualified for this office. Their independence must be beyond doubt. They are appointed for a term of six years by the Council, acting unanimously after consulting the European Parliament, but when the first appointments are made, four members of the Court of Auditors, chosen by lot, are appointed for a term of office of four years only.

The members of the Court of Auditors are eligible for reappointment. They elect the President of the Court of Auditors from among their number for a term of three years, and he or she may be re-elected. The members must, in the general interest of the community, be completely independent in the performance of their duties; they must neither seek nor take instructions from any government or from any other body. They must refrain from any action incompatible with their duties.

A member of the Court of Auditors may be deprived of his office or of his right to a pension or other benefits in its stead only if the Court of Justice, at the request of the Court of Auditors, finds that he no longer fulfils the requisite conditions or meets the obligations arising from his office. The Council, acting by a qualified majority, determines the conditions of employment of the President and the members of the Court of Auditors and in particular their salaries, allowances and pensions. It also, by the same majority, determines any payment to be made instead of remuneration. The provisions of the Protocol on the Privileges and Immunities of the European Communities applicable to the judges of the Court of Justice also applies to the members of the Court of Auditors: Article 247.

The court of Auditors examines the accounts of all revenue and expenditure of the Community; it also examines the accounts of all revenue and expenditure of all bodies set up by the Community in so far as the relevant constituent instrument does not preclude such examination. The Court of Auditors provides the European Parliament and the Council with a statement of assurance as to the reliability of the accounts and the legality and regularity of the underlying transactions. It draws up an annual report after the end of each financial year which is forwarded to the other institutions of the Community and published, together with replies of these institutions to the observations of the Court, in the Official Journal of the European Communities.

The Court of Auditors may also, at any time, submit observations, in the form of special reports, on specific questions and opinions at the request of one of the other institutions of Community. It adopts its annual reports, special reports or opinions by a majority of its members. More generally, it assists the European Parliament and the Council in exercising powers of control over the implementation of the budget: Article 248.

4

Judicial Review in the European Community I: Direct Actions against Member States

4.1 Introduction

4.2 Actions by other Member States

4.3 Actions by European Community institutions

4.4 Actions by individuals against national authorities for breach of Community law

4.1 Introduction

The Member States of the Community are under a duty, imposed by Article 10 of the EC Treaty, to ensure that all appropriate measures are taken at national level to comply with their Community obligations. This obligation requires Member States not only to adopt Community measures into national law but also to eliminate any obstacles which would impair the effectiveness of Community law, particularly where such obstacles would deny the proper exercise of Community rights by private individuals.

To ensure that Member States do not evade this obligation, the EC Treaty creates a structure to allow Member States to be brought before the European Court for alleged infringements of European Community law. The primary means of enforcing Community obligations against Member States is by means of a direct action. All Member States and the European Commission are empowered to bring direct actions against Member States accused of failing to comply with the legal requirements of their Community obligations.

Private individuals have no standing to bring direct actions against Member States. Under the EC Treaty, this right is the exclusive prerogative of other Member States and the European Commission. Therefore, if a private party believes that its rights have been infringed by a national measure which contravenes Community law, it cannot initiate proceedings directly in the European Court. But this omission in the EC Treaty is partially compensated by two factors, one of which is a procedure contained in the EC Treaty itself and the other is the creation of a new right in the recent decisions of the European Court.

First, as we shall see in Chapter 6, individuals may challenge national measures in national courts as being contrary to European law and seek a ruling from the European Court through the preliminary ruling procedure. This process allows the dispute to be brought to the attention of the European Court through indirect means, ie via legal proceedings in a national court. The European Court has frequently declared that national measures brought to its attention through this procedure are incompatible with European law.

The second mechanism is that national courts are now subject to a duty to provide redress to private parties who are successful in establishing injury caused by the failure of national authorities to comply with their Community obligations. Private parties may now claim damages from national authorities, in domestic courts, for breaches of Community law when certain conditions are satisfied. Again this is an indirect procedure which acts as a substitute for the inability of private parties to bring direct actions.

In this chapter, discussion will focus mainly on the rights of other Member States and Community institutions to initiate proceedings against Member States in the European Court. These proceedings are referred to as direct actions, and the only other form of direct actions – proceeding brought at first instance to the attention of the European Court – is against Community institutions.

Consideration will also be given in this chapter to actions by private individuals against national authorities for breach of Community law. While private individuals are denied the right to initiate direct proceedings, their right to seek damages in national courts against Member States is sufficiently analogous to actions against Member States to warrant inclusion in this section.

However, it must be borne in mind that while actions by Member States and Community institutions against Member States are brought in the European Court, actions by private individuals are initiated in the national courts of the Member State alleged to have infringed Community law.

4.2 Actions by other Member States

Article 227 of the EC Treaty allows Member States to bring actions directly before the European Court of Justice if they believe another Member State has failed to meet its obligations under the Treaty. The Court exercises exclusive jurisdiction over all disputes between Member States arising out of the subject-matter of the Community Treaties. Member States are expressly prohibited from resolving these disputes by any other means or in another forum: Article 292 EC Treaty.

Initiating proceedings against another Member State is perceived, in diplomatic terms, as a confrontational course of action, and to mitigate this impact Article 227 contains a number of procedural steps designed to avert such confrontation. The function of these steps is to bring the matter to the attention of the Community authorities, and inside the area of concern of the Community, thereby interposing the interests of the Community between those of the two Member States involved in the dispute.

The steps which must be exhausted before a Member State can bring a dispute to the attention of the Court are as follows:

1. The Member State alleging the violation must bring the dispute to the attention of the European Commission.
2. The Commission is required to deliver a reasoned opinion on the subject-matter of the dispute after allowing the parties an opportunity to submit arguments.
3. Only after the Commission has delivered this opinion, or has failed to do so within the prescribed period of three months from notification of the matter, can the Member State bring the matter to the attention of the Court.
4. If the Commission indicates that it has no intention of pursuing the matter further, the complaining state may initiate proceedings itself.

In the event that these steps are not exhausted, it is extremely unlikely that the Court would be prepared to recognise the standing of a Member State trying to bring a matter to its attention by this route.

In practice, this right has rarely been exercised. In the one completed action to date, France brought proceedings against the United Kingdom for violations of Community law caused by the introduction of conservation measures without proper consultations with the European Commission: *France* v *United Kingdom (Re Fishing Mesh)* Case 141/78 [1979] ECR 2923. The Court found against the United Kingdom and ordered the repeal of the offending measure.

The common reason cited for infrequent recourse to direct actions before the court between Member States is the effect that such actions have on the diplomatic relations between the states involved. On the whole, it is diplomatically preferable to have the Commission institute proceedings on the basis of a complaint from another Member State than for the complaining state to confront the accused state directly in the European Court.

For this reason, actions against Member States are most frequently raised by the Commission, either acting on behalf of Community interests or on the basis of a complaint received from another Member State.

However, this is not to say that such a course of action is never threatened by Member States against each other. In fact, such proceedings are often threatened. For example, in 1990 the United Kingdom threatened to take France to the European Court under the inter-state procedure after the French government threatened to restrict imports of cars manufactured in the United Kingdom by Japanese companies. France claimed that the cars in question failed to satisfy the Community rules of origin and were not therefore Community goods entitled to unrestricted entry into the French market-place.

The French government also alleged that Japanese investment in the UK was in reality an indirect means of circumventing French quotas on the importation of Japanese vehicles. In reply the British government claimed that at least 80 per cent of the cost of the vehicles in question was incurred in the United Kingdom, a proportion which clearly satisfied the rules of origin adopted under the EC Treaty.

Eventually the French government agreed to allow the vehicles into France as Community goods. It is clear that France would have been unable to succeed in its claims had the matter been brought to the attention of the European Court, and this fact, at least in part, accounted for its backdown from confrontation.

A more recent illustration of such a tension has occurred in 1993–1994 when the German government unilaterally threatened to introduce import restrictions on consignments of beef from the United Kingdom on the grounds of the threat posed by so-called mad cow disease (BSE). The British government countered with the prospect of bringing a direct action to the European Court. The European Commission eventually sided with the United Kingdom and informed the German government that if it adopted unilateral measures, without adequate scientific evidence of the dangers posed by BSE, it would bring proceedings in the European Court on behalf of the European Community.

4.3 Actions by European Community institutions

Article 226 reads:

> 'If the Commission considers that a Member State has failed to fulfil an obligation under this treaty, it shall deliver a reasoned opinion on the matter after giving the state concerned the opportunity to submit its observations. If the state concerned does not comply with the opinion within the period laid down by the Commission, the latter may bring the matter before the Court of Justice.'

The duty of the Member States to fulfil obligations arising from or under the treaties is derived both from the general rule of public international law, pacta sunt servanda, and from specific provisions of Community law itself.

The duty to carry out Community obligations falls upon the Member States as such and not upon their various internal organs and agencies since it is the Member States, each taken as a whole, that are the subjects at Community level. It follows that a Member State cannot justify its failure to fulfil its Community obligations by invoking the provisions, procedures and practices of their internal legal or constitutional orders, such as the principle of the separation of powers, unforseeable practical circumstances and difficulties, governmental crises or dissolution of Parliament, or even the slowness of the ordinary legislative process.

An example of the inability of a Member State to attribute failure to implement Community law to lower government agencies or provincial government arose in *EC Commission* v *Belgium (Re Failure to Implement Directives)* Case C–225/86 [1989] 2 CMLR 797. In this case, the Belgian central government was constitutionally unable to compel the compliance of a provincial government with Community measures for the management of waste. An action was brought by the European Commission in the European Court and the decision went against Belgium. Due to these constitutional limitations, the Belgian government could not implement the Court decision and a second case was brought by the Commission, this time for implementation of the original decision.

The Court held that the constitutional inability of a government to implement a decision of the Court in its territory was not a defence to the action. This handicap could not be allowed to absolve the Member State of its responsibilities under Community law.

Preliminary procedure

Before instituting proceedings against a Member State before the European Court, the Commission must comply with the requirements of a compulsory preliminary procedure. Failure to do so will result in the Commission's action being held inadmissible. The procedure has three purposes:

1. To enable the Commission to ascertain the precise nature and extent of the infringement alleged.
2. To provide the Member State concerned with an essential guarantee in respect of its right of defence.
3. To give both parties the opportunity of clarifying in co-operation with one another sometimes complex legal solutions, and thus reaching an amicable solution.

The procedure is as follows:

1. The Commission is required to communicate to the Member State concerned a written statement of complaints clearly specifying, on the one level, the grounds on which the Commission considers that state to have failed to fulfil an obligation under the treaty and, on the other, the obligation broken.
2. At the same time the Commission must invite the state to submit its observations. This constitutes the Member State's guarantee of the right of defence, which need not be taken up by the state concerned, but which is an essential formal requirement. This right has the consequence that where the Commission changes the subject matter of its complaint it must set in motion the preliminary procedure again.
3. Following any dialogue between the Commission and the Member State, and assuming that no solution is found, the Commission delivers a reasoned opinion on the matter, fixing a period of time within which the Member State is required to comply with it. This reasoned opinion sets out the legal and factual grounds on which the Commission considers the Member State at fault, and specifies the measures required to end the infringement.

As a matter of general practice, the Commission takes some care to provide exhaustive reasoning in its opinion. However, the opinion need not, as a matter of law, contain more than a certain minimum of information.

A Member State that is subject to an investigation by the Commission is required to co-operate at every stage in the investigation. In particular, Member States are required to respond promptly to preliminary enquiries dispatched by the Commission and to questionnaires sent in the more formal parts of the investigation, and to respond to the formal pre-litigation reasoned opinion: *EC Commission* v *Greece (Re Electronic Cash Registers)* Case C–137/91 [1992] 3 CMLR 117.

This duty of co-operation stems from Article 10 of the EC Treaty, and failure to co-operate is in itself a breach of Community law even if the investigation, or the proceedings before the Court, reveals the existence of no substantive violation of Community law.

Member States are entitled to limited legal protections when the Commission initiates proceedings under this authority. The Commission must, for example, follow the correct pre-litigation procedure, with due respect for time limits, or the action will be inadmissible. Further, the scope of the application under Article 226 is circumscribed by the pre-litigation notification intimated by the Commission to the Member State. New matters which are not included in the notification cannot be brought into the proceedings by the Commission at the contentious stage of the proceedings: see *EC Commission* v *Denmark (Re Taxation of Imported Motor Vehicles)* Case C–52/90 [1994] 2 CMLR 885.

Enforcement procedure

Action before the Court of Justice

If the Member State concerned does not comply with the reasoned opinion within the period laid down by the Commission the latter may institute proceedings against the state before the Court of Justice. The application made by the Commission to the Court must be based on the same facts, grounds and issues on which the reasoned opinion has been based, and in respect of which the Member State has been given an opportunity to present its observations.

The judicial proceeding is essentially an objective proceeding, the sole purpose of which is to obtain a declaration to the effect that the state has failed to fulfil a certain obligation within a given period of time.

It follows from an objective concept of default that the Court of Justice has to establish its existence without examining the question of culpability on the part of the Member State, and irrespective of any political, economic, social or legal difficulties that the Member State may have had, justified or unjustified, in fulfilling its obligation.

Consequences of successful action

Under the original terms of the EC Treaty, if the Court of Justice finds against a Member State, it does not, strictly speaking, pass a sentence but delivers a purely declaratory judgment which merely notes the fact that a Member State is in default. This judgment had no executory force and neither the European Commission nor the Court was able to impose sanctions to compel the offending Member State to redress its behaviour.

In the past, the Commission was therefore continually compelled to bring proceedings against Member States failing to implement Court decisions for violations of their Community obligations under Article 10 of the EC Treaty which requires Member States to respect their Community obligations.

This position has been radically changed by the amendments made to Article 228 of the EC Treaty by the Treaty on European Union.

After the European Court has ruled against a Member State in a direct action brought by the European Commission, the Commission is empowered to specify a fine for non-compliance if the terms of the judgment are not implemented within a time period specified by the European Commission.

The European Commission has considerable control in the exercise of this power. In particular, it is responsible for: (a) determining that the Member State has failed to comply with the terms of the decision and commencing the second proceedings for the enforcement of the judgment; (b) deciding the time limits within which a Member State should implement a decision; and (c) quantification of the fine which should be imposed by the Court which should be 'appropriate in the circumstances'.

In the event that the European Court confirms the determination of the Commission – which will be in the overwhelming majority of these cases – the Court is authorised to impose either a lump sum fine or a penalty payment.

The Commission has now adopted guidelines on how these fines will be calculated. Three principles will be applied to this determination – the seriousness of the violation, the duration of the infringement and the need to achieve a deterrent effect by preventing the repetition of the violation.

The starting point for calculating a fine is a basic amount of 500 ECU per day which applies for every day beyond the deadline for compliance. This sum is then multiplied by two co-efficients. The first relates to the seriousness of the violation which is evaluated on a scale of between 1 and 20. The Commission has already drawn up rules to establish the seriousness of the violation. The second relates to the duration of the violation. In this context, the Commission will judge the degree of goodwill demonstrated by the recalcitrant States on a scale of between 1 and 3.

As a final stage, this amount will be multiplied by a constant factor designed to express a Member State's ability to pay the fine. This factor is determined by reference to each Member State's gross domestic product and the number of votes which it can cast in the Council of Ministers. These constants very from 1.0 for Luxembourg to 26.4 for Germany. The UK has been given a factor of 17.8 while France and Italy have been given the figures of 21.1 and 17.7 respectively.

4.4 Actions by individuals against national authorities for breach of Community law

The EC Treaty did not envisage the possibility of individuals bringing direct actions against Member States, and there is no express provision to allow such actions to be brought immediately to the attention of the European Court. Similarly, for a considerable time, the English courts have held the view that actions against the United Kingdom government and its agencies in the English courts could only succeed under the traditional heads of tortious injury, such as breach of a statutory duty. Infringements of Community law by the British government and its agencies were widely believed not to give rise to such liability.

The European Court has, however, introduced a concept of liability for violations of Community law by Member States, and it is clearly the policy of the Court to extend this remedy to individuals.

In the landmark case *Francovich* v *Italian Republic* Case C–6/90 [1991] ECR 5357, the European Court upheld the existence of a duty in European law to make reparation for injury caused by a state failing to comply with its obligations.

The facts of this case were essentially that Italy had failed to transpose a directive requiring the setting up of a scheme to compensate individuals in the event of the insolvency of their employers. The directive was intended to provide a minimum level of protection in the event that employers became insolvent and were unable to pay the wages of their employees. The plaintiff was made unemployed and was unable to recover her unpaid wages. She was also unable to claim under the scheme implemented under the directive because Italy had not incorporated the directive into Italian law. In fact, Italy had already been found in violation of Community law for failing to do so in an earlier direct action: *EC Commission* v *Italy (Re Failure to Implement Directives)* [1989] ECR 143.

The plaintiff raised an action in the Italian courts against the government to establish liability for failure to implement the Community directive and causing injury as a result of the omission. The Italian courts referred the question of state liability for failure to comply with Community law to the European Court under the preliminary reference procedure.

The European Court held that Member States were under an obligation to ensure the full effect of Community law and to guarantee the rights of private individuals under Community law. The effectiveness of these rights would be significantly undermined if individuals were denied compensation when their rights had been infringed by the illegal actions of Member States. Therefore, the Court continued, Member States were liable to compensate individuals for any injury sustained for violations of Community law where the breach of duty could be imputed to the behaviour of the Member State.

This liability is not, however, unlimited, and three conditions must be demonstrated before it can be established:

1. The purpose of the Community measure must have been to create rights conferred on private individuals.
2. The content of those rights must be identifiable from the content of the measure.
3. There must exist a causal link between the failure by the Member State to comply with Community law and the injury sustained by the private individual.

The Court left open the exact mechanism in each Member State for the vindication of such rights. Each Member State is responsible for ensuring the existence of a mechanism of compensation but has a certain degree of discretion in selecting the most appropriate method. As a minimum requirement, the Court stated that the substantive and procedural conditions for establishing liability on this basis could not be less favourable than those relating to similar claims under national law. At the same time, the procedure itself should not be organised in such a fashion as to render it excessively difficult, or practically impossible, for these rights to be exercised.

Confirmation whether the first two of the three requirements for establishing the liability of Member States are satisfied may be obtained by a national court through the preliminary reference procedure. By requesting a ruling from the European Court of Justice, a national court can confirm the compatibility of the national measures with Community law. Thereafter, it is for the national court to decide whether, on the basis of the facts presented, a causal connection exists between the violation of Community obligations and the injury sustained by the parties: see, for example, *Paola Faccini Dori* v *Recreb Srl* Case C–91/92 [1994] ECR I–3325.

Many of the outstanding questions not initially elaborated on by the Court in *Francovich* have been addressed in *Brasserie du Pêcheur SA* v *Germany* and *R* v *Secretary of State for Transport, ex parte Factortame and Others* Joined Cases C–46/93 and C–48/93 [1996] 1 CMLR 889, in which the Court set out a number of detailed applicable principles.

The applicant in *Brasserie du Pêcheur* was a French company claiming damages against Germany because the company was forced to discontinue exports, after the German authorities ruled that the product was not in conformity with the German beer purity law (Reinheitsgebot). This law required all beer products to be manufactured using only four ingredients and prohibited the use of additives in the production of beer. These statutory requirements had been declared incompatible with Article 28 of the EC Treaty by the ECJ after proceedings had been initiated by the European Commission (*EC Commission* v *Germany (German Beer Purity Law)* Case 178/84 [1988] ECR 1227).

In *Factortame*, the applicants claimed that the UK government was liable to them in damages because of injury sustained as a result of the application of the Merchant Shipping Act 1988. This statute had tightened the requirements for registering vessels in the UK shipping register mainly to prevent so-called quota-hopping by non-UK EU fishermen. The effect of this statute was to discriminate against non-UK nationals and was therefore contrary to Article 10 of the EC Treaty.

The Court was asked to clarify the conditions under which Member State liability accrued in light of the principles first developed in *Francovich*.

The ECJ first reiterated the basic rule that, in principle, Member States may be liable to private individuals for damage sustained as a result of a serious infringement of a directly effective provision of Community law. The right to reparation was simply the necessary corollary of the denial of these rights. Further, such liability could attach to a Member State as a result of the act or omission of any organ of the state including the legislature.

The Court reiterated the three conditions which must be satisfied to establish liability, but added that the breach of Community obligation must be sufficiently serious. In gauging whether a breach was sufficiently serious, the Court prescribed a set of factors which should be examined. These included: the clarity and precision of the rule allegedly breached; the degree of discretion conferred on national authorities to implement the provision; whether or not the damage inflicted was intentional or involuntary; whether the error of law was excusable; and the position taken by the Community institutions in the matter.

Applying these principles, the Court held that neither breach of Community law was excusable. In the case of Germany, the infringement was clear and unambiguous from the established case-law of the Court. In the case of the UK, the nationality restrictions imposed under the Merchant Shipping Act were manifestly contrary to Community law. In these circumstances, both countries were held liable to the plaintiffs.

The Court held, however, that national courts were responsible for assessing the actual levels of reparation which had to be paid as a result of an infringement of Community law by a Member State. The criteria applied for this assessment must not be less than for similar claims based on domestic law and must not make a successful claim impossible or excessively difficult.

In its judgment, the Court provided greater precision on the application of the basic concept of Member State liability for breaches of Community law. A number of issues did, however, remain outstanding including the degree of clarity and precision of the measure and seriousness of a breach. Further elaboration of some of these points was rendered in the Court's decisions in the *British Telecommunications plc* case and the *R v Ministry of Agriculture, Fisheries and Food, ex parte Hedley Lomas (Ireland) Ltd* case.

R v Ministry of Agriculture, Fisheries and Food, ex parte Hedley Lomas (Ireland) Limited Case C–5/94 [1996] 2 CMLR 391 concerned UK legislation prohibiting the export of live sheep to Spain based on allegations of inhumane treatment by Spanish slaughter-houses. Proceedings were raised for a declaration that the ban was contrary to EC law and that the UK was liable in damages for the injury sustained by the plaintiffs. Since the violation concerned an established principle of Community law, namely Article 29 of the EC Treaty, the breach of law was sufficiently serious as to establish liability. The Court paid particular attention to the fact the breach arose from a situation where the UK was not required to make a decision on the nature of national legislation required to implement its Community obligations. Indeed, the UK appeared to have deliberately legislated on this subject despite the clear terms of its Community obligations.

On the other hand, where there is a degree of ambiguity in the principle of Community law being applied, the Court has been more lenient. For example, in *British Telecommunications plc* Case C–392/93 [1996] ECR I–1631, BT initiated proceedings against the UK government for allegedly failing to properly implement the EC Directive on public procurement in the telecommunications sector. On the point of establishing liability, the Court held that the Directive was capable of more than one interpretation despite the fact that the Court itself favoured an interpretation which differed significantly from that of the United Kingdom. Since the provision was capable of more than one construction, the United Kingdom could not be held to have committed a manifest or sufficiently serious breach of Community law.

5

Judicial Review in the European Community II: Direct Actions against European Community Institutions

5.1 Introduction

5.2 Article 230 actions

5.3 Grounds for review under Article 230

5.4 Procedure for initiating review under Article 230

5.5 Actions for failure to act under Article 232

5.6 Actions for damages under Article 288

5.1 Introduction

To safeguard the rights of both Member States and private individuals, and to protect the rights of Community institutions relative to each other, an extensive system of judicial review for the acts of Community institutions has been created under the EC Treaty. The function of this system is to ensure that the Community institutions behave within their respective competencies as specified in the Treaty.

In order to provide effective remedies against any abuse of competence, relief is provided in the form of direct actions for the review of measures adopted by Community institutions. In other words, a Member State, another Community institution and, in certain circumstances, private individuals can apply directly to the European Court for review of such actions.

This system for judicial review is complex and elaborate, but it may be broken down, for the sake of simplicity, into three separate types of action:

1. Actions for the review of the legality of acts of Community institutions: Article 230 EC Treaty.
2. Actions for failure to act: Article 232 EC Treaty.
3. Actions for damages: Article 288 EC Treaty.

By far the most significant type of action is that for judicial review under Article 230. This provision forms the basis for the vast majority of actions brought against Community institutions. Therefore the greatest part of this chapter will tackle this subject, although consideration will be given later to the other two types of action.

5.2 Article 230 actions

Article 230 states:

'The Court of Justice shall review the legality of acts adopted jointly by the European Parliament and the Council, of acts of the Council, of the Commission and of the European Central Bank, other than recommendations and opinions, and of acts of the European Parliament intended to produce legal effects vis-à-vis third parties.

It shall for this purpose have jurisdiction in actions brought by a Member State, the Council or the Commission on grounds of lack of competence, infringement of an essential procedural requirement, infringement of this Treaty or of any rule of law relating to its application, or misuse of powers.

The Court shall have jurisdiction under the same conditions in actions brought by the European Parliament, by the Court of Auditors and by the European Central Bank for the purpose of protecting their prerogatives.

Any natural or legal person may, under the same conditions, institute proceedings against a decision addressed to that person or against a decision which, although in the form of a regulation or a decision addressed to another person, is of direct and individual concern to the former.

The proceedings provided for in this Article shall be instituted within two months of the publication of the measure, or of its notification to the plaintiff, or, in the absence thereof, of the day on which it came to the knowledge of the latter as the case may be.'

The above provision has two major roles:

1. It provides a judicial means of controlling the legality of the binding acts of the Community institutions.
2. It offers legal protection to those who are subject to the legislative and executive competence of the Community, especially those individuals whose rights and interests may be adversely affected by the illegal conduct of the institutions.

The action therefore displays elements of judicial review of the 'constitutionality' of legislation and judicial review of executive action. The former is achieved by requiring the Court to check the objective conformity of secondary Community law with the treaties in their guise of Community constitutions. The latter is realised by empowering the Court to annul Community measures within the framework of individual fact-related complaints brought by a defined set of plaintiffs. The former allows the Court to act as the guardian of legality, the latter as the defender of private interests deemed worthy of protection.

Scope of the measures that may be reviewed under Article 230

The scope of measures that are subject to review depends, in the first place, on the identity of the party bringing the proceedings. For this purpose, applicants can be classified into two groups:

1. Member States and Community institutions; and
2. Private parties.

Member States and Community institutions

The ambit of Community acts which are actionable is to a certain extent determined by the identity of the person bringing the action. If the applicant is a Member State, the Council or the Commission, the acts which are subject to review are not specified by the article. The Court is, however, given jurisdiction to review the legality of all acts of the Council and Commission other than recommendations and opinions. Two considerations must be borne in mind: first, the act generally complained of must be binding on the applicant, and second, in order to determine whether this is so, the Court will look at the substance of the act, its subject matter, context and legal effect, rather than its form and designation. It seems, therefore, that any measure which is designed to lay down a course of action binding on any of the Community subjects in Member States may be challenged by a Member State; the Member States are presumed to have an interest in the legality of all Community acts.

In *Italy* v *EC Council* Case 166/78 [1979] ECR 2575 it was held that every Member State, regardless of its position at the time of adoption, may challenge a Council regulation – and presumably every other act as well.

According to the original terms of Article 230, Member States, the Council and the Commission are privileged applicants, and their standing to bring actions to challenge such measures is presumed. No reference was made in the original provision to the right of the European Parliament to bring actions against other Community institutions, and in a series of cases the European Parliament was refused standing to do so by the Court of Justice.

The Court subsequently reversed itself on the matter in *European Parliament* v *EC Council (Re Tchernobyl)* Case C–70/88 [1992] 1 CMLR 91. Having regard to the institutional balance within the Community, the Court held that the Parliament was able to proceed under Article 230 if two conditions were satisfied. First, the Parliament must demonstrate 'a specific interest in the proceedings'. Second, the action must seek to safeguard the powers of the Parliament and must be based exclusively on the infringement of those powers; see also *European Parliament* v *EC Council (Re Students' Rights)* Case C–295/90 [1992] 3 CMLR 281. This formula was adopted into the revisions made to Article 230 by the Treaty on European Union.

Private parties

In order to establish standing to bring a direct action to the attention of the

European Court to challenge a Community measure, private individuals must establish the existence of three separate facts:

1. The measure must be 'a decision'.
2. The measure must be of individual concern to the applicant.
3. The measure must be of direct concern to the applicant.

All of these conditions must be satisfied before a private party will have standing to challenge a Community measure under Article 230(4).

A decision. Only decisions of Community institutions may be challenged by private parties under this provision. But the concept of 'decision' in this context is not identical to that contained in Article 249, namely a measure 'binding in its entirety upon those to whom it is addressed'. Rather, the concept has a broader definition. For example, measures that take the form of regulations may be considered decisions, if certain conditions are met, for this purpose. In other words, a measure need not take the strict legal form of a decision to be challengeable under Article 230(4).

Individual concern. The Court first considered the meaning of the phrase 'direct and individual concern' in *Plaumann* v *EC Commission* Case 25/62 [1964] CMLR 29 where the act challenged was a decision addressed to a Member State. The Court decided, for no really apparent reason, to consider 'individual concern' first and held:

> 'Persons other than those to whom a decision is addressed may only claim to be individually concerned if that decision affects them by reason of certain attributes which are peculiar to them by reason of circumstances in which they are differentiated from all other persons and by virtue of these factors distinguishes them individually just as in the case of the person addressed. In the present case the applicant is affected by the disputed decision as an importer of clementines, ie by reason of a commercial activity which may at any time be practised by any person and is not therefore such as to distinguish the applicant in relation to the contested decision as in the case of the addressee.'

The similarities between the criteria used here and those used for distinguishing a decision are obvious, but two features in particular stand out.

First, there is the repeated reference to the importance of showing that the applicant is affected in the same way as the addressee of the decision. Second, there is a clear allusion to the comparison with the objective application of regulations, by reason of a commercial activity which may at any time be practised by any person.

Nothing in later cases suggests that the Court intended anything other than assimilation of the notion of direct and individual concern with the criteria for defining a decision. Indeed, it seemed to regard them as interchangeable, sometimes looking first at the nature of the act, sometimes looking first to the question of 'individual concern'. From cases where the latter approach was adopted, it might well be deduced that the Court necessarily had assimilated the two ideas, for what would have been the point in examining the potentially broader notion first, coming to an affirmative decision on that point, and then rejecting the appeal because the act nevertheless did not amount to a decision because of a narrower definition of individual for that purpose.

Direct concern. The concept of direct concern has a somewhat different meaning and significance according to whether the contested measure is a decision addressed to a Member State, a decision addressed to another natural or legal person, or a decision taken in the form of a regulation. In all cases, however, it is clear that the criterion of 'directness' is not used simply to measure the gravity of the impairment of the applicant's rights or interests. Nor is it intended to refer merely to a casual connection, which may be both direct and indirect, between the challenged act and the rights or interests impaired. Rather, it expressed the fact that the decision produced immediate, automatic and inevitable – not merely possible – disadvantageous legal effects upon the applicant.

Thus the difference between direct and indirect concern is characterised, on the one hand, by the absence or presence of an intermediary with an independent power of decision between the authority taking the measure and the results that follow from it, and on the other hand by the inevitability or mere probability with which those results follow from that measure.

Generally, a decision, irrespective of its form or addressee, will concern the applicant directly if it imposes a disadvantage on, or denies an advantage to, a class of persons of which the applicant is a member, or, conversely, grants an advantage to, or terminates a disadvantage which had been imposed on, the applicants' competitors, if these results follow automatically and necessarily from the decision. Where, however, the results are merely likely to follow, but depend upon the intervention of certain persons or upon the fulfilment of certain conditions, there will be no direct concern.

So, for example, where a number of companies apply for licences to import goods into the European Community, and the Commission then makes a decision on these licences, the companies are directly and individually concerned. The leading cases on this point are now: *L'Etoile Commerciale* v *EC Commission* Cases 89 and 91/86 [1988] 3 CMLR 564, *ARPOSOL* v *EC Council* Case 55/86 [1989] 2 CMLR 508, and *Sociedade Agro-Pecuaria Vincente Nobre Lda* v *EC Council* Case 253/86 [1990] 1 CMLR 105. On the other hand, where the allocation of such licences is at the discretion of national agencies, allocating future quotas to companies not traditionally importing these products, direct concern is more difficult to prove: see *Calpak* v *EC Commission* Case 789/79 [1981] 1 CMLR 26.

It is extremely important to note that, from a procedural perspective, private parties who can demonstrate direct and individual concern in a Community measure, and who decline to initiate direct proceedings against the Community institution on this basis, cannot later challenge the validity of the measure by bringing proceedings in a national court. In such circumstances, the European Court will decline to answer a preliminary reference from the national court because private individuals who have direct rights of action should exercise these rights as opposed to indirect rights exercised by way of proceeding through a national court: *TWD Textilewerke Deggendorf GmbH* v *Germany* Case C–188/92 [1994] ECR I–833.

5.3 Grounds for review under Article 230

In direct actions for annulment the Court has been given jurisdiction to declare acts void only where the alleged defect(s) correspond to one or more of the following four specified grounds of illegality upon which the annulment can be based:

1. Lack of competence.
2. Infringement of an essential procedural requirement.
3. Infringement of the treaties or of any rule of law relating to their application.
4. Misuse of powers.

Broadly speaking, the first and second grounds enable such formal and procedural defects to be invoked as are neither negligible nor so grave as to lead to absolute nullity, while the third ground provides the means for questioning the act's substantive legality. It is, therefore, the most important and most general of all grounds. By contrast, the fourth ground relates not to the act's objective formal or material legality but to the subjective intention of the institution in adopting it.

Lack of competence

Lack of competence as a ground of action gives effect to the general principle that a measure is invalid if it originates from a body which does not possess the requisite powers for its adoption. The Community institutions will act outside their competence whenever they exercise a power which has not been conferred upon them by Community law. This may arise in three different circumstances:

1. Where an institution (Council or Commission) exercises a power not transferred to the Community from the Member States or acts in an area not placed under Community competences.
2. Where an institution exercises a power conferred upon another institution, or upon two institutions jointly and exercised without the other.
3. Where an institution exercises a Community competence in relation to a non-Member State or its subjects in circumstances not authorised by general international law.

Infringement of an essential procedural requirement

This ground of action gives effect to the general requirement that in the preparation, adoption, presentation and communication of their measures public authorities must observe certain basic rules as to form and procedure, infringement of which may have as a consequence, depending upon its nature and degree of seriousness, either that no binding measure will come into existence at all or that the measure will suffer from such a defect as to lead to its absolute nullity, or more usually to its annulment. In order to have an effect on the validity of a measure, the infringement must be of an 'essential' procedural requirement.

What amounts to an 'essential requirement' depends to a large extent both on the nature and purpose of the measure and on the degree of legal protection required by its addressee. Thus more detailed and stricter requirements apply to individual measures affecting the legal position of private persons.

Generally speaking, procedural requirements where infringement usually constitutes a ground for action may be divided into three groups:

Preparation

There are two main types of infringement: the first is the failure to consult the various consultative bodies where consultation is required by a provision of primary or secondary Community law, and the second the failure to give parties whose interests may be perceptibly affected by a measure the opportunity to make their points of view known before the measure is fully adopted: see *SA Roquette Frères* v *EC Council* Case 138/79 [1980] ECR 3333.

A recent illustration of a measure being annulled for reasons of inadequate preparation occurred in *Germany* v *European Commission (Re Construction Products)* Case C–263/95 [1998] 2 CMLR 1235. Council Directive 89/106 sets down procedures for the attestation of the conformity of certain construction products to mandatory technical specifications. This is carried out by a standing committee of representatives of each Member State, acting in conjunction with Commission. Under the terms of the Directive, the Commission submitted proposals for approvals to the Permanent Representation offices of the Member States as well as the committee representatives.

Germany sought the annulment of an approval decision on the grounds that the German version of the draft measure had not been sent to its Permanent Representative nor the German member of the Commission within the time period specified. The Commission had acknowledged the delay in sending the German version but had circulated the English version of the draft decision in time to the German delegation. On this basis, it proceeded to adopt the approval decision, exercising its powers to do so under delegated powers.

The Court held that the failure to send the German version to the German delegation, within the appropriate time limits, constituted an infringement of an essential procedural requirement justifying the annulment of the Commission's approval decision. The English version of the proposed measure could not be considered as an adequate substitute for the German language version. The Commission was bound to strictly adhere to the procedural requirements specified in the Directive granting it delegated powers. See Chapter 16, section 16.2, for further details.

Form

As regards the form of the measure, while insignificant formal irregularities are irrelevant, the giving of no, or insufficient, reasons for the adoption of a measure will always constitute an infringement of an essential procedural requirement, inadequate reasoning being treated for this purpose as equivalent to the total absence of reasoning. Reasons are required by Article 253 of the EC Treaty.

Communication of the measure

Broadly speaking, a statement of reasons is deemed adequate when it sets out, in a concise but clear and relevant manner, all the essential legal and factual considerations upon which the operative part of the measure is based and thus enables both the parties concerned and the Court to discover the principal reasons which have led the institution to the adoption of the measure. General considerations which apply without distinction to other cases, or which are limited to repeating the wording of the treaties, or refer to 'information collected' without specifying it, or which are otherwise vague and inconsistent, are not enough. In other words, the statement of reasons must be such as validly to substantiate the measure. It must enable the Court clearly to recognise the facts and considerations held by the institution to be decisive and to determine whether on the basis of those facts and considerations the measure is well-founded or unfounded in law. In short, it must be capable of being reviewed judicially.

Infringement of the treaties or of any rule of law relating to their application

Undoubtedly this is the most general and the most important of the four grounds of action. The main difference between this third ground and the others is that while the first, second and fourth grounds enable the Court to control the formal validity of Community measures and the subjective intentions of the institutions in taking them, the third ground provides the only legal basis for reviewing the objective and substantive legality of those measures – their material conformity with the rules and principles of Community law.

The broad reference to the treaties and to any rule of law relating to their application virtually encompasses the whole body of written and unwritten Community law. In order to ascertain what are the rules whose infringement constitutes a ground for annulment, one must therefore look into the primary, secondary and tertiary sources of Community law. While there is no problem in identifying the basic Community treaties, certain difficulties might arise in defining the concept of 'rules of law relating to their application'. Broadly speaking, this concept refers to general and abstract rules which are binding upon the institutions, generally arising from the secondary legislation.

Misuse of powers

It follows from both the functional nature of the Community's legal existence and the attributed nature of the institutions' competences that the powers conferred upon the latter are strictly purpose-bound – they can be exercised only for the general and particular purposes for which they have been granted. Misuse of powers occurs if the institutions use their powers for a purpose other than the one for which those powers have been given. In order to establish misuse of powers it is necessary first to uncover the real intentions of the institutions, that is, the subject pursued by them in taking the measure challenged, and, second, to show that this object is different from the one which they ought to have pursued under the treaties.

Misuse of the powers must be distinguished from the other grounds of action, especially from lack of competence and infringement of the treaties. Such a distinction is easy to make if it is borne in mind that misuse of powers can only exist if the following two conditions are cumulatively fulfilled:

1. The institutions must be in possession of the requisite powers to act in the given case.
2. Those powers must be discretionary.

Where the requisite power is missing the institutions cannot 'misuse' it, that is, use it for a wrong purpose; where it is present but can only be used in a certain way strictly specified by the treaties it cannot be misused either, it can only be used illegally or not used at all. The former restriction, where power is missing, constitutes a case of lack of competence; the latter, where the conditions laid down by the treaties are disregarded, one of infringement of the treaties.

By its very nature, it is difficult to prove misuse of powers. On the one hand the institutions enjoy the presumption of innocence, being presumed to have pursued legitimate objectives in their actions unless and until the opposite is proved. On the other hand what needs to be proved is their subjective interests and motives which are not usually recognisable from the act itself; nor are they easily ascertainable by any other usual means, especially by private parties who may not have access to the relevant documents.

5.4 Procedure for initiating review under Article 230

Prescription and limitation for actions

Article 230(5) of the EC Treaty states:

> 'The proceedings provided for in this Article shall be instituted within two months of the

publication of the measure, or of its notification to the plaintiff, or in the absence thereof, on the day on which it came to the knowledge of the latter, as the case may be.'

This is supplemented by Article 81(1) of the Rules of Procedure of the European Court:

'The period of time allowed for commencing proceedings against a measure adopted by an institution shall run from the day following the receipt by the person concerned of notification of the measure or, where the measure is published, from the fifteenth day after publication thereof in the Official Journal of the European Communities.'

No problem is raised in identifying the limitation period for actions for the annulment of regulations. This is because Article 254 of the Treaty renders the publication of regulations obligatory, and it has been held that the publication of a regulation has immediate effect.

Actions for the annulment of decisions and directives are not so straightforward in this respect since these need not be published. All that is required is that they be notified to their addressees. If the act is neither published nor notified to the plaintiff, then there seems no difficulty in holding that time begins to run from the date of the plaintiff's knowledge of the latter.

However, if the decision or directive is either published or notified to the plaintiff or both, problems arise. This is because it is not clear from the test of Article 230(5) whether the criterion of publication applies to these and, if so, whether it takes precedence over the criterion of notification. The problem arose in *Milchwerke Heinz Wöhrmann* v *EC Commission* [1962] ECR 501, an action by certain German companies for the annulment of various decisions addressed to the German government. The decisions had been published several months before the lodging of the action with the Court. In the view of the Advocate-General the interpretation of Article 230(5) was clear: 'If the application is directed against a measure which has been published, the period runs from the publication of the measure.' He thus declared the action inadmissible. The Court merely held that the periods began to run at the latest on the publication of the German measures implementing the EC decision in the *Bundesgesetzblatt*, the German equivalent to the *Official Journal*. In each case this resulted in a declaration that the action was inadmissible. The case is thus inconclusive on this point.

The Court of First Instance considered the effect of procedural irregularities in the notification of decisions, excusable error in delaying to initiate proceedings, and unforeseeable circumstances or *force majeure*: *Bayer AG* v *EC Commission* Case T–12/90 [1993] 4 CMLR 30. In this case, the applicant argued each of these grounds as justifying its delay in initiating proceedings within the time-limits set in Article 230(5).

According to the decision of the Court, a delay can only be justified on the grounds of irregularity of the notification if fault for the irregularity lies with the relevant Community institution.

The second plea, that of excusable error, was also rejected by the Court as being inapplicable unless the applicants could demonstrate to the satisfaction of the Court that they took all steps within their power to avoid any error causing delay.

Finally, the Court considered that, for the concept of *force majeure* to apply, there must exist abnormal difficulties, independent of the will of the persons seeking to rely on the plea and apparently inevitable, even if all due care is taken.

It may be gathered from the above that delay in initiating actions after notification has been dispatched is difficult to justify to the Court, and the Court itself is rigorous regarding the application of this requirement.

Consequences of successful action

Continuity of legislation and administrative action requires that acts of the institutions which are formally in force shall in principle be carried out as long as a judgment of the European Court of Justice has not held them illegal.

If the action is well-founded, the Court of Justice can declare the act concerned to be void, thus reversing the legal position. The annulled act is regarded as if it had never existed in law, and the parties to the dispute must be restricted to their original position.

When a particular provision is severable from the rest of the measure, partial annulment is possible, even to the extent of deleting certain words from the challenged act. In the case of a regulation, if the Court of Justice considers it necessary the EC Treaty authorises it to state which of the effects of the regulation it has declared void.

Where there is partial annulment, the unannulled parts of the act must be regarded as confirmed by the European Court. If the unannulled parts are reproduced in a subsequent measure they have the benefit of res judicata and, if reproduced, cannot be contested by a further action for annulment.

The obligation of the institutions to comply with the Court's judgment does not include an obligation on the part of the Communities to make good any damage that may have been caused by the annulled act. Such damage may be recovered by means of separate action under Articles 235 and 288. Although illegality of a Community act as established by a judgment of annulment may be an important factor in establishing the Community's non-contractual liability, it ensures in itself neither the admissibility nor the success of such an action for damages. The Court cannot order the Commission to adopt a measure to replace the annulled one: *British-American Tobacco (BAT)* v *EC Commission* Cases 142 and 156/84 [1988] 4 CMLR 24.

Although the obligation to give effect to the Court's judgment of annulment is imposed by the treaties only on the institution whose acts has been declared void, the erga omnes effect of such a judgment may require third parties to take appropriate actions. The annulment of a Council regulation may entail for the Commission or the Member States the obligation no longer to apply the measures adopted by them in its implementation, and even to repeal such measures formally in the interests of legal certainty. The same obligation may arise for a Member State in respect of a Community dictate or decision annulled by the European Court which has been implemented by national measures. These implementing measures, having lost their legal foundations, must be regarded as illegal.

5.5 Actions for failure to act under Article 232

Action for failure to act

It would obviously be unsatisfactory if Community institutions were subject to judicial control only in respect of their positive actions while they could evade the obligations imposed upon them by simply failing to act. An action for annulment provides adequate remedy only against the illegal positive conduct of the institutions and is not suitable to compel an institution to act. For this purpose the action for failure to act is available. These two forms of action may, in fact, be envisaged as the two sides of the same coin: they constitute, in a broader sense, the two aspects of the same general remedy, a review by the European Court of the legality of the institution's conduct.

In order to afford effective protection they should, in principle, form a 'watertight' system in the sense that any illegal behaviour of the institutions can be challenged through one procedure or another. Thus an action for a failure to act should in theory be always available where an action for annulment is not: for example, in situations where an institution duly called upon to take action in fulfilment of an obligation fails to adopt, within a prescribed period of time, a formal, even if adverse or unsatisfactory, act, which itself is in turn subject to an action of annulment. The institution's complete silence, or response by an informal act not subject to annulment, should open the way for an action for failure to act.

In practice, however, such a watertight system does not exist under the provisions of the EC Treaty. This is due to the fact that an institution may prevent an action for failure to act by adopting an informal act which is not, at the same time, subject to annulment. This arrangement considerably weakens the legal protection which the action for failure to act ought, by its nature, to afford.

On the other hand, the two procedures are mutually exclusive of each other; the range of application of one ends where that of the other begins. An action for failure to act cannot be made parallel to, or in substitution for, an action for annulment for a purpose for which the latter is the proper remedy – for example, to bring about the annulment of an act which can no longer be challenged in annulment proceedings because the time-limit for the latter has expired. Similarly, an action for failure to act is no longer available where the institution requested to act responds within the proper time-limit by a formal, even though adverse or unsatisfactory, measure. Against this an action for annulment is the only remedy.

Concept of failure to act

Under the EC Treaty, a failure of the Council or Commission to act is subject to judicial review only in so far as it constitutes an infringement of the treaty. Accordingly, failure to act means the omission of an act the application of which is obligatory upon the institution: *Borromeo* v *EC Commission* Case 6/70 [1970] ECR 815. The institution must be under a clear legal obligation to take a certain action so that the failure to take action constitutes a breach of duty. A failure to exercise a mere discretionary power or to take a measure dictated by mere considerations of expediency is not sufficient. This type of negative conduct is not subject to judicial control: *Eridania* v *EC Commission* Case 10/68 [1969] ECR 459. The failure to act must, in other words, be illegal.

In practice, in order for an action to succeed, it is not enough to refer in general terms to a violation of the treaty. The applicant must specify the exact provisions of Community law which require the Council or Commission to take the measure sought. The provisions founded on must impose upon the institutions a particular obligation to take, and at the same time create a corresponding subjective right in the applicant to demand, the requested measure. The general duty of the Commission under Article 211 to ensure that Community law is observed by all those subject to it, individuals as well as Member States, is too general an obligation to serve as a basis for an action for failure to act. It does not confer upon individuals enforceable rights to demand particular measures. Reliance on Article 211 alone will not, therefore, ensure admissibility of action. It is, moreover, doubtful whether interested parties possess an abstract right, enforceable by action for failure to act, to demand prompt and due consideration, as distinct from, or in addition to, the taking of a specified measure, whenever they make a complaint to an institution.

The categories of measures which are the subject matter of the obligation to act and whose omission constitutes an actionable failure to act, differ according to whether the applicant is a Member State or institution, or a private party. The European Court has stated generally that the concept of an act that can be the subject of an action is the same for the purposes of both actions for annulment and actions for failure to act, since both actions are in fact only different aspects of one and the same legal remedy. It is, however, thought that this statement is correct only where the applicant is a private party. In the case of Member States and institutions as applicants, while an action for annulment is not available against non-binding acts such as recommendations and opinions, no such limitation exists for failure to act. The latter is thus open in respect of any act, binding or non-binding, which the Council or Commission has failed to take, provided that the inaction constitutes an infringement of Community law.

Action for failure to act is admissible only if the requirement for an obligatory preliminary procedure has been complied with. Briefly, as a first step, the institution concerned has to be called upon to act. In this respect it is necessary that the prospective applicant should put the institution formally on notice to act. This is achieved only by indicating to it with unequivocal clarity the acts which it is required to take, and by advising it of the applicant's intention to go to court, or at least to use 'all means of appeal', should it refrain from acting. Requests that do not amount to this will not suffice. The institution then has two months within which to act. If within the two months the institution has not defined its position, the action may be brought within a further period of two months.

Definition of position

Definition of position in this context means an express declaration of the view taken by the institution of the subject matter of the request and the merits of the case. For example, the Commission's reply to a request asking it to initiate Article 226 proceedings against a violated law amounts to a definition of position and, if notified within the prescribed time-limit, is sufficient to prevent an action. That is so even if the reply itself is not a binding act and is, therefore, not subject to annulment. It follows that a reply which in the final analysis constitutes a refusal to act in the way requested may amount to a declaration of position and may stop an action.

Nevertheless, an interim reply which merely informs the applicant that his request is being studied, and which does not involve any clarification of attitude on the substantive issues of the request, does not amount to a definition of position. Even an indication to the effect that, in the Commission's view, there is no possibility of bringing an action on the basis of the applicant's request amounts in itself to a mere statement of an opinion and does not constitute a taking of position in response to the request. That is so even if such an indication implies a refusal to act on the part of the institution. An implied refusal does not equal a taking of position; rather it is the typical case for which the action for failure to act is provided.

In contrast, a brief statement to the effect that the Commission is 'not under any obligation to adopt any measure' with respect to the request does, even if not reasoned, constitute, as an express refusal to act, a definition of position. A clear distinction must be made between an express refusal to act and a failure to act, even though implying a refusal to act, ie between an expressed intention – even though negative – and the total lack of any expression of intention. The former does, and the latter does not, constitute a definition of position.

The adoption of an act different from the one sought or deemed necessary by the interested parties, or the adoption of a negative decision, does not fall within the concept of failure to act: *National Carbonising* v *EC Commission* Cases 109 and 114/75 [1977] ECR 381.

Consequences of successful action

An action for failure to act is not an action for annulment – that is, annulment of an implied decision of refusal inferred from the silence of the institutions – but an action for a declaration. The Court is asked to establish, first, the dilatoriness of the institution in defining its position with regard to the applicant's request, and, second, that this constitutes an infringement of Community law. All that the Court can do is examine whether the treaties or secondary legislation impose a clear obligation to take the requested measure and whether, if so, that obligation has been fulfilled. It follows that the applicant cannot request, and the Court cannot order, specific measures to be taken by the Council or the Commission. In fact the indication of such measures in the application is inadmissible, and still less can the Court's judgment itself be regarded as a substitute for such measures. Nevertheless, the applicant will attain practically the same result, since in the case of a successful action the institution whose failure to act has been declared contrary to Community law is required by the treaties to take the necessary measures to comply with the judgment of the Court of Justice.

Since the legal effect of the judgment flows not merely from the operative part but also from the decisive grounds on which it is based, the institution must take the judgment as a whole into account, including any relevant observations made by the Court, in establishing what measures are necessary to comply with it. A mere reading of the judgment will indicate the measures by the adoption of which alone it is possible to terminate the infringement. Should the institution still fail to take the required measures, another action for failure to act is the only remedy. The obligation of the Council and Commission to comply with the Court's judgment is clearly separated from the obligation of the Communities to make good any damage that may have been caused by the institution's inaction. This obligation is governed entirely by the principles laid down by Article 288(2) and forms no part of the institution's duty to execute the court's judgment rendered in the action for failure to act.

5.6 Actions for damages under Article 288

Article 288(2) of the EC Treaty provides:

'In the case of non-contractual liability, the Community shall, in accordance with the general principles common to the laws of the Member States, make good any damages caused by its institutions or by its servants in the performance of their duties.'

It is apparent that, in the course of the normal performance of their tasks, Community institutions may commit certain acts or omissions which cause material damage to those subject to their jurisdiction and to third parties. This is particularly so where such activities take place predominantly in the economic sphere where even a limited measure of improper intervention may have far-reaching harmful effects.

The Treaty has deliberately and carefully separated, both substantially and procedurally, the power of the European Court to review the legality of Community action from the power to establish liability for the consequences of such action. Consequently, the action for damages should be seen as a distinct and independent form of judicial recourse.

General conditions for liability

The EC Treaty does not determine in precise terms the general conditions for, and the limits of, the Community's non-contractual liability which forms the legal basis for an action for damages. Article 288 refers, generally, to the non-contractual liability of the Communities which is to be determined 'in accordance with the general principles common to the laws of the Member States'.

This reference is to the various national laws concerning administrative (governmental) liability rather than to general (civil law) liability. It is clear that by referrring to the broad concept of common general principles the treaties deliberately left it to the European Court to work out, by a combination of comparative and creative activity, the general conditions for the non-contractual liability of the Community.

Broadly speaking, four conditions must be satisfied before the Community's' liability for damages may be established. These are as follows:

1. There must exist an injury.
2. There must be causal connection between the injury alleged and the conduct with which the institutions are charged.
3. The conduct of the institutions must be illegal.
4. The conduct of the institutions must be culpable (wrongful).

Nature, proof and assessment of injury

Broadly speaking, in order to establish the liability of the Community, there must exist a damage which is certain and specific, proved, and quantifiable.

The damage must have crystallised by the time that the claim for compensation is made and must be clearly specified by the applicant: *Lesieur v EC Commission* Cases 67–85/75 [1976] ECR 391. Not only must the damage be certain but it must also be specific, affecting the applicant's interests in a special and individual way. The normal disadvantages inevitably following from a financial arrangement or scheme set up for the benefit of all Community undertakings operating in a particular sector, or for the benefit of the public at large and affecting all commercial operators by virtue of general and objective criteria, cannot constitute an 'injury' giving a right to compensation. Otherwise it would be possible for individual undertakings virtually to cancel the effects of the scheme by claiming as damages the amount whereby they are disadvantaged by its operation.

Generally the onus to prove an injury allegedly suffered lies with the injured party. He must provide conclusive evidence as to the existence and exact amount of the damage, to enable the Court to make the necessary assessment and award appropriate compensation.

Causal connection

The existence of an injury cannot in itself establish the liability of the Community. It is also necessary that the injury should have been caused by the conduct of

Community institutions or servants. The causal connection between the wrongful act or omission and the damage alleged must be direct, immediate and exhaustive. It must be proved by the applicant, and in the absence of such proof the action will be dismissed as unfounded.

Illegality of institutions' conduct
The non-contractual liability of the Community covers damages caused by their institutions or servants 'in the performance of their duties'. The institutions perform their duties basically in two different ways:

1. By carrying out ordinary official activity necessary for the putting into operation or supervision of legal measures.
2. By enacting legal measures in the exercise of their quasi-sovereign powers.

These different methods of performance give rise to two different types of liability. As far as the first method is concerned, the claim for compensation will be founded upon the restricted concept of official fault involving negligent or defective administration, bad organisation or lack of supervision. In such situations the question of liability can be, and usually is, disengaged from that of legality and is examined separately.

The position is more complex where the damage alleged has occurred as a direct result of a binding Community measure or a failure to take such a measure. In such a case the question of liability is usually dependent upon, and therefore inseparably linked to, that of the legality of the measure or default.

Under the EC Treaty there is in principle nothing to prevent the question of the illegality of an act or a measure on which an action is based from being raised within the framework of such an action or, alternatively, in an action for annulment brought simultaneously.

Culpability of institutions' conduct
Generally, the system of Community liability created by the treaties is based on the concept of subjective, not objective, liability. This means that, in addition to the objective illegality of the injurious act or omission, the subjective criteria of culpability on the part of the institutions in committing it must also be shown to exist. The illegal act or omission must constitute an official fault, a wrongful conduct, on the part of its author. It is precisely the factor of culpability that endows the illegal act or omission with an element of default. Were it otherwise, the circumstances in which liability can be invoked and those in which illegality may be alleged would become indistinguishable. As a result, an action for damages could be brought on exactly the same grounds as an action for annulment or for failure to act, despite their very different legal consequences and despite the very different limitations imposed on the right of private parties to institute each actions.

A culpable conduct may consist of, for example:

1. the enactment of an improper Community measure;
2. the incorrect application of an otherwise lawful provision, in a situation or in a way in which this is justified because the requisite conditions have not been fulfilled;
3. inadequate supervision of the execution of Community provisions by the Member State or other institutions set up for that purpose:.

To these general propositions must be added the qualification that, if the damage complained of results from legislative measures which involve choices of economic policy, then the institution concerned will only be liable if there is a serious enough breach of a superior rule of law for the protection of the individual: *Zuckerfabrik Schöppenstedt* v *EC Council* Case 5/71 [1971] ECR 975.

Time

Proceedings are time-bound five years after the occurrence giving rise to the action, but the applicant must become aware of the occurrence before time starts to run: *Adams* v *EC Commission* Case 145/83 [1985] ECR 3539.

6

Preliminary Ruling Jurisdiction of the European Court of Justice

6.1 Introduction

6.2 Jurisdiction of the European Court

6.3 Interpretation of Community law

6.4 Optional references

6.5 Compulsory references

6.6 The form and procedure for a reference

6.7 Legal effects of preliminary rulings

6.1 Introduction

Article 234 of the EC Treaty sets out the Court's jurisdiction to give preliminary rulings. This jurisdiction fulfils two different but equally important functions:

Legal integration

Legal integration within the Community is directly relevant to the attainment of the fundamental Community objectives. Since this latter process is to take place within a strictly defined legal framework, it can only be successful if accompanied or preceded by a corresponding legal integration.

'Legal integration' has two aspects:

1. That Community law should be uniformly applied.
2. That it should be uniformly interpreted throughout the Member States (a necessary precondition).

To ensure this, the treaties have placed the interpretation of Community law and the determination of the validity of the acts of institutions within the exclusive jurisdiction of the Court of Justice. At the same time they empower and, in the case of courts and tribunals of last resort, require national courts to invoke that jurisdiction wherever this becomes necessary in the cause of the application of Community law by them.

Although primarily it aims to avoid divergences in the interpretation of that law, it also tends to ensure uniformity and effectiveness in its application by providing the national courts with a means of eliminating any obstacles that might undermine such differences within the legal systems of Member States.

The procedure for preliminary rulings, although designed to channel to the European Court any dispute concerning the interpretation and validity of Community law that may arise in the national courts, does not superimpose the European Court upon the national courts. The system implies a spirit of collaboration between the two courts, requiring joint efforts to ensure the uniform interpretation and effective application of Community law.

In exercising its preliminary ruling jurisdiction the European Court is strictly limited to the interpretation of Community law and to the determination of the validity of the acts of institutions, while leaving the application of that law to the national courts.

The task of the European Court is thus restricted to assisting the national courts, within the framework of questions put to it, in resolving a particular dispute.

Legal protection to individuals

The second function of preliminary rulings is that of affording additional legal protection to individuals by complementing and completing the system of remedies made available to them in the form of direct actions.

For this purpose they can be used both in situations where no other remedies exist at all, and in situations where other remedies do exist but fail to afford adequate protection. The former is the case where redress is sought against a Member State violating the Community rights of individuals by adverse national measures or practices. The latter arises where the complaint is directed against a Community institution but the bringing of an action is excluded for one reason or another.

The importance of preliminary rulings may be shown by the fact that, for various reasons, by far the majority of cases come before the Court of Justice on references from the national courts. In addition, the Court has formulated some of the most fundamental concepts and principles of Community law in the framework of the preliminary ruling procedure, such as, for example, the doctrines of the direct applicability and the supremacy of Community law.

6.2 Jurisdiction of the European Court

Under Article 234 the Court of Justice has jurisdiction to give preliminary rulings concerning three distinct areas:

1. The interpretation of the Treaties and the acts of the institutions.
2. The determination of the validity of the acts of the institutions.
3. The interpretation of the statutes of bodies established by acts of the Council.

These provisions place a double limitation upon the jurisdiction of the Court of Justice:

1. The Court of Justice may only consider the interpretation and validity of Community law, not domestic or general international law.
2. The Court is concerned with an abstract 'interpretation' and 'determination of the validity' of Community law. It is not concerned in the 'application' of the law to particular facts, cases and situations. That task is the sole province of the national courts. Thus questions are posed and answered in the abstract. However, since the abstract interpretation of Community law always takes place in the context of concrete cases which are the subject of litigation, the distinction between interpretation and application is a particularly delicate one.

Subject to the above, the jurisdiction of the Court is dependent solely upon the existence of a valid request for a preliminary ruling from a national court or tribunal. The Court of Justice has no jurisdiction to determine whether the request for a ruling is necessary to enable the national court to give judgment – that is solely a matter for the national courts.

The European Court also has jurisdiction to decide whether the requirements of the preliminary reference itself satisfy the terms of Article 234 of the EC Treaty. In particular, the Court has had to deal with the following questions:

1. Whether a body in national law is a 'court or tribunal for the purposes of Article 234': see *Pretore Di Salo* v *Persons Unknown* Case 14/86 [1989] 1 CMLR 71.
2. Whether a reference is premature or may have the effect of precluding a later reference from the same court in the same case.
3. If the question asked is too vague, or general, or involves questions of national law.
4. If a preliminary ruling was competent in the event that a higher court had already ruled on the matter: see *Society for the Protection of Unborn Children (Ireland)* v *Grogan* Case C–159/90 [1991] 3 CMLR 849.

In general, the Court has demonstrated a great deal of flexibility in these matters and has been willing to accept references from even the lowest tribunals or quasi-tribunals. Similarly, when a question referred to it is too vague or general, the Court at least until recently reworded the reference.

Also, when a national court has asked questions involving the interpretation of national law, the Court has skilfully elicited the issues of Community law from the reference and answered these without ruling on the issue of national law.

6.3 Interpretation of Community law

Limitation of Community law

'Community law' in this context embraces the following:

1. The 'basic' Community treaties – in other words, the EC, Euratom, Merger, Budgetary and Accession Treaties, all as amended by the Single European Act and the Treaty on European Union.
2. Those treaties concluded between the Member States which have been expressly brought within the Court's jurisdiction such as, for example, the Convention of the Mutual Recognition of Companies and Legal Persons of 1968, interpretation of which is entrusted to the Court of Justice by means of separate protocol.
3. The interpretation of treaties and agreements which the Communities have concluded with third states and international organisations.
4. The interpretation of all acts of the Community institutions, regardless of whether or not they have binding force and are directly applicable in the technical sense of the term. It thus embraces not only regulations, directives, decisions, recommendations and opinions of the Council and Commission but also the judgment and orders, as well as the rules of procedure, of the Court of Justice, and joint acts of the Council and the representatives of the government of the Member States.

Limitation to interpretation

The limitation of the Court's role to interpretation in principle prevents it from taking cognisance of, conducting investigations into or settling disputes between the parties concerning the assessment of the facts involved. Similarly, the Court has no authority to find that a concrete factual situation meets the conditions laid down in a Community provision and that therefore certain legal effects follow. The only course allowed to the Court is to define the scope of the letter and spirit of Community provisions while remaining at the level of generalisation.

The Court has, in addition, no jurisdiction to apply the law to a particular person, case or situation, to rule on the merits of the main action or on any disputed issue, or to act as a supreme court to reconcile conflicting decisions given by the courts of the different Member States. Nor can it decide upon the compatibility of a national law or administrative practice with Community law, nor upon how the former should be brought into conformity with the latter. In other words, it cannot settle conflicts between the two legal systems. This would amount to the application of Community law to a particular case, which the Court is entitled to do only in a direct action brought against the Member State whose law is in question. It is therefore always a matter for the national court in the main action to apply to the particular case before it the rules of Community law as interpreted by the European

Court, and to reach a decision on the question of compatibility in the light of the interpretation laid down in the Court's ruling.

Generally, though, the Court is reluctant to decline jurisdiction. Where, for example, a question as formulated by the national court is not limited to the pure interpretation of Community law but contains elements involving the application of that law, or the interpretation, application or compatibility of national law, the Court is prepared to extract from its wording that core which alone pertains to the interpretation of Community provisions and to give a ruling on it only.

Finally, although the European Court is not in principle permitted to go outside the scope of the questions referred to it by the national court, it is not rigidly bound by the terms of reference. In the interest of an exhaustive and proper clarification of the matter it may depart from the order of questions, may give supplementary interpretations, and may have regard to all provisions which are relevant to the issues raised provided that it does not enter the area of the application of national law.

6.4 Optional references

The procedure to obtain a preliminary ruling can be set in motion only by a court or tribunal of a Member State. Generally, the power of the court is optional, except in the case of courts or tribunals against whose decisions there is no judicial remedy under national law, where it is compulsory.

In practice, when a reference is made to it the European Court, in order to ascertain if it is properly seized of the question, must first satisfy itself as to whether the body submitting the request is a 'court or tribunal' of a Member State. The body should:

1. Represent the power of the state, being properly and permanently set up under national law.
2. Exercise a judicial function, settling disputes according to rules of law.
3. Follow an adversarial procedure similar to those used in ordinary courts of law, one which ensures its independence and impartiality as well as the proper hearing of the parties.

Thus specialised bodies on the periphery of the ordinary judicial structure may also be entitled to submit preliminary questions. In the UK, the reference procedure is open, in addition to the ordinary civil and criminal courts, to administrative tribunals such as that of the National Insurance Commissioner or the Employment Appeal Tribunal.

The power to refer is largely unfettered. The national courts may freely decide whether to refer or not, what legal issues and at what stage of the proceedings to refer. Their decision and the reasons for it are not subject to review by the European Court. The only prerequisites for an exercise of that discretion are:

1. that a question involving interpretation or consideration of the validity of provisions of Community law should be raised before them; and
2. that they should consider a preliminary ruling on that question to be necessary to enable them to give judgment.

Such a question is raised as soon as plausible arguments are put foward which raise prima facie a reasonable doubt upon the meaning, scope, effect or validity of a Community provision or upon the compatibility with it of a national measure or practice.

A preliminary ruling on such a question becomes necessary where a court assesses on the one hand that the clarification of the question is essential to the determination of the issue before it and, on the other hand, that it itself would be unable to perform that without the help of a ruling: *Bulmer* v *Bollinger SA* [1974] 2 CMLR 91.

Although Article 234 gives the national courts discretion to refer a question to the European Court it is obvious that the cause of legal uniformity across the Community is helped by allowing the European Court the opportunity to decide on the interpretation and validity of Community law rather than such matters being considered in ten separate national legal institutions.

6.5 Compulsory references

If a question concerning the interpretation or the validity of Community provisions is raised in a case pending before a court or tribunal of a Member State against whose decisions there is no judicial remedy under national law, that court or tribunal is obliged to bring the matter before the Court of Justice.

The object of this rule is to prevent a body of national case law not in accord with the rules of Community law from coming into existence in any Member State. It follows that the compulsory reference should not be limited to particular courts, such as the House of Lords, or to a class of court which stands at the summit of the judicial hierarchy. The obligation to refer should apply to any court, whether of first, second or last instance, whose ruling on an issue of Community law in a particular case is not subject to ordinary appeal for any reason whatever, and whose decision is final in the sense that it does not give rise to any review of the case on the request of either of the parties as regards either the facts or the law.

In *Hoffman-La Roche* v *Centrafarm* Case 107/76 [1977] ECR 957 the European Court considered the question of whether the highest appeal court in the case or the highest court in the country should be the court 'against whose decision there is no judicial remedy under national law'. The case concerned interlocutory judgments which were later not to be final, but in so finding the Advocate-General argued for the highest court in the case:

'It seems to me therefore that, in order that the court may fully and effectively discharge its task of uniformly protecting the rights which the Community legal system has created in favour of individuals, it is reasonable to regard the courts, at every level, as under a duty to seek a preliminary ruling in the course of any proceedings which must of necessity result in a final decision.'

Initially, some decisions in the UK courts appeared to follow a different line: that the only courts from which a reference is compulsory are those from which there is no appeal – the highest court in the land. In England a party who wants to appeal to the House of Lords must obtain leave to proceed there. That leave can be refused. What then is the position of the Court of Appeal? It may be the last instance and it may not.

The discretion of the Court of Appeal is, in fact, not complete; it should take account of the possibility that appeal to the House of Lords might be impossible and should, therefore, in principle, make the reference itself. However, as long as it grants leave to make an appeal to the House of Lords, the Court of Appeal is legally not a court against whose decision there is no judicial remedy and, therefore, there is no strict legal obligation to refer. The House of Lords is obviously under an obligation to refer questions concerning the validity or interpretation of Community law to the ECJ, subject to principles established by the European Court in *CILFIT Srl* v *Minister of Health* Case 283/81 [1982] ECR 3415; see also *SA Magnivision NV* v *General Optical Council* [1987] 2 CMLR 887. Equally, if the Queen's Bench Divisional Court refuses to certify a point of law for consideration by the House of Lords then it is a final court.

In *CILFIT* v *Minister of Health*, the European Court laid down guidelines on when a court of final instance need not refer a question of interpretation to the European Court for a preliminary reference. Such a court does not have to refer a matter if the question has already been decided by the European Court. This discretion applies only 'where previous decisions of the [European] Court have already dealt with the point of law in question, irrespective of the nature of the proceedings which led to those decisions even though the questions at issue are not strictly identical'.

At the same time, the Court also established a number of guidelines to ensure that a national court cannot abuse the doctrine of acte clair as elaborated in the *CILFIT* decision. The doctrine of acte clair is simply the principle that a court need not to make a reference if the point of Community law is capable of clear interpretation and application. Where a court decides not to refer a question due to an earlier precedent, special consideration must be given by that court to the 'characteristic features' of Community law and the particular difficulties which are encountered in its interpretation and application. Special considerations require a court to bear in mind the following factors:

1. European legislation is drafted in several different languages all of which are equally authentic and proper interpretation often involves comparison of texts with different language versions.

2. Community law has acquired its own terminology and legal concepts do not necessarily have the same meaning in Community law as in national law.
3. Every provision of Community law has to be placed in its proper context and interpreted in light of the system established by the Treaties having regard to both its objectives and to the state of the law at that particular point: see *Litster* v *Forth Dry Dock and Engineering Co* [1989] 1 All ER 1134.

The House of Lords has adopted these principles in numerous case, for example in *R* v *Secretary of State for Employment, ex parte Equal Opportunities Commission* [1994] 2 WLR 409. When dealing with whether or not a reference to the European Court was necessary in the particular circumstances of this case, Lord Keith of Kinkel stated that the applicable principles of Community law were clear from existing ECJ rulings and that the court was entitled to apply these established principles without assistance from the European Court.

As a related matter, in practice there are other circumstances in which a reference to the European Court by a national court under Article 234 is essential if a satisfactory resolution of a question of Community law is to be obtained. The European Court has exclusive authority to declare an act of a Community institution invalid, and such jurisdiction cannot be exercised by national courts and tribunals. Consequently, if a question concerning the validity of a Community measure is raised before a national court or tribunal, that matter must be referred to the European Court for consideration. The Court addressed this matter in *Firma Foto-Frost* v *Hauptzollamt Lübeck-Ost* Case 314/85 [1988] 3 CMLR 57, by pointing out that, although Article 234 allowed national courts against whose decision there was a judicial remedy to refer a question to the European Court, it did not address the issue of whether these courts could declare acts of Community institutions invalid.

The Court then went on to declare that national courts were incapable of declaring acts of Community institutions void. Article 234 was designed to facilitate the uniform application of Community law, and this requirement is most acute when the validity of a Community act is in question. Divergences between courts in the Member States as to the validity of Community measures would place in jeopardy the unity of the Community legal order and detract from the fundamental requirement of legal certainty. This conclusion was supported by the system of judicial protection established by the treaty which allowed challenges to Community measures under a separate provision, Article 230. Therefore, in these circumstances, a reference to the European Court must be made. The Court has subsequently reaffirmed that national courts have no power to declare an act of a Community institution void without the intervention of the Court under the preliminary reference procedure: see *Angelopharm GmbH* v *Freie und Hansestadt Hamburg* Case C–212/91 [1994] ECR I–171.

6.6 The form and procedure for a reference

To enable the European Court to arrive at a useful interpretation, the referring court is generally expected to indicate the factual and legal context which has given rise to the request for reference and into which the interpretation is to be placed. The European Court of Justice is not concerned with adjudication of the facts, nor is it concerned with academic exercises. For example, in *Meilicke* v *ADV/ORGA FA Meyer AG* Case 83/91 [1992] ECR 4871, the Court rejected a reference from a German court concerning a dispute that had not yet arisen between the parties but had been the subject of proceedings in the national court to resolve a hypothetical and abstract point of law. Further it must be satisfied there is a real dispute between the parties: *Foglia* v *Novello* Case 104/79 [1980] ECR 745.

In more recent cases, the European Court has adopted a much more rigorous approach than before in deciding whether or not to accept a reference from a national court. The Court has become increasingly intolerant of lax references probably due to its increased case load. So, for example, where the facts specified by a national court in a preliminary reference are inadequately stated, the European Court may find that there is an inadequate factual basis for a useful interpretation of Community law: *Pretore Di Genoa* v *Banchero* Case C–157/92 [1993] ECR 1085

As regards the form of reference, neither the treaties nor the statutes and rules of procedure of the Court of Justice lay down, expressly or by implication, any particular requirements. Some guidelines have been supplied by the European Court in *Pretore Di Salo* v *Persons Unknown* Case 14/86 [1989] CMLR 71:

1. Ideally the facts of a case should be settled before the Article 234 reference so that the Court could then take into account the facts and the law which were relevant to the reference.
2. A national court was in the best position to decide at what stage in the proceedings a reference was necessary, so this should not restrict the discretion of the national courts.
3. A second reference may be made under Article 234 in respect of the same case.

In the United Kingdom special rules have been laid down concerning the form in which and the procedure according to which references are made. The main common features of the rules applicable to the English courts are as follows:

1. An order referring a question to the European Court may be made by the court of its own motion or on the application of either party.
2. An order must set out in a schedule the request for the preliminary ruling of the European Court. The court may give directions as to the manner and form in which the schedule is to be prepared.
3. The proceedings in which an order is made will normally be stayed until the European Court has given its ruling.
4. A copy of the order is to be sent to the Register of the European Court always

through the Senior Master of the Supreme Court (Queen's Bench Division) no matter which court has made the order.

6.7 Legal effects of preliminary rulings

The judgments of the European Court given in reference proceedings are in principle subject to the normal operation of the res judicata rule. Accordingly, a preliminary ruling is binding on the national court which has requested it – including all lower and higher courts that may be called upon to adjudicate in the same case – but, strictly speaking, only to the particular case and in respect of the parties to that case (inter partes). Thus the court before which the main action is pending is required to defer to the ruling as regards the points of law in which the European Court has given its decision.

Nevertheless, it follows from the nature and the purpose of the preliminary ruling system, and from the special relationship between the European Court and the national court on which it is based, that the latter remains free to draw from the Court's ruling the relevant legal conclusions necessary for a definitive settlement of the case. It remains free even to the extent of not drawing any conclusions at all, for example if it discovers afterwards that the consultation was not necessary and that it can give a decision on other grounds. Also, the national court remains free to assess whether it is sufficiently enlightened by the ruling of the Court, or whether certain doubts still remain which necessitate the re-submission of the same or further questions.

Generally, there is nothing to prevent a court, if it so desires, from making a new reference even though the issues involved have already formed the subject of a preliminary ruling in the very same proceedings or in a similar earlier case. In such situations the European Court must give a new judgment, but if the question is identical with that already settled, and no new factor is presented, the Court will refer the national court to the previous judgment.

Again in recent time the European Court has attempted to cut back on its workload by rendering judgments in similar or related cases by issuing one principal judgment and cross-referring to that judgment in subsequent decisions. For example, in *Rochdale Borough Council* v *Anders* Case C–306/88 [1993] 1 All ER 520, the Court declined to issue a fresh judgment in the case, which was virtually identical in terms of both fact and law to an immediately preceding case. Even though the UK court had informed the European Court in the reference that at least one point remained unsettled, the European Court considered that all four points had been adequately settled. In the circumstances, the Court cited its earlier judgment and declined to issue a full report.

Although in theory the effect of the preliminary ruling is strictly inter partes, in practice it may have an erga omnes effect. For example, an interpretative ruling which defines the meaning, scope and effect of a Community rule is, in practice, authoritative even beyond the individual case which has given rise to it.

When the preliminary ruling deals with the direct applicability of a Community provision, once established the rule cannot change and a ruling must necessarily have a definitive effect. On the other hand, where the Court is concerned with the validity of an act the legal consequences may be strictly inter partes. As a rule, the Court does not examine and confirm the validity of an act in general, but strictly in relation to the specific arguments and complaints raised in the order for reference as amplified by the submission of the parties.

If the Court confirms the validity of the act then the effect is inter partes. If the court declares an act invalid, although the ruling does not make the act in question null and void this is usually the practical consequence. A measure which is invalid with respect to one person must be regarded as invalid with respect to all. It is inconceivable that such an act could ever be enforced, either by the Community institutions or by the national authorities, in any future situation.

7

Sources of Community Law and Principles of Interpretation

7.1 Introduction

The Community Treaties themselves nowhere define what the sources of Community law are to be. Unlike the statute of the International Court of Justice, which enumerates the sources of international law which that court is called upon to apply, the Treaties give instruction to the European Court of Justice in very broad terms only, requiring it to ensure that in the interpretation and application of the Treaties 'the law' is observed: Article 220 EC Treaty.

The sources of European Community law and, in a broader context, the law of the European Union, may be classified into three broad categories, namely primary, secondary and tertiary sources.

There are two primary sources of European law:

1. The Treaties creating the European Union; and
2. Treaties entered into by the European Community with third states.

91

The European Community Treaties, as amended from time to time and especially by the Treaty on European Union, form the constitution of the organisation and are the ultimate source of legal authority. They sit at the top of the hierarchy of legal norms. International agreements entered into by the European Community with third states, if directly enforceable, form a second category of rules that may be classified as a primary source mainly because such rules prevail over secondary and tertiary sources.

Article 249 of the EC Treaty identifies the secondary sources of Community law which consist of the acts of the Community institutions. These are collectively known as secondary legislation and consist of the following:

1. regulations;
2. directives; and
3. decisions.

As a residual category, there are a number of tertiary sources, the legal authority for which lies not in the Community Treaties but mainly in the jurisprudence of the European Court. These sources fill any legal vacuum created by any omission in the Treaties. The following are the most significant tertiary sources:

1. Acts adopted by the representatives of the governments of the Member States meeting in Council;
2. The case law of the European Court of Justice;
3. National laws of the Member States;
4. General principles of law; and
5. Principles of public international law.

At this stage, it is also useful to consider an ancillary subject, namely the interpretation of Community law. This subject concerns the manner in which these sources and principles are applied by the European Court and the courts of the Member States in decisions involving questions of Community law. Therefore, after consideration of the sources of Community law, discussion of the principles of interpretation will follow.

7.2 The Treaties establishing the European Community

These Treaties are those establishing the Community, as supplemented or amended by other treaties and acts, including the Treaties of Accession and now the Treaty on European Union, together with the Treaty of Amsterdam and its protocols. In the United Kingdom these various agreements are included in the concept of 'European Community Treaties' under the European Communities Act 1972, and a special procedure is laid down for the participation of the United Kingdom therein. Within the framework of Community law, the Treaties – ECSC, EC, Euratom, the Treaty on European Union and the Amsterdam Treaty – are 'self-executing' in that they become law on ratification by the Member States. Generally there is no derogation from the obligations imposed by them, unless grounds for derogation are provided. There is little ground for stating that derogation will be allowed by reference to the principles of international law.

The Treaties define the territorial scope of their application (see, eg, Article 299), but interestingly they have been held to have extra-territorial effect. In *Re Wood Pulp Cartel* Case 89/85 [1988] 4 CMLR 901, the Court upheld fines imposed on suppliers of wood pulp whose registered offices were in Canada, Sweden, Finland and the USA. The basis of this decision was the so-called 'effects principle' of international law which allows states to extend the jurisdiction of their courts to acts which have effects within their territory when implemented. In this case, the fixing of the international prices of wood pulp on the world market was the anti-competitive practice being attacked.

7.3 Treaties entered into by the European Community with other states

Each of the three principal European Community Treaties authorises the European Community to enter into international agreements with third states, or groups of states, as well as with certain types of international organisations. The nature and contents of the agreements must fall within the scope of the competence of the European Community, and commonly take the form of free trade agreements and association agreements.

Since association agreements are a preliminary step towards membership of the European Community, these treaties often contained detailed arrangements and rights even for individuals. Similarly, a number of free trade agreements contain provisions concerning the customs treatment of goods flowing between the parties. When the terms of such agreements are sufficiently precise, the agreements themselves may be capable of providing a source of directly applicable principles of Community law: see *Demirel v Stadt Schwäbisch GmbH* Case 12/86 [1989] 1 CMLR 421.

In order to constitute a formal source of Community law, capable of being enforced in the European Court or in national courts, the provisions being relied on must be capable of direct effect. The case *Hauptzollamt Mainz* v *Kupferberg* Case 104/81 [1982] ECR 3641 provides an illustration of the application of the principle of direct effect to treaties entered into by the European Community with other states. A German importer was charged duties on imports of Portuguese port which were later reduced by the German Finance Court which applied Article 21 of a trade agreement between Portugal and the European Community. This agreement prohibited, on a reciprocal basis, discriminatory internal taxation between imported and domestic products. The German tax authorities appealed against this decision, and a preliminary reference was made to the European Court for a ruling.

The Court held that the terms of the agreement could be given direct effect if the following conditions were satisfied:

1. The provision being relied on was sufficiently precise and unconditional;
2. The provision was capable of conferring individual rights; and
3. National courts or tribunals could enforce the obligation created.

There has been a series of cases developing each of these requirements: see *Polydor* v *Harlequin Record Shops* Case 270/80 [1982] 2 ECR 329; *Pabst and Richarz KG* v *Hauptzollamt Oldenburg* Case 17/81 [1982] 4 ECR 1331; and *Fediol* v *EC Commission* Case 70/87 [1991] 2 CMLR 489.

These requirements were also discussed by the European Court in *SZ Sevince* v *Staatssecretaris van Justitie* Case 239/90 [1992] 2 CMLR 57. This case concerned the legal effects of a series of decisions made by a Council of Association established under the Turkish-EC Association Agreement and Additional Protocol. The applicant relied on a number of provisions of these decisions to challenge an order of a Dutch court deporting him. This order, it was claimed, was contrary to the right of free movement of persons contained in the relevant provisions of the Council decisions.

The Court held that a provision in an agreement concluded by the European Community with a non-Member country must be regarded as being directly applicable when, regard being had to its wording and to the purpose and nature of the agreement itself, the provision contains a clear and precise obligation. This obligation could not, however, be subject, in its implementation or effect, to the adoption of any subsequent measures. In other words, the same criteria that apply to the direct effect of treaties apply to a determination as to whether a decision of an organisation to which the European Community is a party has direct effect.

7.4 Secondary legislation

The expression 'secondary legislation' is a collective term comprising all the acts of the two 'law-making' bodies, the Council and the Commission, which these two institutions can adopt under the terms of the treaties in their capacity as European Community institutions, and which create enforceable rights and obligations for European Community subjects.

The 'secondary' nature of this legislation implies that it is derived from, limited by and hierarchically subordinate to the primary sources. This means, in general, that a secondary Community law, whatever its title or nature, cannot legally have the aim and the effect of amending, repealing or altering the scope of a primary treaty provision. It also means, in particular, that the law-making power of the two institutions is subject to two important limitations, non-observance of which entails the invalidity or illegality of the resulting act and renders it liable to annulment by the European Court.

The institutions may act only in order to carry out their tasks in accordance with the provisions of the Treaties and within the limits of their respective powers as conferred upon them by the Treaties. These limitations reflect the reluctant transfer of sovereignty from the Member States to the European Community institutions.

Regulations

In substance regulations are of a truly legislative nature, creating rights and obligations directly and uniformly applicable throughout the whole European Community both to the Member States and to individuals within the Member States. They enter into force on the date specified within them.

By the express provisions of the Treaties, regulations have the following four characteristic features: they are of general application; they are binding in their entirety; they are directly applicable; and they are applicable in all Member States.

General applicability

It follows from the essentially legislative nature of a regulation that it is applicable not to an individual case or situation, nor to a limited number of defined or identifiable persons, but to objectively determined situations, and involves immediate legal consequences in all the Member States for categories of persons defined in a general and abstract manner.

Binding in their entirety

This is what distinguishes a regulation from a directive, which is binding upon the Member State to which it is addressed only as to the result to be achieved while leaving to the national authorities the choice of form and method. By contrast, Member States must give effect to a regulation in its entirety.

Direct applicability

This concept is considered in greater depth later. Briefly, it has three aspects in relation to regulations:

1. Regulations are incorporated automatically into the law of each Member State, and the legal force of the regulation lies in the measure itself, independently of any implementing legislation: *Bussone* v *Ministry of Agriculture* [1978] ECR 2429.
2. Generally speaking regulations are automatically implemented, although Community regulations occasionally require Member States to enact supplementary national legislation, eg, to provide penalties or sanctions for failure to respect the terms of the regulation: *Anklagemyndigheden* v *Hansen and Son* Case C–326/88 [1990] ECR 2911.
3. Regulations may create individual rights and obligations, enforceable in the national courts.

Applicability in all Member States

Community law requires the simultaneous and uniform application of regulations in all Member States. Consequently, Member States are prohibited from adopting any method of implementation that may jeopardise such application and that would result in a different or discriminatory treatment of European Community citizens according to national criteria.

In addition to these four particular characteristics, it follows from the fundamental principle of the supremacy of the European Community legal system as a whole that directly applicable provisions of regulations must enjoy the same priority over the national laws of the Member States as directly applicable provisions of the Treaty itself enjoy. Article 253 indicates that regulations, as well as directives and decisions, must be reasoned and refer to any proposals or opinions which were required to be obtained, and failure to comply with this requirement may lead to an annulment action under Article 230.

Directives

The EC Treaty places two different courses of action at the institutions' disposal to enable them to carry out the European Community's tasks. One is for them to lay down, in direct implementation of the Community Treaties, uniform common rules directly applicable throughout the European Community. For this the legislative means is the regulation.

The second is for them to call upon the Member States to exercise their own legislative powers, either for the purpose of adapting their laws to common standards laid down by the institutions, mainly in areas where the diversity of national laws could adversely affect the establishment or functioning of the Common Market, or for the purpose of carrying out the obligations arising from the Treaties. For this, the legislative form is the directive which accordingly provides an indirect means for the implementation of the Treaties.

While a regulation is applicable to Member States and individuals alike, a directive is primarily intended to create legal relationships between the European Community and the Member State to which it is addressed. It is binding upon such States, but only as to the result to be achieved, while leaving to the national authorities the choice of form and method. Directives must be notified to those to whom they are addressed and take effect upon notification: Article 191(3).

Generally directives provide no directly enforceable rights for individuals, but, as will be seen, individuals may acquire rights under the directive if the Member State fails to implement the directive within the time limit.

Other measures

Decisions

Decisions represent the most versatile and least readily definable form of secondary legislation. The term 'decision' may describe a legally binding measure taken in a specified form and having specific legal effects, as well as a non-binding informal act laying down a programme, a declaration of intention or guidelines which, in order to generate legal effects, must be implemented by further legislative measures. Its most striking feature is that it is binding only upon those to whom it is addressed. A decision therefore is characterised by the limited number of persons, identified or identifiable, to whom it is applicable.

Recommendations and opinions

Recommendations and opinions differ from regulations, directives and decisions in that, on the one hand, they have no binding force and, on the other, they may be issued by the Council and Commission on any matter dealt with in the Community Treaties at any time when the institutions consider it necessary and not only upon an express authorisation granted in specific cases. Although not binding in law, recommendations and opinions carry considerable political and moral weight.

7.5 Acts adopted by the representatives of the governments of the Member States meeting in Council

The Council of the European Communities exercises two different kinds of function. Primarily, it is a European Community institution set up under the Community Treaties and endowed with specific powers and competencies.

It is also the setting in which the representatives of the governments of the Member States concentrate their activities and decide on principles and methods of joint action. When it is acting in its first function, as an organ of the European Community, its measures fall within the concept of secondary legislation.

When meeting as the representatives of the governments of the Member States the Council cannot pass Community measures, as the authority does not arise from the 'basic' Treaties. Instead, the acts are usually referred to as 'decisions and agreements adopted by the representatives of the governments of the Member States meeting in Council'.

The legal nature of these acts is ambiguous, falling within both Community law – and forming a source of it – and international law. Their nature as international agreements between sovereign states – albeit dealing with Community-related subject matter – generally prevents these acts from being subject to the European Court's judicial review.

However, in *Luxembourg* v *European Parliament* Case 230/81 [1983] CMLR 726, where Luxembourg challenged the Parliament's decision to establish its seat in

Strasbourg and Brussels, the Court attributed to decisions of the representatives of the Member States the same legislative effect as a decision of the Council as a Community institution has.

The advantage of this form of decision-making is that it provides a quick and simple way for the Member States to take action in areas outside European Community competencies. At the same time it has the disadvantage of enabling the Council to take action in disregard of the conditions and procedures laid down by the Treaties in situations where in reality it might have acted as a European Community institution, and this might upset the institutional balance within the European Community.

7.6 The case law of the European Court of Justice

Technically speaking, unlike the position in the common law countries, in the Continental civil law systems the doctrine of the binding force of precedents does not apply. Since the European Court is modelled upon the Continental courts, it is generally not bound by its own previous decisions: contrast *European Parliament* v *EC Council (Re Common Transport Policy)* Case 13/83 [1985] ECR 1513 with *European Parliament* v *EC Council (Re Tchernobyl)* Case C–70/88 [1992] 1 CMLR 91. The context of the binding force of the Court's judgment is governed instead by the principle concerning res judicata.

However, it may be expected that wherever the Court has given a leading judgment it will be unlikely to depart from it in subsequent cases without strong reasons, even though it retains the right to do so. Certainly the case law of the European Court reveals a remarkable consistency of adjudication on both substantive and procedural issues: see *Procureur de la République* v *Chiron* Cases 271–274/84 [1988] 1 CMLR 735.

Wherever the Court interprets a provision, clarifies a concept or defines a rule, its judgment inescapably has an effect going beyond the individual case.

The Court has often ventured into a form of law-making, eg, by recognising the European Community's treaty-making power in the field of transport, or by extending the concept of a prohibited abuse of a dominant position to mergers and acquisitions.

7.7 National laws of the Member States

The division between national and Community powers and competencies inevitably prevents the national laws of the Member States from forming a formal source of Community law. Nevertheless there are two specific situations where the Court does apply, or at least calls upon, rules and concepts of municipal law.

The first is where Community law expressly or by implication refers to the laws of the Member States. This is normally the case where the nationality, personal status or legal capacity of individuals, or the status, legal capacity or representation of legal persons or of entities without legal personality, is in question. The question whether the condition is fulfilled is decided by the application of the relevant municipal law.

The second is where Community law has developed in the legal systems of the Member States, and here the European Court turns for guidance to the laws of those states, particularly where there is a gap in Community law.

7.8 General principles of law

Except for the single case of non-contractual liability (Article 288), the European Court is not directed by any explicit Treaty provision to apply the 'general principles of law' in deciding disputes submitted to it.

However, it is generally recognised that 'the law' which the Court is directed to apply includes the general principles of law of the legal systems of the Member States which the Court will incorporate into the common law of the European Community. A number of such general principles of law have been recognised.

Protection of fundamental human rights

In *Stauder* v *City of Ulm* Case 29/69 [1970] CMLR 112 an Article 234 reference was made by a German court which was hearing a claim that a European Community measure involved an infringement of fundamental human rights. The European Court gave an interpretation which was consistent with the principles of Community law and the protection of fundamental human rights, an implicit acknowledgement which was followed by the explicit formulation in *Internationale Handelsgesellschaft GmbH* v *EVGF* Case 11/70 [1970] CMLR 255.

In this case in the course of judgment it was stated that 'respect for fundamental human rights forms an integral part of general principles of law protected by the Court of Justice. The protection of such rights, while inspired by the constitutional traditions common to the Member States, must be ensured within the framework of the structure and objectives of the [the European Community].' To the 'constitutional traditions', 'international treaties for the protection of human rights' were added as guidelines which should be followed: *Nold* v *EC Commission* Case 4/73 [1974] 2 CMLR 338. This was obviously a reference to the European Convention for the Protection of Human Rights and Fundamental Freedoms to which all Member States are parties: see *R* v *Kirk* Case 63/83 [1985] CMLR 522 for an example of the application of the ECHR (Article 7).

The matter has been adjudicated by a competent court and may not be perused further [handwritten annotation]

Taking effect from a date in the past [handwritten annotation, left margin]

Legal certainty

In *Da Costa en Schaake* v *Nederlandse Belastingadministratie* Cases 28–30/62 [1963] CMLR 224, Advocate-General Lagrange stated: 'The rule that res judicata binds only the particular case is the weapon which permits the Court to do this [alter its view of the law]. Of course they should only use this weapon prudently, on pain of destroying legal certainty' – so establishing legal certainty as one of the general principles of Community law. The principle was invoked by the court in *Defrenne* v *Sabena* Case 43/75 [1976] 2 CMLR 98 as a major ground for refusing to allow retrospective direct effect to Article 141.

The principle would appear to embody the concept of respect for legitimate expectations and the principle that European Community measures may not have retroactive effect: *EC Council* v *European Parliament* Case 34/86 [1986] 3 CMLR 94, and *R* v *Kirk* (above). It must be noted, however, that where the purpose to be achieved demands it, and where the legitimate expectations of concerned parties are respected, a measure may be held to be retroactive: *Amylum* v *EC Council* Case 108/81 [1982] ECR 3107.

Proportionality

This principle involves the notion that administrative measures must be proportionate to the aim to be achieved. It was first mooted in the *Internationale Handelsgesellschaft* case and taken further in *Balkan Imp-Exp GmbH* v *Hauptzollampt Berlin-Packhof* Case 5/73 [1973] ECR 1091.

The principle has been applied also in other than purely economic areas. In *Lynne Watson and Alessandro Belmann* Case 118/75 [1976] ECR 1185 it was found that the suggested deportation of Watson from Italy by the authorities was a measure disproportionate to the crime committed, which was failure to comply with administrative requirements. The conclusion of the Court was also an illustration of the jealousy with which the Court regards basic rights given by the Treaty, here the right of free movement of workers under Article 39.

Protection of legitimate expectations

In *Mulder* v *Minister of Agriculture and Fisheries* Case 120/86 [1989] 2 CMLR 1, the European Court held that a farmer who had entered into an undertaking not to supply milk for five years to the market organisation which distributes milk throughout the European Community was entitled to resume production upon the expiry of this commitment and that the European legislation which deprived the farmer of this right was void on the ground that it impinged upon the principle of legitimate expectation.

Equality

Equality was acknowledged in *Ferrario* Case 152/81 [1983] ECR 2357 as one of the basic principles of Community law. Its application may be seen most frequently in cases involving discrimination on grounds of nationality and gender.

Legal professional privilege

In *AM & S Europe Ltd* v *EC Commission* Case 155/79 [1982] ECR 1575 it was acknowledged that the principle whereby written communications between lawyer and client are privileged would be upheld in Community law. The principle is, however, confined to communications between an independent lawyer and his or her client and does not extend to in-house lawyers or lawyers from non-Member States.

7.9 Public international law

The extent to which public international law may be regarded as a source of Community law is determined by the dual nature of the European Community as, on the one hand, entities established by treaties under international law and, on the other hand, autonomous bodies with quasi-sovereign powers creating their own autonomous legal order which is distinct from both international and national law.

This first aspect implies that, to the extent to which the European Community possess legal personality under international law, they are in principle subject to the rules of that law. It is international law that governs their external relations, whether treaty or other relations with third countries and international organisations, for in the exercise of their external powers, such as treaty-making power, and of their internal powers with an external effect, the European Community must conform with public international law. So it forms part of the 'law', the observance of which it is the task of the European Court to ensure.

7.10 Principles of interpretation

The obvious need for judicial interpretation of legal texts has developed certain rules and methods of interpretation in all national, international and supranational courts. The difference is in accentuating one or other of these methods, depending on the nature of the text to be interpreted and on the legal system in which the interpretation is to take place.

The general pattern of interpretation followed by the European Court is to examine in turn the wording, general scheme and spirit of the provision in question as well as its position in the system of the European Community Treaties and the function of the provision in the light of the Treaty's objectives.

Where the provision is an act of secondary legislation it is examined in the light of the spirit, system and objectives of both the act itself and the relevant Treaty provisions under which the act was adopted.

Generally, where upon examination of its wording the Court finds that a provision is absolutely clear and unequivocal, no further interpretation is necessary. The text may then be applied as it stands. Where, however, literal interpretation fails to give a definite answer or leads to a conclusion which runs counter to common sense, to the basic principles of Community law or to its rational application, the court looks beyond the text to equity, the 'spirit of the law', and, to a lesser extent, to the real or presumed intention of the legislator.

Perhaps most importantly, a provision is interpreted according to its position in the system of the Treaty (systematic interpretation) and in the light of its own, as well as the Treaty's, purposes and objects (teleological interpretation). In the practice of the European Court these two methods appear as two sides of the same coin and are therefore usually employed simultaneously. They represent a dominant, and without doubt the most characteristic, feature of the court's own particular way of interpretation.

In practice, the use made by the Court of Justice of the various methods of interpretation discussed above is subordinate to the operation of three fundamental principles of overriding importance. These principles are designed to ensure that the specifically supranational nature of the Community's legal system is duly taken into account, and given effect to, in the interpretation of its individual provisions. These are the principles of uniformity, effectiveness, and protection of individual rights.

The principle of uniformity

The requirement of uniform interpretation and application of Community law throughout the Member States is essential to the autonomous and supranational character of Community law.

It follows that undefined terms appearing in European Community texts which are also used in the national laws of the Member States (eg 'worker', 'public policy') must be presumed to have an independent Community meaning which must prevail over any different or conflicting meaning attributed to them in other legal systems. They must therefore be interpreted according to independent Community criteria, by reference, in the first place, to the scheme, object and purpose of the Community text in which they occur and, in the second place, to the general principles of Community law.

The principle of uniformity further requires that Community texts of general application, for example regulations or directives and decisions addressed to the Member States, should be interpreted in the light of their versions in the official languages of the Community. All these versions being equally binding, no single one of them can be regarded as the solely authentic text. In cases of divergences between the various translations, an attempt must be made to derive a meaning common to them all from the scheme, object and purpose of the provision. In the absence of such a meaning, preference must be given to the interpretation that is least onerous for European Community subjects, provided that it suffices to achieve the purpose covered by the text. This is on the assumption that the legislator did not intend to impose stricter obligations or confer less rights in some of the Member States than in others.

The principle of effectiveness

This principle has the effect that, where there are various alternatives, preference must be given to an interpretation that tends to prevent the effectiveness or validity of basic European Community rules from being undermined.

Therefore, the various exceptions and obligations allowed by the Treaties in such fundamental provisions as, eg, those relating to the free movement of workers must be interpreted and applied restrictively.

Also, since in principle integration under the EC Treaty is of a comprehensive character, and is not to take place separately according to economic sectors, particular provisions relating to individual sectors must be interpreted narrowly by reason of their exceptional nature.

Finally, the principle of effectiveness enables such implied powers to be attributed to the European Community institutions as are necessary for a proper and effective implementation of the provisions of the treaties.

The principle of the protection of individual rights

This principle applies to the interpretation of both substantive and procedural provisions of European Community law.

In the context of substantive law, it applies so that where a provision is silent or obscure it must be given a meaning that is the least unfavourable to individuals, affording them the widest possible freedom of action that is still compatible with European Community interests in general and with the purpose of that provision in particular.

Similarly, with regard to procedural requirements, the provisions of the European Community Treaties enabling individuals to bring actions in the European Court in defence or enforcement of their substantive European rights should not be interpreted restrictively to the detriment of the person concerned. This obviously does not then result in an interpretation which would disregard the clear limitations placed by the European Community Treaties on the system that they have created for the legal protection of individuals.

Principles of interpretation and national courts

It is not only the European Court that is bound to apply the teleological approach to the interpretation of Community legislation. National courts are also required to adopt this method of construction. Within the United Kingdom this raises considerable problems for courts that have for some considerable time employed the literal approach to the interpretation of statutes.

The United Kingdom courts are obliged to apply a teleological approach not only to the interpretation of treaty Articles but also to regulations and directives. Difficulties arise when a European Community directive is enacted into United Kingdom law by an instrument that has the appearance of a normal statute or order in council. In *Litster* v *Forth Dry Dock and Engineering Co* [1989] 2 WLR 634, the House of Lords upheld an appeal, on a point of construction of a statutory instrument giving effect to a directive, on the ground that the lower courts had erroneously interpreted the instrument in a literal fashion instead of adopting the proper teleological approach.

8

Fundamental Principles of European Community Law

8.1 Introduction

8.2 Direct applicability and direct effect

8.3 The primacy of European Community law

8.4 Equal pay

8.5 Prohibition of discrimination on the grounds of nationality and other factors

8.6 The principle of subsidiarity

8.1 Introduction

European Community law operates on the basis of a number of principles which can accurately be described as fundamental to the operation of the Community legal system itself. These principles have played an orchestrating role in the evolution of Community law and lie at the heart of the present system.

The five fundamental principles are:

1. The principles of direct applicability and direct effect, which can be considered together.
2. The principle of the supremacy of Community law over national law.
3. The principle of equal pay.
4. The principle prohibiting discrimination on the grounds of nationality.
5. The principle of subsidiarity.

Two of these principles – those of direct applicability/direct effect and the supremacy of Community law – were not originally stated in the EC Treaty and have been developed in the jurisprudence of the European Court. The third and fourth are specifically stated in the Treaty, but even these have been extensively developed both by the Court and in secondary legislation.

The final principle, that of subsidiarity, was inserted as Article 5 of the EC Treaty by the Treaty on European Union and supplemented by a Protocol added by the Treaty of Amsterdam.

8.2 Direct applicability and direct effect

General

Direct applicability is the quality which enables a provision of Community law to become a part of the national law of a Member State without the necessity of legislation – it is incorporated directly in the corpus of national law: see Article 249 EC Treaty and its reference to the direct applicability of regulations

Direct effect means that a provision of Community law can be interpreted by the Court as being able to create rights which any natural or legal person may enforce against the state and sometimes against other persons. The right once established must be protected by the national courts: see *Van Gend en Loos* v *Netherlands* Case 26/62 [1963] CMLR 105; [1963] ECR 1.

Although the Court uses the terms interchangeably, it is proposed in the following discussion to adhere to the definitions above. The two qualities will be discussed in relation to the various types of European Community law.

The application of the principles to types of European Community law

Treaty Articles

No provision of the EC Treaty expressly authorises the use of individual Treaty provisions as a reservoir of legal principles which can be relied on for the creation of individual rights, but from the very formation of the European Community the European Court has sought to achieve this objective. In *Van Gend en Loos* v *Netherlands* (above) the Court held that where a provision of the Community Treaties imposes a clear and unconditional obligation on a Member State, unqualified by any reservation reserving the right of legislative intervention, such a provision may be capable of direct effect. This process establishes private rights for individuals which are enforceable in municipal courts.

Three specific conditions are therefore required for a provision of a European Community Treaty to have direct effect:

1. The provision being relied on must be clear and precise: see *Gimenez Zaera* v *Instituto Nacional de la Seguridad Social* Case 187/85 [1987] ECR 3697.
2. The term must be unqualified and not subject to the intervention of the state authorities for its operation: see *Sociaal Fonds voor de Diamantarbeiders* v *Brachfeld & Chougol Diamond Co* Cases 2 and 3/69 [1969] ECR 211.
3. The obligation must not confer a discretion on either a Member State or a Community institution to act: see *Salgoil SpA* v *Italian Ministry for Foreign Trade* Case 33/68 [1968] ECR 453.

The principle of direct effect has also been expressly acknowledged in a number of cases concerning the UK courts: see *R* v *Goldstein* [1983] 1 WLR 151; [1983] 1 All ER 434 and *Garden Cottage Foods Ltd* v *Milk Marketing Board* [1984] AC 130.

The principle applies most frequently in the relationship between private individuals and national authorities. Thus it can act as a means of establishing a defence to an action or as a ground for an action: see *Brown* v *Secretary of State for Scotland* Case 197/86 [1988] ECR 3205. This is known as the quality of vertical direct effect and operates in the relationship between a private individual and the national authorities.

Some provisions, because of their nature, have been recognised by the Court as having a wider effect in that they can be invoked against other individuals: this is known as a horizontal effect in that they impose obligations on other individuals.

The Treaty provisions regarding the competition rules applicable to undertakings, for example, can clearly be invoked before the national courts by one undertaking against another: see *Nissan France* v *Garage Sport Auto* Case C–309/94 [1996] ECR I–677.

Similarly, Article 141 EC Treaty, which provides that 'each Member State shall ensure and subsequently maintain the application of the principle that men and women should receive equal pay for equal work', has been held to apply 'not only to the action of public authorities, but also ... to all agreements which are intended to regulate paid labour collectively as well as contracts between individuals': *Defrenne* v *Sabena* Case 43/75 [1976] 2 CMLR 98; [1976] ECR 455, a case which provided the court with an opportunity to widen its view on direct application.

This horizontal effect giving rights to individuals inter se, which the Court has accorded to some treaty provisions, gives a new scope to 'direct effect' as it has been generally understood since *Van Gend en Loos*.

It is clear that, although the Court makes up for failures on the part of the institutions and the states by giving direct effect to provisions when the period within which they should have been implemented has expired, it sets limits to this procedure by refusing to accord this effect to provisions which it considers too general and indeterminate in scope for any clear rules to be inferred.

A limitation on the principle of allowing retroactive application of direct effect is that the Court has refused to adopt a policy decision giving direct effect to a Treaty provision. Thus, in *Defrenne*, the Court held that the direct effect of Article 141 applied only from the date on which the judgment was rendered, except as regards those litigants who had already instituted legal proceedings; see also *Barber* v *Guardian Royal Exchange Assurance Group* Case C–262/88 [1990] 2 CMLR 513.

In *Blaizot et al* v *University of Liège* Case 24/86 [1989] 1 CMLR 57, the European Court outlined its policy towards the non-retroactive application of treaty Articles. This case involved the payment of university fees which the Belgian government refused to allow in the case of a French national studying in a Belgian university. The student challenged this decision on the basis of the prohibition on discrimination on the grounds of nationality contained in Article 12 of the EC Treaty.

The Court held that the non-payment of the fees of European Community nationals was contrary to Article 12, but as regards the retroactive payment of fees to other Community nationals by the Belgian government, it observed:

'... in determining whether or not to limit the temporal effects of a judgment it is necessary to bear in mind that, although the practical consequences of any judicial decision must be weighed carefully, the Court cannot go so far as to diminish the objectivity of the law and compromise its future application on the grounds of the possible repercussions which might result, as regards the past, from a judicial decision'.

In the circumstances of the case, the Court precluded any re-opening of past investigations into this matter, thereby effectively preventing the retroactive application of the principle.

Regulations

Article 249(2) of the EC Treaty reads as follows: 'A regulation shall have general application. It shall be binding in its entirety and directly applicable in all Member States.' A regulation is capable of both horizontal and vertical effect, which means that regulations can impose obligations on individuals as well as the state. Observe the formula from the case of *Politi* v *Italian Ministry of Finance* Case 43/71 [1971] ECR 1039. In dealing with Article 249(2) the Court recognised that: 'By reason of their nature and their function in the system of the sources of European Community law, regulations have direct effect and are, as such, capable of creating individual rights which national courts must protect.'

A note of warning must be sounded here, as direct applicability does not necessarily mean directly effective, for it was pointed out by Advocate-General Roemer in the case of *Leonesio* v *Italian Ministry of Agriculture and Forestry* Case 93/71 [1972] ECR 287 that the exact legal effect of a provision will depend on whether an implementation discretion was left to national authorities and to what extent the provision had to be completed by national provisions.

On occasion, Community regulations confer on Member States discretion as to the method of implementation and sometimes even a choice of obligations. Similarly, often regulations which require penal sanctions do not specify a particular penalty and this is left to individual Member States. In such cases, national legislation is enacted to support the regulation with the necessary measures.

Where Member States are required to implement national legislation to supplement a regulation, they are obliged to implement the regulation unless otherwise instructed. Thus, in *EC Commission* v *United Kingdom (Re Tachographs)* Case 128/78 [1979] ECR 419, the European Court held the United Kingdom to be in violation of its Community obligations by failing to incorporate a regulation in its entirety. Community regulations are intended to be directly applicable, and Member States are prohibited from implementing such measures in an incomplete and selective manner so as to render abortive those aspects of the legislation which the Member States oppose.

Directives

Directives, said in Article 249(3) EC Treaty to be 'binding, as to the result to be achieved, upon each Member State to which it is addressed, but shall leave to the national authorities the choice of form and methods', are not directly applicable but may have 'vertical' direct effect.

In the case of *Franz Grad* v *Finanzampt Traustein* Case 9/70 [1970] ECR 825 the Court gave judgment on the combined effect of a decision that value added tax was incompatible with other turnover taxes and the directive instituting VAT. It held that:

> 'Although it is true that, by virtue of Article [249], regulations are directly applicable and therefore by virtue of their nature capable of producing direct effects, it does not follow from this that other categories of legal measures mentioned in that Article can never produce similar effects ...'

It would be incompatible with the binding effect attributed to directives by Article 249 to exclude in principle the possibility that persons affected may invoke the obligations imposed by a directive. Particularly in cases where, for example, the Community authorities by means of a directive have imposed an obligation on a Member State or all the Member States to act in a certain way, the effectiveness, *l'effet utile*, of such a measure would be weakened if the nationals of that state could not take it into consideration as part of Community law.

However, it was not until *Van Duyn* v *Home Office* Case 41/74 [1974] ECR 1337 that the Court gave a ruling on the direct effect of a provision in a directive taken in isolation. The Court was asked to give a ruling on the right of an individual before a national court to claim the benefit of Article 3(1) of the Directive No 64/221 co-ordinating provisions concerning immigration regulations. This Article provides: 'Measures taken on grounds of public policy or of public security shall be based exclusively on the personal conduct of the individual concerned.'

The case concerned a European Community national, a member of the Church of Scientology, who had, on this ground, been forbidden access to British territory where she wished to take up employment. The Court repeated in full the findings it had made in *Franz Grad* v *Finanzampt Traustein* (above). It went on to examine the nature, the subject matter and the terms of the provision in question and concluded that the latter gave rise to rights enforceable at law for the benefit of individuals.

It is clear that the key concept is and remains the existence of discretionary powers with the Member States. Direct effect only exists in so far as there is no such power when the directive in question has not been implemented by the state within the period prescribed for its implementation: *Ratti* Case 148/78 [1979] ECR 1629. The case of *Marshall* v *Southampton and South-West Area Health Authority* (*Teaching*) (*No 1*) Case 152/84 [1986] 1 CMLR 688 is an example of this. It was held that the state could not defend itself on the grounds of its own failure to implement a directive (No 76/207). The effect, of course, was that a 'vertical' action, against the state, could be brought by an individual, notwithstanding that an 'arbitrary and unfair distinction' would be created between state employees and private employees.

The case begged the question as to what exactly is the state acting as an employer for the purposes of such an action. Indeed what is the state and its emanations? In *R* v

London Boroughs Transport Committee [1990] 1 CMLR 229 it was held that since a local authority exercises governmental power it was an emanation of the state. The width of the interpretation of emanation fell to be considered in the Court of Appeal in the case of *Foster and Others* v *British Gas plc* [1988] 2 CMLR 697, where Lord Donaldson MR held that although the Court of Justice in *Marshall* had held that the health authority was the 'state', the question was really a matter for the English courts.

Inevitably this case went on appeal to the House of Lords, which tabled an Article 234 reference to the Court of Justice (Case C–188/89 [1990] 3 All ER 897). It was held that provisions of a directive, if they are capable of being directly effective, may be relied upon against an entity which provides a public service under the control of the state and which has powers in excess of those which result from the normal rules applicable in relations between individuals. The legal form of the entity does not matter. Accordingly Article 5(1) of Directive 76/207 could be relied on against British Gas. For the application of this ruling see [1991] 2 All ER 705.

Improper or incomplete implementation of a directive may also occur if a state does not allow individuals to fully exercise the rights conferred by the directive. For example, in *Marshall* v *Southampton and South-West Area Health Authority (No 2)* Case C–271/91 [1993] 3 CMLR 293, the European Court held that an upper limit for compensation on a claim brought in a national court by a private individual exercising their Community rights under a directive was tantamount to improper implementation of the measure. In the circumstances, the Court held that Member States were obliged to give full effect to Community measures by providing effective and real relief to those whose Community rights were infringed.

A Member State cannot rely on the principle of direct effect to impose duties upon individuals if the state in question has failed to implement the directive within the required period. Thus, the European Court rejected an attempt by the Dutch authorities to prosecute a trader for stocking mineral water containing additives which were prohibited by a Council directive which the Dutch government had failed to implement: *Officier van Justitie* v *Kolpinghuis Nijmegen BV* Case 80/86 [1989] 2 CMLR 18.

In this case the Court observed that, according to Article 249(3) of the EC Treaty, the obligations contained in a directive exist only in relation to 'each Member State to which it is addressed'. A directive is therefore binding only on states and may not by itself impose obligations on individuals. Consequently, the Court held that '... a Member State which has not adopted the implementing measures required by the directive within the prescribed period may not plead, as against individuals, its own failure to perform the obligations which the directive entails.'

While the Court of Justice has refused to recognise the concept of the 'horizontal direct effect' of directives, it has sought to achieve the same effect as the adoption of the principle would have brought about through other means. Instead of concentrating on the relationship between individuals and the state, the Court has diverted its attention to the obligations of Member States under Article 10 of the EC Treaty.

In a series of cases, most notably *Von Colson* v *Land Nordrhein-Westfalen* Case 14/83 [1984] ECR 1891, and more recently *Marleasing SA* v *La Comercial Internacional de Alimentacion SA* Case C–106/89 [1992] 1 CMLR 305, the Court has relied on the obligation of Member States under Article 10 to interpret national law in a manner consistent with unimplemented directives.

Article 10 requires Member States to take 'all appropriate measures ... to ensure fulfilment of the obligations arising out of this Treaty'. In *Marleasing* the Court was required to answer the question whether Directive 68/151 on company law harmonisation, which had not been implemented in Spain, could be relied upon to override a provision of Spanish law allowing the nullity of a company on the ground of lack of consideration. The directive exhaustively enumerated the grounds on which the incorporation of a company could be declared void. Spanish law therefore contradicted Community law, but the directive remained unadopted.

The Court held that the national law must be interpreted in conformity with the directive, and any attempt to dissolve a company on grounds other than those set out in the directive was incompatible with Community law. This decision was reached on the basis of a point of interpretation, namely, that Spanish law must be interpreted in a manner consistent with Community law.

The impact of this decision has been to give restricted horizontal direct effect to directives in an indirect manner. While the Court expressly rejected the possibility of directives having horizontal direct effect, its method of interpretation arrived at the same effect.

International agreements concluded by the Community

In view of its decisions on direct effect, the Court was logically bound to admit that the provisions of international agreements concluded by the Community could be invoked by courts and tribunals as elements of Community law.

It did so in the *Bresciani (Daniele) Conceria* v *Amministrazione delle Finance* Case 87/75 [1976] ECR 129, a judgment concerning the scope of an article in Yaounde Conventions I and II referring to a provision in the EC Treaty which itself has direct effect.

The Court did not merely point to the existence of the particular article. It set the provision in the context of the association agreements to which it belonged. It observed that the provision on customs duties on imports was, for the European Community, an obligation unqualified by any reservation, either implicit or explicit. Only the associated states could ask for consultations on the subject to be opened, and this imbalance in the benefits, normal in agreements of this kind, did not have the result of robbing the provision of direct effect in the relations between the Member States and individuals.

The Court has also recognised the direct effect of provisions in international agreements similar to those contained in the EC Treaty which did occur in agreements establishing free trade zones between the Community and non-member states, such as the agreements concluded with European countries.

The Association Agreement between the European Community and Portugal has been the subject of two cases which should here be noted, the first concerning provisions similar to Articles 28–30 of the EC Treaty in the context of copyright, and the second concerning a provision similar to the prohibition on discriminatory internal taxation in Article 90 of the EC Treaty in the context of port wine. In *Polydor* v *Harlequin Record Shops* Case 270/80 [1982] 2 ECR 329 the Court did not decide whether provisions similar to Articles 28–30 were of direct effect but held that the interpretation by the Court of Articles 28–30 of the EC Treaty could not be transposed to the EC/Portugal Agreement since the objectives of the two treaties were different, the latter only being intended to establish a customs union while the former was designed to go further and unite national markets into a single common market. In *Haupzollamt Mainz* v *Kupferberg* Case 104/81 [1983] CMLR 1 the Court held that Article 21 of the EC–Portugal agreement was of direct effect because of the specific object of Article 21 in the system of rules laid down by the agreement and its terms, and not because of the nature or status of the agreement. But it gave a more restrictive interpretation to Article 21 than it has given to Article 90 of the EC Treaty.

The British courts also considered the doctrine of direct effect as it applies to international agreements entered into by the European Community. In *R* v *Secretary of State for the Home Department, ex parte Narin* [1990] 2 CMLR 233, the Court of Appeal was asked to decide whether a provision in an additional protocol to an Association Agreement between the European Community and Turkey had direct effect. The plaintiff argued that a deportation order made out against him was inconsistent with a provision in this treaty analogous to Article 39 of the EC Treaty which creates the right of free movement of persons. If this treaty provision were given direct effect, the deportation order could not be carried out since such action would interfere with the Community rights of the plaintiff.

Sir Nicholas Browne-Wilkinson observed that, according to the jurisprudence of the European Court:

'A provision in an agreement concluded by the Community with non-Member countries must be regarded as being directly applicable when, regard being had to its wording and the purpose and nature of the agreement itself, the provision contains a clear and precise obligation which is not subject, in its implementation or effects, to the adoption of any subsequent measure.'

After consideration of the structure, evolution and content of the additional protocol, the Court concluded that the protocol did not have direct effect because the article upon which the plaintiff relied did not satisfy these criteria. Therefore the provision did not confer rights on individuals which could be exercised in the English courts.

The status of a national rule contrary to a community rule with direct effect

In the Court's view, national law contrary to a European Community rule with direct effect cannot be applied by the courts, but it is for the legal system in each state to decide the legal procedure by which this result is to be achieved.

The Court stated in *Luck* v *Hauptzollampt Köln-Rheinau* Case 34/67 [1968] ECR 115 that the national court must not apply a national rule conflicting with a European Community provision having direct effect. The same solution was repeated in *Lorenz* v *Germany* Case 120/173 [1973] ECR 1471 and in *Simmenthal* v *EC Commission* Case 92/78 [1979] ECR 777, where we read:

> 'The relationship between provisions of the Treaty and directly applicable measures of the institutions on the one hand and the national law of the Member States on the other is such that those provisions and measures by their entry into force render automatically inapplicable any conflicting provision of current national law. The recognised right of the domestic order to choose the most appropriate procedure for ensuring the direct effect of Community law must be reconciled with the fact that its provisions are an immediate source of rights and obligations for all concerned.'

At the very least, national courts must refrain from applying contrary earlier law. The courts will be able to go further and, for example, declare the contrary provisions null and void where the national law affords them such power.

By virtue of the primacy of Community law, the 'blocking effect' of directly applicable provisions is also apparent with regard to subsequent national law. As has been seen, this may occur with provisions implementing a directive. In the *Simmenthal* judgment, the Court strongly emphasised that directly applicable provisions of Community law had the effect of preventing the 'valid adoption of new national legislative measures to the extent to which they would be incompatible with Community provisions'. Such acts being invalid, the national courts cannot give effect to them.

The limits of direct effect

Although, to repeat the Court's words once again, 'direct applicability ... means that the rules of European Community law must be fully and uniformly applied in all the Member States from the date of their entry into force and for so long as they continue in force', the principle of the states' so-called procedural autonomy may result in differences in the actual application of European Community law.

It is for national courts to ensure that their subjects benefit from the legal protection arising from the direct effect of European Community law: see *Rewe-Zentralfinanz AG and Rewe-Zentral AG* v *Landwirtschafiskammer für das Saarland* Case 33/76 [1977] 1 CMLR 533. In doing so, the national courts must apply the rules of domestic procedural law.

The absence of any co-ordination of domestic procedural rules necessarily entails the existence of different limitation periods, and therefore a certain divergence in the actual application of Community law. It is possible that similar observations might be made with respect to the system of national penalties for infringements of European Community law and the procedure for bringing actions. There is no doubt that in these matters there is a wide divergence between the various domestic systems. The obligation to co-operate incumbent on the Member States by virtue of Article 10 of the Treaty seems quite inadequate to meet these divergences which are rooted in history. Only co-ordinating actions initiated by the European Community or spontaneously by the Member States with a view to the approximation of national laws can, in the long term, reduce these differences.

8.3 The primacy of European Community law

General

It was in *Costa* v *ENEL* Case 6/64 [1964] 3 CMLR 425 that the Court established its doctrine of the primacy of European Community law.

The facts behind the case were simple: an individual was claiming before his local court – the guidice conciliatore of Milan – that the law nationalising production and distribution of electricity was incompatible with the EC Treaty. The local court referred several questions to the Court of Justice for a preliminary ruling. The Italian government maintained that the proceedings were totally inadmissible because, in the case in question, the Italian court was only entitled to apply the nationalisation law and not the Italian national law ratifying the EC Treaty, since the latter law was earlier. This argument was based on a judgment given by the Italian constitutional court in a case between the same parties. The decision had aroused legitimate concern in European Community circles.

It is understandable that the Court of Justice decided to take a stand on the problem. In any case, the procedural objection raised left it no option. The judgment in *Costa* v *ENEL* plays the same role with regard to primacy as the judgment in *Van Gend en Loos* (see section 8.2, above) with regard to direct effect. Primacy is the corollary of the Court's conception of the Community legal order as being 'integrated into the legal systems of the Member States and binding on their courts'.

The Court in its judgment in the *Costa* case emphasised the unlimited duration of the Community, the autonomy of Community power, both internally and externally, and especially the limitation of competence or transfer of powers from the states to the European Community. The close connections between direct effect and primacy are clear. These twin pillars of the Community legal order are necessarily implied by the refashioning of powers entailed in the establishment of the European Community.

The Court was determined to show that the 'words and spirit of the treaty' necessarily implied that 'it is impossible for the states to set up a subsequent unilateral measure against a legal order which they have accepted on a reciprocal basis'. It is not possible to repeat here the textual arguments. It should be pointed out, however, that the Court found the primacy of Community law confirmed by the wording of Article 249 EC Treaty under which regulations have 'binding' force and are 'directly applicable to all Member States'. In so doing, the Court emphasised afresh the connection not only between direct applicability and primacy but also between the latter and the legislative power conferred on the European Community. The Court pointed out that this provision, which is not qualified by any reservation, 'would be meaningless if a state could unilaterally nullify its effect by means of legislative measures which could prevail over European Community law'. Any claim that a state might have to give precedence to a later law over a regulation was moreover rendered absurd simply by the fact that a subsequent regulation could put an end to this inconsistency.

The Court was thus able to reach a conclusion in *Costa* in words which have become classic and have had considerable influence in national decisions:

> 'It follows from all these observations that the law stemming from the Treaty, an independent source of law, could not, because of its special and original nature, be overridden by domestic legal provisions, however framed, without being deprived of its character as Community law and without the legal basis of the Community itself being called into question. The transfer by the states from their domestic legal system to the Community legal system of rights and obligations arising under the treaty carries with it a permanent limitation of their sovereign rights against which a subsequent unilateral act incompatible with the concept of the Community cannot prevail.'

The Court's ruling is addressed directly to national courts. Its decisions cannot be regarded as an expression of the practical necessity which has always led international courts to assert the superiority of the law they are applying over national law, the latter being sometimes treated as simply a question of fact. This dualism is not appropriate in the relations between the Community legal order and the national orders. It gives a poor idea of the co-ordination between them, which finds expression especially in the machinery for seeking preliminary rulings. Thus when the Court rules that domestic law cannot override Community law, it is referring to proceedings before national courts. This is even clearer in *Simmenthal* (above) where the court concluded:

> 'Every national court must, in a case within its jurisdiction, apply European law in its entirety and protect rights which the latter confers on individuals and must accordingly set aside any provision of national law which may conflict with it, whether prior or subsequent to the Community rule.'

Primacy is not an obligation which it is incumbent upon the founder of the constitution or the legislator to implement. It is a rule to be applied by the courts.

This rule is unconditional. It is also absolute in the sense that it applies to every rule of domestic law, whatever its standing, even if it is a constitutional rule. Suggested discreetly in the *Costa* judgment, as appears in the passage quoted above, the principle of the primacy of Community law over national constitutions has been developed and amplified in later judgments.

In *Internationale Handelsgesellschaft GmbH* v *Einfuhr und Vorratsstelle für Getreide und Futtermittel* Case 11/70 [1970] ECR 1125 the judgment repeated word for word one of the grounds of judgment in *Costa* v *ENEL* and added:

'The validity of a Community measure or its effect within a Member State cannot be affected by allegations that it runs counter to either fundamental rights as formulated by the constitution of the state or the principles of a national constitutional structure.'

Furthermore, in *EC Commission* v *EC Council (Re ERTA)* Case 22/70 [1971] CMLR 335 the Court went further and ruled that Community law was supreme not only over domestic law but also over a Member State's obligations to other states.

United Kingdom

In the United Kingdom, the European Communities Act 1972, as amended by the European Communities (Amendment) Acts 1986, 1993 and 1998, makes all Community law provisions which are directly effective part of national law: s2(1). Further, s2(4) states: 'any enactment passed or to be passed, other than one contained in this Part of this Act, shall be construed and have effect subject to the foregoing provisions of this section'. This has been held by some to mean that the national courts must interpret Community law 'in accordance with the principles laid down by and any relevant decision of the European Court' (s3(1)), and so acknowledge the supremacy of Community law. It has been further contended that the foregoing places a duty on the national courts to interpret national laws so as to give effect to provisions of Community law. This proposition relies on the judgment in *Von Colson* v *Land Nordrhein-Westfalen* (above), part of which states that national courts are required to interpret national law in the light of the wording and purpose of the directive.

As regards the principle of the supremacy of Community law, the English courts have tried hard to reconcile the doctrine of the supremacy of Community law with that of the principle of parliamentary supremacy. There was little doubt that Community law prevailed over pre-1972 British legislation because the 1972 Act incorporated all existing Community law at that date into United Kingdom law. The courts were therefore prepared to accept that Community law overruled pre-1972 statutes: see *Shields* v *E Coomes (Holdings) Ltd* [1979] 1 All ER 456.

In *R* v *Secretary of State for Transport, ex parte Factortame (No 1)* [1989] 2 WLR 99 the House of Lords was compelled to decide whether the application of a statute of Parliament enacted after 1972 could be suspended pending an application to the European Court for a decision concerning the consistency of the legislation in question with Community law. The applicants were companies incorporated in the United Kingdom but owned mainly by Spanish nationals. These companies had been created for the purpose of acquiring ownership of fishing vessels registered in the United Kingdom. The statutory requirements for registering vessels as British were altered by the Merchant Shipping Act 1988 and the Merchant Shipping (Registration of Fishing Vessels) Regulations 1988. In particular, conditions relating to nationality were introduced in order for an applicant to register a vessel as a British ship. The applicants maintained that these conditions violated the principle of non-discrimination and deprived the applicants of enforceable Community rights.

The Divisional Court of the Queen's Bench decided to request a preliminary reference on the question from the European Court, and, on a motion by the applicants for interim relief, the court ordered that, pending a decision from the European Court, the contested parts of the statute were to be disapplied and the Secretary of State should be restrained from enforcing the legislation. The Court of Appeal, on appeal by the Secretary of State, set aside the order made by the Divisional Court for interim relief. The applicants appealed to the House of Lords.

In the House of Lords, Lord Bridge of Harwich declared that, in the absence of an overriding principle of Community law allowing national courts to suspend the application of national law, the British courts would be unable to provide effective interlocutory relief to protect putative rights. No such doctrine existed in British constitutional law, and it was up to the European Court to establish such a principle if Community obligations were to be protected. The House of Lords therefore asked the European Court whether or not a national court was obliged to grant interim suspension of an Act of Parliament pending a decision by the European Court.

In reply to this reference, the European Court declared:

'Any provision of a national legal system and any legislative, administrative or judicial practice which might impair the effectiveness of Community law by withholding from the national court having jurisdiction to apply such law the power to do everything necessary at the moment of its application to set aside national legislative provisions which might prevent, even temporarily, Community rules from having full force and effect, are incompatible with [the principles of Community law]': *Factortame (No 2)* Case C–213/89 [1990] 3 CMLR 1.

Community law was therefore to be interpreted as meaning that a national court must set aside any measure of national law which precludes it from granting interim relief to protect rights established under Community law.

Upon receiving this judgment from the European Court, the House of Lords reconsidered the issue and granted interim relief to the applicants. As Lord Bridge conceded in this later judgment: 'Under the 1972 Act it has always been the duty of a United Kingdom court, when delivering final judgment, to override any rules of national law found to be in conflict with any directly enforceable Community law': *R* v *Secretary of State, ex parte Factortame (No 3)* [1990] 3 WLR 818, 857.

The implications of this series of decisions are not absolutely settled, but a number of preliminary points may be made. First, the British courts have widely acknowledged that national legislation enacted prior to the 1972 Act is inapplicable if inconsistent with Community law. Second, the British courts have power, by virtue of the European Court decision in *Factortame,* to suspend temporarily the application of an Act of Parliament. Third, any further extension of this power must emanate from the jurisprudence of the European Court. Fourth, the British courts will continue to apply the doctrine of parliamentary sovereignty to cases not involving issues of Community law. Finally, as the jurisprudence of the European Court now stands, the British courts have no explicit authority to suspend permanently the application of an Act of Parliament that is inconsistent with Community law.

The English courts have accepted the implications of the *Factortame* decision gracefully. Indeed Lord Bridge, in that decision, once the reference to the European Court was returned to the House of Lords for implementation, felt obliged to make the following observation:

> 'Some public comments on the decision of the Court of Justice, affirming the jurisdiction of the courts of the Member States to override national legislation if necessary to enable interim relief to be granted for the protection of rights under Community law, have suggested that this was a novel and dangerous invasion by a Community institution of the sovereignty of the United Kingdom Parliament.
>
> But such comments are based on a misconception. If the supremacy within the European Community of Community law over the national law of Member States was not always inherent in the EEC Treaty it was certainly well established in the jurisprudence of the Court of Justice long before the United Kingdom joined the Community. Thus, whatever limitation of its sovereignty Parliament accepted when it enacted the European Communities Act 1972 was entirely voluntary': *R v Secretary of State for Transport, ex parte Factortame (No 3)* [1990] 3 WLR 818.

8.4 Equal pay

General

Article 141 is the base article providing that 'men and women should receive equal pay for equal work'. The Article defines pay as 'basic or minimum wage or salary and any other consideration in cash or in kind'. The Article expands on the definition by providing:

> 'Equal pay without discrimination based on sex means:
> 1. That pay for the same work at piece rates shall be calculated on the basis of the same unit of measurement;
> 2. That pay for work at time rates shall be the same for the same job.'

'Pay' was defined in *Garland* v *British Rail Engineering* (*BREL*) Case 12/81 [1982] ECR 359 as 'any consideration whether immediate or future provided that the worker receives it, albeit indirectly, in respect of his employment from his employer'.

Not surprisingly, since the Article was for a long time the keystone of the Community's Social Policy, it is directly effective: *Defrenne* v *Sabena* Case 43/75 [1976] ECR 455. But the road to that conclusion was not an easy one. The first years of the Article's life did not lead to any great rush towards its implementation, a situation which concerned the European Commission. This led to the adoption of Directive 75/117, the Equal Pay Directive.

Defrenne v *Sabena* posed the following questions: does Article 141 introduce directly into the law of each Member State the principle that men and women should receive equal pay for equal work so that workers are entitled to institute proceedings before national courts to ensure its observance, and if so, from when? Has Article 141 become applicable in the internal law of the Member States by virtue of measures adopted by the authorities of the European Community (if so, from when?), or must national legislatures be regarded as alone competent in this manner? The Court ruled that Article 141 could be relied on before the national courts but could not be relied on to support claims prior to the judgment except by those who had already brought legal proceedings.

Thus direct effect was established and extended vertically and horizontally. Again in *Defrenne*: 'In fact since Article 141 is mandatory in nature [it] applies not only to the action of public authorities but also ... to contracts between individuals.'

The Court closed off its options by stating in the judgment that:

> 'For the purposes of the implementation of these provisions a distinction must be drawn within the whole area of application of Article 141 between, firstly, direct and overt discrimination which may be identified solely with the aid of the criteria based on equal work and equal pay referred to by the Article in question, and, secondly, indirect and disguised discrimination which can only be identified by reference to more explicit implementing provisions of a Community or national character.'

The 'direct and overt' discrimination could be found by referring to legislative provisions, collective agreements and the legal analysis of them, and clear situations where men and women received unequal pay for equal work carried out in the same establishment. In order to avail of Article 141 in the national courts, the applicant had to show 'direct and overt discrimination.' This proposition was echoed in *Macarthys* v *Smith* Case 129/79 [1980] ECR 1275.

The distinction created discomfort, not least for Advocate-General Warner who expressed dissatisfaction in his opinions in *Jenkins* v *Kingsgate (Clothing Productions) Ltd* Case 96/80 [1981] ECR 911 and *Worringham and Humphreys* v *Lloyds Bank* Case C69/80 [1981] ECR 767. He acknowledged that Article 141 did not have direct effect in all circumstances, but he limited the circumstances where it was not directly effective to those where the national courts could not apply it simply by reference to the criteria laid down in the Article as a result of which either Community or national legislation was required.

The Court took note, and in the judgment in the *Worringham and Other* v *Lloyds Bank* Case C69/80 [1981] ECR 767 it said that the Article would apply to *all* forms of discrimination which could be identified solely with the help of the equality criteria laid down in the Article itself.

Article 141 applies regardless of whether an employee is employed on a part-time or a full-time basis. Further, where discrimination is being perpetrated on the basis of a distinction between full-time and part-time workers, where the majority of one or other of these categories is predominantly of one gender, discrimination contrary to Article 141 may exist. As the European Court held in *Nimz* v *Freie Und Hansestadt Hamburg* Case C–184/89 [1992] 3 CMLR 699, where there is a significantly disproportionate ratio between part-time and full-time workers, with one gender being discriminated against, there is a violation of Article 141 unless the discrimination can be justified on the basis of 'objectively justified factors'.

This interpretation of Article 141 has also been applied by the House of Lords in *R* v *Secretary of State for Employment, ex parte Equal Opportunities Commission* [1994] 2 WLR 409. In this case, the applicants sought judicial review of the terms of the Employment Protection (Consolidation) Act 1978 in light of Article 141 of the EC Treaty. The statute limited the right to claim compensation for unfair dismissal and redundancy payments to employees working more than a certain number of hours each week. Since the majority of part-time workers in the United Kingdom are in fact female, the applicants took the view that the UK legislation indirectly discriminated against female employees in conflict with Article 141 as applied by the European Court.

Lord Keith of Kinkel laid down the test which must be satisfied to establish the consistency of national laws with the terms of Article 141. Any differentiation in pay must be justified on the basis of 'objectively justified factors' unrelated to any form of discrimination based on a distinction on gender. He then proceeded to reject the contention, made on behalf of the government, that the distinction between full-time and part-time workers made under the 1978 Act could be justified objectively as an attempt to strike a fair balance between the interests of employers and employees. Since this rationale could not be objectively justified, the effect of the law was to create discrimination between genders contrary to Article 141.

Directive 75/117 and implementation in the United Kingdom

Directive 75/117 is stated to be 'on the approximation of the laws of the Member States relating to the application of the principle of equal pay for men and women'. Article 1 of the Directive gives a restatement of the general provision of Article 141, while adding to the principle the meaning that there must be equal pay for the same work *or for work to which equal value is attributed.*

Paragraph 2 of Article 1 states that if a job classification system is used to determine pay it must be based on the same criteria for both men and women and must be drawn up in such a way as to exclude discrimination on grounds of sex.

Article 2 requires Member States to introduce 'such measures as are necessary' to facilitate the bringing of claims by employees who consider themselves wronged.

Article 4 provides that Member States should ensure that provisions in collective agreements, wage scales, wage agreements or individual contracts contrary to the principle of equal pay should be annulled or amended.

Article 7 states that Member States should ensure that employees are aware of provisions adopted under the Directive.

It has been submitted that the Directive merely repeated what was already provided by Article 141, and that a Member State could not be in violation of its treaty obligations by failing to implement it: *EC Commission* v *Luxembourg* Case 58/81 [1982] ECR 2175. The Court did not uphold this proposition and stated that simply because the Directive reiterated the provisions in the Treaty Article it did not mean that the Directive was invalid. *Defrenne* acknowledged that Directive 75/117 did not affect Article 141 but provided 'further details regarding certain aspects of the material scope of Article 141'.

The relevant implementing legislation in the UK, the Equal Pay Act 1970 amended by the Sex Discrimination Act 1975, provided that the only method of evaluating 'works to which equal value is attributed' was a job classification system: see Article 1(2) of Directive 75/117. A classification system could not be introduced under UK law without the consent of an employer. This situation led to a Commission action under Article 226 against the United Kingdom: *EC Commission* v *United Kingdom (Re Equal Pay Directive) (No 1)* Case 61/81 [1982] ECR 2601. The United Kingdom objected that the concept of equal work of equal value was too vague to be applied by the courts. The European Court of Justice disagreed and stated that the UK was in breach of its treaty obligations by failing to introduce measures enabling all employees 'who consider themselves wronged by failure to apply the principle of equal pay for men and women for work to which equal value is attached and for which no system of job classification exists to obtain recognition of such equivalence'.

Directive 76/207 and implementation in the United Kingdom

Directive 76/207 concerns the implementation of the principle of equal treatment for men and women regarding access to employment, vocational training and promotion and working conditions. Article 2, paragraph 1, provides 'no discrimination on the grounds of sex directly or indirectly'. Article 2 in paragraph 2 of the Directive provides that the Directive 'will be without prejudice to the right of the Member State to exclude from its field of application those occupational activities ... where ... by their nature or the context in which they are carried out, the sex of the worker constitutes a determining factor'.

Article 3 provides that there should be no discrimination in selection criteria for access to all jobs or posts at all levels, and paragraph 2 of the Article states that Member States have to take the measures necessary to ensure that any laws or provisions in collective agreements or individual contracts are abolished, annulled or amended.

Article 4 refers to a similar duty on the Member States in the area of training and retraining. Article 5 places an identical duty on them regarding working conditions, including the conditions governing dismissal, ensuring thereby that men and women enjoy the same conditions.

An action under Article 226 was brought against the UK for failing to implement the Directive properly. There were three grounds of action argued by the Commission before the European Court of Justice, namely:

1. The relevant UK legislation did not provide that rules of undertakings or rules governing independent occupations were to be declared void or amended.
2. The relevant UK legislation provided that the prohibition of discrimination did not extend to employment in a private household or where the number of persons employed by an employer did not exceed five.
3. UK law allowed discrimination in access to the training and occupation of midwives: *EC Commission* v *United Kingdom (Re Equal Pay Directive) (No 2)* Case 165/82 [1983] ECR 3431.

The UK adduced the following defences:

1. Collective agreements are not normally legally binding, and if there were any collective agreements they would be rendered void by s77 of the Sex Discrimination Act of 1975.
2. The 1975 Act attempts to reconcile the principle of equal treatment and the principle of respect for family life.
3. Personal sensitivities were important in certain professions, see Article 2(2) of 76/207, and the occupation of midwife was one such.

None of these defences was upheld and the Court found the UK in breach of its obligation to properly implement Community directives.

Directive 79/7

The Directive deals with the progressive implementation of the principle of equal treatment for men and women in matters of social security, which include, according to Article 3, statutory schemes which provide protection against sickness, invalidity, old age, accidents at work, occupational diseases and unemployment. The Directive will not apply to provisions concerning survivors' benefits or family benefits.

Article 7 excludes from its scope the determination of pensionable age for the purposes of granting old-age and retirement pensions and the possible consequences for other benefits. Directive 86/378 provides for equal treatment in occupational social security schemes. Directive 86/613 concerns equal treatment in self-employment; it is an extension of 76/207 to the self-employed.

Article 141 and the directives through the cases

As was stated above in the remarks about *Defrenne* v *Sabena*, Article 141 is directly effective. The subsequent cases reveal two tendencies on the part of the Court:

1. To interpret Article 141 widely.

2. To try to deal with any relevant action before it on the basis of the Article and not to regard the Directives.

Macarthys v *Smith* (above) affords an example of the Court's wide interpretation. Here the plaintiff received £10 per week less in a job than a male predecessor. The Court said that the Article was not confined to comparison of jobs being done simultaneously but also successively.

Worringham and Others v *Lloyds Bank* (above) assisted understanding of the notion of pay. Here the bank contributed to a pension scheme available to all employees except women under 25 years of age. This was contrary to Article 141. The ambit of the Article was advanced further in *Jenkins* v *Kingsgate* (above) where part-time workers received a lower hourly rate than their full-time co-workers. If the differential was based solely on the grounds of sex, then the Court considered that it would be contrary to Article 141. The Court also pointed out that there might be other objective reasons for the differential. The facts of the case disclosed that there was only one woman working full time.

Article 141 has effect after retirement: *Garland* v *BREL* (above) held that providing post-retirement travel concessions to men but not to women was discriminatory. Article 141 even extends to equal pay for work of unequal value where discrimination is shown: *Murphy* v *An Bord Telecom Eireann* Case 157/86 [1988] ECR 445. Ms Murphy and her women co-workers claimed that they were entitled to the same pay as a male co-worker. On evaluation it was found that the women were performing work of *higher* value than their male counterparts. The Irish court held that it was not 'like work' so the Article did not apply, although there was discrimination on the grounds of sex in the rates of pay. On an Article 234 reference the ECJ said that Article 141 did not, prima facie, cover equal pay for work of unequal value. But to hold this would be absurd as it would mean that workers could do work of higher value than the work performed by the opposite sex and be paid less on the grounds of sex. Article 141 must be interpreted to apply to the facts of the present case.

Regarding Directive 76/207 the major case is *Marshall* v *Southampton and South-West Hampshire Area Health Authority (No 1)* (above). Ms Marshall was employed by the authority as a dietician. She was dismissed by the authority on reaching the age of 62 despite her stated willingness to continue until she was 65 years of age. The authority had a policy of 'retiring' employees at the age when state pensions would be granted, which according to the Social Security Act 1975 would be 60 for women and 65 for men. Ms Marshall claimed she had lost financially and had lost the satisfaction she derived from her work. She claimed that the Authority's behaviour amounted to unlawful sex discrimination contrary to Community law and the Sex Discrimination Act 1975.

The Court considered Article 5 of Directive 76/207 and the word dismissal. It noted that *Burton* v *British Railways Board* Case 19/81 [1982] ECR 555 (see also *Beets Proper* Case 267/84 [1986] ECR 706) stated that 'dismissal' should be given a wide interpretation. The ECJ therefore stated that an age limit for compulsory dismissal fell within the term. Against this interpretation had to be placed the fact that Directive 79/7 in Article 7(1)(a) allowed for discrimination in determination of pensionable age. The court stated that this latter provision applied only in the sphere of social security and to the determination of pensionable age for the purposes of granting old-age and retirement benefits. The Court held that the case fell to be considered under Directive 76/207 Article 5. It stated: 'Dismissal of a woman solely because she had reached the qualifying age for a state pension where that age was different for men and women constituted discrimination on the grounds of sex.' The Court further held that Directive 76/207 enjoyed vertical direct effect.

Some of the controversy in the area of pensionable ages is now laid to rest in *Barber* v *Guardian Royal Exchange Assurance Group* Case C–262/88 [1990] 2 CMLR 513, where it was decided that men and women are to be treated equally in occupational pension schemes. The Court decided this on the basis of Article 141 of the Treaty, which ensures that the freedom of a state to determine state pension ages provided by Directive 79/7 is no longer sustainable.

Another important case concerns the dismissal of a female employee on account of her pregnancy, and whether such dismissal constitutes a violation of the terms of the Directive. In *Webb* v *EMO Air Cargo (UK) Limited* Case C–32/93 [1994] 2 CMLR 729, the European Court held that Directive 76/207 prohibited the dismissal of a female employee who was unable to fulfil the terms of her employment contract due to her absence for maternity leave. The Court found that the leave for her condition could not be equated to a period of absence attributable to a comparable medical condition in a male employee which would justify dismissal. The Court's judgment was, in part, influenced by the fact that Community legislation is due to be implemented to protect female employees from dismissal.

The European Court has also had to decide the issue of the compatibility of affirmative discrimination programmes with Article 141 and the related directives. In *Kalanke* v *Freie Hansestadt Bremen* Case C–450/93 [1995] ECR I–3051, the Court considered the legality of a law enacted to promote positive discrimination in the appointment of staff to certain public positions. The aim of the legislation was to raise the number of female staff in these positions. In essence, where two employees or job applicants had the same qualifications or the same levels of experience, the female employees were to be appointed to the post. The applicant was a candidate who had not been appointed to a position as a result of this legislation.

The Court held that Community law prohibited the operation of such programmes insofar as they discriminated in favour of female employees. National rules which guarantee women absolute and unconditional priority for appointments or promotion exceed the objective of equal opportunities between genders which is the objective of Community law in this field. The legislation was too excessive in its structure and had the direct effect of unconditionally discriminating against men.

Article 226(4) was added by the Amsterdam Treaty to allow positive discrimination programmes in favour of underrepresented genders in specific areas of employment. This new provision is intended to overrule the European Court's decision in *Kalanke* v *Freie Hansestadt Bremen*, above.

The Council has also adopted Council Directive 98/52/EC on the extension to the United Kingdom of Directive 97/80/EC on the burden of proof in cases of discrimination based on gender. The Directive was adopted in December 1997 under the Protocol on Social Policy annexed to the Maastricht Treaty but did not apply to the United Kingdom by virtue of its opt out of the Social Chapter. Other provisions of Directives 97/80 and 98/52 aim to ensure that measures taken by the Member States to implement the principle of equal treatment are made effective. The principle of equal treatment means that there must be no discrimination whatsoever based on gender, either directly or indirectly. Indirect discrimination exists where an apparently neutral provision, criterion or practice disadvantages a substantially higher proportion of the members of one gender and is not objectively justified.

8.5 Prohibition of discrimination on the grounds of nationality and other factors

Article 12 of the EC Treaty, as amended, establishes the fundamental principle that 'any discrimination on the grounds of nationality shall be prohibited'. The application of this fundamental principle is confined to the exercise of the rights contained in the EC Treaty. In other words, this obligation, imposed on the Member States, extends to all activities within the scope of the EC treaty and, in particular, to the exercise of the rights of the free movement of goods, persons, services and capital. The same obligation is repeated in many subsequent provisions of the Treaty which emphasises the importance of the article as a fundamental principle of Community law.

This fundamental principle has a number of important effects. For example, the obligation precludes Member States from levying tariffs, customs duties or charges having an equivalent effect on goods imported from other Member States. Similarly, no Member State can impose, either directly or indirectly, any form of internal taxation on the products of other Member States in excess of that imposed on identical or similar domestic products.

The same requirement extends to the supply of services. Member States cannot discriminate between domestic and Community suppliers of services. In fact, the European Court has extended the principle of non-discrimination not only to the freedom to supply services but also the freedom to receive services: see *Cowan* v *Trésor Public* Case 186/87 [1990] 2 CMLR 613.

In practice, any right or obligation created under national law which is extended to nationals, but denied to Community nationals engaged in the same economic activities, is capable of infringing the obligation to refrain from discrimination on the grounds of nationality. This is demonstrated by *Collins* v *Imtrat Handelsgesellschaft mbH* Case C–92/92 [1993] 3 CMLR 773, in which the European Court considered the compatibility of a German law preventing unauthorised recordings with Article 12. This protection was afforded to German nationals but denied to the nationals of other Community countries. In other words, while German artists could prevent unauthorised recording of their performances, non-nationals were denied access to such remedies.

The Court held that the EC Treaty, and the rights and duties created by virtue of that treaty, applied to rights protected by copyright laws. Article 12 therefore extended to the exercise of such rights and, since that provision has direct effect, an individual is entitled to rely on its terms to prevent discrimination on the grounds of nationality in the application of copyright laws. Since the German copyright statute distinguished between nationals and other Community nationals, it amounted to an infringement of European Community law.

Article 13, inserted by the Treaty of Amsterdam, gives the Council of Ministers power to adopt legislation to prohibit discrimination based on sex, racial or ethnic origin, religion or belief, disability, age or sexual orientation. As regards discrimination on the grounds of sex, there is an overlap with Article 141. However, the other grounds on which discrimination will be prohibited are innovations as far as Community law is concerned.

8.6 The principle of subsidiarity

Article 5 provides:

> 'The Community shall act within the limits of the powers conferred upon it by [the EC Treaty] and of the objectives assigned to it therein.
>
>   In areas which do not fall within its exclusive competence, the Community shall take action, in accordance with the principle of subsidiarity, only if and in so far as the objectives of the proposed action cannot be sufficiently achieved by the Member States and can therefore, by reason of the scale or effects of the proposed action, be better achieved by the Community.
>
>   Any action by the Community shall not go beyond what is necessary to achieve the objectives of [the EC Treaty].'

It should be noted at the outset that this principle applies only when the European Union is acting within its competencies under the EC Treaty as amended, and not under its newly acquired competencies such as the common foreign and security policy and the provisions on justice and home affairs.

The functioning of this principle requires the European Commission to demonstrate that there is a genuine and legitimate need for every initiative or proposal. Three preliminary issues must be settled before a proposed measure or policy satisfies this test:

1. identification of the Community dimension of the subject matter to be regulated;
2. isolation of the most effective means of regulating the matter given the means

available under the EC Treaty to the European Community and the Member States respectively; and

3. confirmation of some tangible and identifiable real added value of common action as opposed to isolated national action on the part of the Member States.

Once these assessments have been made, the principle of subsidiarity requires that the measures must be proportionate to the aim or objective sought to be achieved. In many respects, this is akin to the general principle of proportionality created by the European Court as a general rule of Community law; the major difference is that the principle has been transformed into a fundamental constitutional principle of European Community law.

The Amsterdam Treaty also inserted a Protocol dealing with the application of the principle of subsidiarity to the EC Treaty. This Protocol defines the application of the principle in far more detail.

From a legal point of view, it is extremely likely that, in the future, measures may be challenged in the European Court for inconsistency with the principle of subsidiarity and, if found incompatible, may be declared invalid in whole or in part. Naturally, the exact implications of the principle and guidelines to govern the application of the rule remain to be elaborated in the inter-institutional agreement. In addition, the European Court will play a critical role in the formulation and shaping of this principle through its future jurisprudence.

9

Free Movement of Goods

9.1 Introduction

9.2 The elimination of customs duties and charges having an equivalent effect

9.3 Quantitative restrictions

9.4 Measures having an equivalent effect to quantitative restrictions

9.5 Exceptions to the prohibitions on quantitative restrictions and measures having an equivalent effect

9.6 Elimination of measures of internal discriminatory taxation

9.7 The internal market programme and harmonisation of national measures

9.8 The right of free circulation of non-Community goods

9.1 Introduction

At its conception, one of the primary purposes of the European Community was the creation of a common market founded on four principles; the free movement of goods, persons, services and capital. While it would be inaccurate to say that the free movement of goods is the most important of these principles, this freedom does provide the structural and doctrinal model for the operation of the other three principles. It is therefore logical to consider this principle before proceeding to examine the others.

In essence, the free movement of goods implies that products manufactured or produced in one Member State can move throughout the Community without having to pay customs duties or charges having an equivalent effect to customs duties and also will not be subject to unfair restrictions when sold in a country other than the country where they were manufactured or produced.

The purpose of this principle is to promote efficiency in production by removing artificial barriers to trade between Member States, allowing producers in different countries to compete directly with each other. This objective is also reinforced by the Community competition policy which is seen as an indispensable element to the creation of a true common market among the Member States.

From the point of view of goods, the legal framework established for achieving this goal can be broken down into four component parts:

1. The abolition of customs duties and charges having an equivalent effect.
2. The elimination of quantitative restrictions and measures having an equivalent effect to quantitative restrictions.
3. The abolition of measures of discriminatory domestic taxation.
4. The right of goods from non-EC countries to circulate freely within the Community once import formalities, customs duties and charges having an equivalent effect have been paid.

These rules form the framework of the legal regime for the free movement of goods.

This structure has been significantly developed through the internal market programme introduced by the Single European Act. A number of measures conceived under this programme are designed to secure the free movement of goods, and this dimension of the programme will be considered later in this connection.

9.2 The elimination of customs duties and charges having an equivalent effect

Customs duties

The six original Member States of the Community agreed to reduce customs duties among them in progressive phases immediately after the EC Treaty came into effect. This involved a series of staggered reductions in the duties that were applicable at that time, eventually culminating in the elimination of all duties, on both import and export transactions, on 1 July 1968.

The nine Member States which have subsequently joined the Community have been required, as a condition of membership, to eliminate all customs duties between them and other Member States over negotiated transitional periods. Any new members in the future will be similarly obliged to remove such barriers to trade. The exact terms of these reductions are specified in the treaties of accession entered into by these states with the Community.

The last remaining customs duties for intra-Community trade, in respect of the accessions of Spain and Portugal, were removed on 1 January 1993. Austria, Finland and Sweden were given no additional transition time to remove customs duties because these were to have been eliminated as part of the EEA Agreement.

Article 25 of the EC Treaty expressly prohibits the re-introduction of any customs duties on imports or exports of goods passing between Community states. This Article states:

> 'Member States shall refrain from introducing between themselves any new customs duties on imports or exports or any charges having equivalent effect, and from increasing those which they already apply in their trade with each other.'

Article 25 is directly effective: *Van Gend en Loos* v *Netherlands* (above). It provides <u>no derogation</u> and falls to be <u>interpreted very strictly by the Court</u>, as in *Sociaal Fonds voor der Diamantarbeiders* v *Brachfeld & Chougol Diamond Co* Cases 2 & 3/69 [1969] ECR 211, where the Belgian authorities imposed a duty on diamonds in order to raise money to benefit <u>Belgian diamond workers</u>. Belgium defended itself by stating that the duty was not imposed for protectionist reasons and therefore Article 25 was not applicable. Belgium is not a diamond producer. It was held that the duty came within Article 25 and was prohibited:

> 'It follows … that customs duties are prohibited independently of any consideration of the purpose for which they were introduced and the destination of the revenue obtained therefrom. The justification for this prohibition is based on the fact that any pecuniary charge – however small – imposed on goods by reason of the fact that they cross a frontier constitutes an obstacle to the movement of such goods.'

Charges having an equivalent effect

Member States are also obliged to eliminate all '<u>charges having an equivalent effect</u> to customs duties', again on both imports and exports, and also to refrain from re-introducing such charges on intra-Community transactions.

<u>No definition of charges having an equivalent effect</u> is elaborated in the Treaty, and interpretation of this term has been left to the European Court. In *EC Commission* v *Italy (Re Statistical Levy)* Case 24/68 [1969] ECR 193 the Court defined the term as follows:

relating to money

> 'Any (pecuniary) charge, however small and whatever its designation and mode of application, which is imposed unilaterally on domestic and foreign goods by reason of the fact that they cross a frontier, and which is not a customs duty in the strict sense, constitutes a charge … even if it is not imposed for the benefit of the state, is not discriminatory or protective in effect and if the product on which the charge is imposed is not in competition with any domestic product.'

This definition has been repeatedly stated by the Court: see *Procureur du Roi* v *Dassonville* Case 8/74 [1974] ECR 837 and *EC Commission* v *Germany (Re Animals Inspection Fees)* Case 18/87 [1990] 1 CMLR 561.

Care must taken with 'pecuniary charge' as in very exceptional circumstances a charge may be held not to be within Article 25, as in *EC Commission* v *Belgium (Re Storage Charges)* Case 132/82 [1983] 3 CMLR 600, where an impost by the customs on imports for storage services, requested by the importer, was not a charge within the ambit of Article 25.

<u>Charges made for services authorised by Community law</u> do not constitute charges having an equivalent effect to customs duties so long as these satisfy four conditions:

1. The charges do not exceed the actual costs of the services rendered.
2. The services in question are obligatory and uniform for all the products concerned in the Community.

3. The services are required by Community law in the general interests of the Community.
4. The services promote the free movement of goods, in particular by neutralising obstacles which could arise from unilateral measures of inspection adopted in accordance with Article 30 of the EC Treaty.

If a contested charge satisfies these four conditions, it cannot be classified as a charge having an equivalent effect and proscribed under Article 25: *EC Commission* v *Germany (Re Animals Inspection Fees)* Case 18/87 [1990] 1 CMLR 561.

9.3 Quantitative restrictions

A quantitative restriction is a national measure which restrains the volume or amount of imports or exports, not by artificially raising the direct cost of importing or exporting (as would be the case with a tariff or export tax) but by placing direct or indirect limits on the physical quantity of imports or exports that may enter or leave a country. The most obvious example of a quantitative restriction is the quota.

Quantitative restrictions between the original six Member States were gradually phased out, and new Members must observe the same obligation: Articles 28–30.

The explicit prohibition on the introduction of quotas is periodically violated by Member States. For example, in 1978 the United Kingdom restricted imports of Dutch potatoes while in the same year France imposed an embargo on sheepmeat from the United Kingdom. Similarly, in 1982, the United Kingdom limited imports of French UHT milk by means of a quota. Each of these actions resulted in litigation in the European Court: *EC Commission* v *United Kingdom (Re Imports of Dutch Potatoes)* Case 231/78 [1979] ECR 1447, *EC Commission* v *France (Re Sheepmeat from the United Kingdom)* Case 232/78 [1979] ECR 2729, and *EC Commission* v *United Kingdom (Re Imports of UHT Milk)* Case 124/81 [1983] ECR 230.

9.4 Measures having an equivalent effect to quantitative restrictions

'Measures' is defined in the preamble to Directive 70/50/EEC as 'laws, regulations, administrative provisions, administrative practices, and all instruments issuing from a public authority including recommendations'. This formulation is further explained in *Procureur du Roi* v *Dassonville* Case 8/74 [1974] ECR 837 and seen in 'judicial action' in *Rewe-Zentral AG* v *Bundesmonopolverwaltung für Branntwein* Case 120/78 [1979] 3 CMLR 337 (the *Cassis de Dijon* case). Here the German authorities imposed a restriction on the sale in Germany of beverages below a minimum alcohol content. The minimum content permissible in Germany for fruit liqueurs was 25 per cent, whereas the cassis was approximately 15 per cent. It was held by the European Court that this restriction was a measure having equivalent effect to an import quota and was therefore prohibited.

An interesting gloss on Article 28 and Directive 70/50 was found in *EC Commission* v *Ireland* Case 249/81 [1983] 2 CMLR 99, where the government's 'Buy Irish' campaign was held to be in breach of Article 28. The Irish government had provided public funds to boost the campaign. The Court found that the campaign was designed to substitute domestic products for imported ones. No account was to be taken of the campaign's failure.

Article 28 and the relevant legislative measures also apply to the activities of local and regional government agencies which are required to respect the terms of such measures. The European Court will not permit any distinction to be drawn between measures enacted at local, regional or national level as long as the enacting authority exercises the necessary legislative competence. A Member State cannot therefore argue that it bears no liability for infringements of Article 28 caused by the actions of such agencies: *Aragonesa de Publicidad Exterior SA and Others* v *Departmento de Sanidad y Seguridad Social de la Generalitat de Cataluna* Joined Cases C–1/90 and C–176/90 [1994] 1 CMLR 887.

The concept of 'measures having an equivalent effect' is not confined to legislation, regulations or administrative practices on the part of national authorities. It extends to rules enacted by regulatory agencies such as professional bodies where these agencies exercise special powers. In *R* v *Pharmaceutical Society of Great Britain* Cases 266 and 267/87 [1989] 2 CMLR 751 the Court observed that 'measures adopted by a professional body on which national legislation has conferred powers may, if they are capable of affecting trade between Member States, constitute "measures" within the meaning of Article [28] of the Treaty'.

In ascertaining whether or not a particular body exercises sufficient authority to establish measures having an equivalent effect to quantitative restrictions, the Court considers, inter alia, the legal status of the body, the requirement of mandatory enrolment, the power to enact rules of ethics, the existence of disciplinary powers, and the sanctions which may be invoked in the event of a failure to respect the rules and regulations of the organisation.

The essence of Article 28 is the element of discrimination in the marketing, sale or distribution of goods between goods of national origin and similar goods of non-national origin. The European Court has stressed the importance of this element after a series of cases brought by traders to challenge national rules restricting trading opportunities but which did not cause this form of discrimination. One of the most important was *Stoke-on-Trent City Council* v *B & Q plc* Case C–169/91 [1993] 1 CMLR 426, where the UK Sunday trading laws were attacked as being contrary to Article 28. In fact the European Court found that no discrimination was caused and therefore the application for relief was unsuccessful.

The propensity of traders to bring actions based on Article 28, even in the absence of any discrimination, caused the Court to react against this trend. In *Keck & Methouard* Cases C–267–268/91 [1993] ECR 6097, the Court held national laws, measures and practices which restrict or prohibit the selling of goods do not hinder trade between Member States contrary to Article 28 if such provisions apply to all affected traders and as long as they affect in the same manner, in law and fact, the marketing of domestic products and those from other Member States. In these circumstances, the application of national laws to the sale of products from other Member States does not ipso facto impede the sale of such products any more than the access of domestic products. Rules fulfilling these requirements therefore fall outside the scope of Article 28.

The Court has followed this precedent in more recent cases. For example, in *Belgapom* v *ITM Belgium SA and Vocarex SA* Case C–63/94 [1995] ECR I–2967, the Court had to consider the legality of a Belgian law which prohibited traders from offering products for sale at a price which lead to an overall loss of profit. A company in Belgium sold bags of potatoes at a price which was less than it had paid the wholesaler and was well below the price charged by its competitors. The company was restrained by a legal order from continuing to sell potatoes at these prices. It replied that such a prohibition infringed Article 28 of the EC Treaty on the grounds that this would also impede the sale of non–Belgian Community products. The Belgian court referred the question of compatibility to the European Court for a ruling.

Following its earlier decision in *Keck & Mithouard*, supra, the Court held that the Belgian legislation concerned 'selling arrangements'. Such laws regulated the sale of products in general and did not, either directly or indirectly, discriminate in favour of domestic producers. Both Belgian and non–Belgian Community goods were subject to the exact same rules. Hence, the law in question fell outside the scope of Article 28 and the law was compatible with Community law.

9.5 Exceptions to the prohibitions on quantitative restrictions and measures having an equivalent effect

Article 30 enumerates the various exceptions to the general rules prohibiting quantitative restrictions and measures of equivalent effect on the free movement of goods. It expressly states:

> 'The provisions of Article [28] shall not preclude prohibitions or restrictions on imports, exports or goods in transit justified on grounds of public morality, public policy or public security; the protection of health and life of humans, animals or plants; the protection of national treasures possessing artistic, historic or archaeological value; or the protection of industrial and commercial property.
>
> Such prohibitions or restrictions shall not, however, constitute a means of arbitrary discrimination or a disguised restriction on trade between Member States.'

There are therefore four express purposes for which Member States may impose quantitative or qualitative restrictions:

1. The protection of public morality, public policy or public security: in *R* v *Henn and Darby* Case 34/79 [1979] ECR 3795 the European Court held that Member

States were justified in imposing restrictions on imports of pornographic material from other States. Such restrictions are not permitted if the materials or matter may legitimately be manufactured within the territory of the Member State imposing the restriction: *Conegate Limited* v *HM Customs & Excise* Case 121/85 [1986] ECR 1007. See also *R* v *Uxbridge Justices, ex parte Webb* [1994] 2 CMLR 288.

2. **The protection of the health of life of humans, animals or plants:** Member States are allowed to introduce measures to protect public health, but these measures must not be unduly restrictive: see *Schumacher* v *Hauptzollamt Frankfurt am Main-Ost* Case C–215/87 [1990] 2 CMLR 465.

3. **Protection of artistic, historic or archaeological treasures:** such restrictions may only be justified when the work remains in the public domain. Once a treasure or work of art is placed on the market or is the subject of a private sale, the exception cannot be invoked.

4. **Protection of industrial or commercial property:** the obvious examples of such restrictions are the laws protecting copyright, patents, trademarks, designs and other intellectual or industrial property rights.

These are the express exceptions contained in Article 30. However, the European Court has derived a number of other exceptions in its jurisprudence on this matter. Most notably, in the *Cassis de Dijon Case* Case 120/78 [1979] ECR 649, the Court expressly observed that:

'Obstacles to movement within the Community resulting from disparities between the national laws relating to the marketing of the products in question must be accepted in so far as those provisions may be recognised as being necessary in order to satisfy mandatory requirements relating in particular to the effectiveness of fiscal supervision, the protection of public health, the fairness of commercial transactions and the defence of the consumer.'

There are therefore another four types of 'mandatory requirements' that states may impose on the free movement of goods:

1. **Fiscal supervision requirements:** these are merely rules to ensure that the currency of a state is not undermined.

2. **Public health:** it is unclear how this requirement relates to the express exemption under Article 30 which provides for the protection of public health. Nevertheless, a Member State is not allowed to prevent the marketing of a product in its territory when it satisfies equivalent standards to that which its rules are intended to ensure.

3. **Fairness of commercial transactions:** these are rules to protect consumers from fraudulent or negligent misrepresentations and deceptive practices: see *GB-INNO-BM* v *Confédération du Commerce Luxembourgeois* Case C–362/88 [1991] 2 CMLR 801.

4. **Consumer protection:** this was the type of measure that *Cassis de Dijon* itself was concerned with. The Court has also developed some precedents in this area, and

one example of such rules are provisions intended to protect the environment: see *EC Commission* v *Denmark (Re Returnable Containers)* Case 302/86 [1989] 1 CMLR 619.

A fifth ground on which mandatory requirements may allow a Member State to introduce restrictions is respect for particular national or regional socio-cultural characteristics. This was the justification given by the European Court in permitting Member States to decide the rules to regulate the opening of shops and stores on Sundays.

In *Stoke-on-Trent City Council* v *B & Q plc* Case C–169/91 [1993] 1 CMLR 426; [1993] 1 All ER 481 the European Court held that rules for such socio-economic purposes fell within the exclusive jurisdiction of Member States to decide subject to the principle of proportionality. The Court expressly stated:

> '... such rules were not prohibited by Article [28] of the EC Treaty where the restrictive effects on Community trade which might result from them did not exceed the effects intrinsic to such rules and that the question whether the effects of those rules actually remained within that limit was a question of fact to be determined by the national court.'

However, the introduction of mandatory requirements is not unconditional. In particular, such measures must not constitute an unjustified or arbitrary means of discrimination: *EC Commission* v *Germany (Re German Sausages)* Case 274/87 [1989] 2 CMLR 733. Also, the restrictions will only be allowable if they are no more widely drawn than necessary and are justified to attain the objective of the measure. In other words, the objectives must be proportionate to the aims to be achieved. For example, in *Italy* v *Nepoli* Case C–196/89 [1992] 2 CMLR 1 the European Court held that national rules limiting the minimum fat content of cheese could not be justified as a mandatory requirement based on consumer protection because consumers could adequately be protected by appropriate labelling of the product.

Finally, the burden of justifying such restrictions rests with the national authorities: *Officier van Justitie* v *Peijper* Case 104/75 [1976] 2 CMLR 271.

Where Community legislation has been enacted to harmonise the legislation of the Member States as regards a particular restriction on the free movement of goods under Article 30, or even under the *Cassis de Dijon* rules, any additional requirements imposed under national law which extend or exceed those contained in the Community measure fall outside the scope of Article 30 and are contrary to Article 28: see *Dansk Denkavit* v *Ministry of Agriculture* Case 29/87 [1990] 1 CMLR 203.

However, it is only when Community legislation provides for complete harmonisation for the purposes of Article 30 that recourse to the protections of that provision is no longer justified: *Oberkreisdirecktor des Kreises* v *Handelsonderneming Moorman* Case C–190/87 [1990] 1 CMLR 656.

9.6 Elimination of measures of internal discriminatory taxation

'No Member State shall impose, directly or indirectly, on the products of other Member States any internal taxation of any kind in excess of that imposed directly or indirectly on similar domestic products.

Furthermore, no Member State shall impose on the products of other Member States any internal taxation of such a nature as to afford indirect protection to other products.

Member States shall, not later than at the beginning of the second stage, repeal or amend any provisions existing when this treaty enters into force which conflict with the preceding rules.'

Of the above-mentioned provisions of Article 90, two are considered as being directly effective, namely Articles 90(1) and 90(2): see *Lütticke* v *Hauptzollampt Saarlouis* Case 57/65 [1971] CMLR 674 and *Fink-Frucht* v *Hauptzollampt München* Case 27/67 [1968] CMLR 228.

Paragraph 1 means that internal taxation may not be imposed on either the finished goods (directly) or the raw materials, or components of goods (indirectly): see *EC Commission* v *United Kingdom (Re Tax on Beer and Wine)* Case 170/78 [1983] ECR 2265, a case which also determined that the words must be construed broadly. An interesting 'broad' interpretation can be found in *Schöttle und Söhne OHG* v *Finanzampt Freudenstadt* Case 20/76 [1977] 2 CMLR 98, where an impost on the transportation of imported goods within the borders of the state was held to be within the meaning of 'indirectly'.

The term 'similar domestic products' has been held to mean goods with a similar or comparable use: *EC Commission* v *Italy* Case 169/78 [1980] ECR 385. Whether goods are similar or not may be determined by the test suggested in *John Walker and Sons* Case 243/84 [1987] CMLR 278, which was that the objective characteristics of the goods should be compared as should the cross-elasticity of consumer demand.

9.7 The internal market programme and harmonisation of national measures

The Single European Act amended the EC Treaty by adding Article 14. This article provided the legal basis for the creation of the internal market within the Community. The internal market is simply the name given to the programme of measures designed to remove national barriers to the flow of goods (as well as persons, services and capital) by creating Community-wide standards for the manufacture, production, marketing and sale of goods.

In 1985, the Commission published a White Paper entitled *Completing the Internal Market*. This document envisaged a programme to achieve the transition to a true internal market in which barriers to trade were minimised. This programme was given effect by the Single European Act.

Article 14 defines the internal market as 'an area without internal frontiers in which the free movement of goods, persons, services and capital is ensured in accordance with the provisions of the [EC Treaty]'. The deadline for the achievement of this goal was set as 31 December 1992.

The internal market programme was designed to remove the major physical, technical and fiscal barriers to trade. The programme involved the adoption of 282 Community measures designed to remove barriers to trade in the areas of customs, tax, public procurement, capital movements, company law, employment, transport and safety standards. The existing disparities in the national laws in these areas were seen as being the primary impediment to the free flow of goods.

From a legal perspective, the greatest obstacle to trade was the existence of the many technical barriers. These included: (a) the diversity of national regulations and standards for testing products for the safety of the consumer; (b) the duplication of product testing and certification (for example, in the pharmaceutical industry); and (c) the reluctance of public authorities in certain Member States to open procurement procedures to the nationals of other Member States.

Substantial Community legislation pertaining to the harmonisation of technical standards, mostly in the form of directives, has been passed to approximate technical standards on products ranging from the alcohol content of certain wines to the level of noise emissions from vehicles. The most heavily Community-regulated sectors are the food and drink, chemical and pharmaceutical industries.

It should be pointed out that the internal market programme was not solely confined to the practical realisation of the free movement of goods. Measures have also been enacted in relation to the free movement of persons, services and capital. But a large proportion of the measures adopted under the programme have been designed to procure the free movement of goods, and this is the rationale for explaining the internal market programme at this juncture.

As noted above, the target set for the enactment of all 282 proposals was 31 December 1992. While the Council was unable to adopt all the measures proposed by the Commission under the programme, around 95 per cent of this total were in fact enacted. Further, while the record varies from Member State to Member State, the vast majority of measures adopted have been implemented into the national laws of the Member States.

Article 14 does not have direct effect, notwithstanding that the programme was due to be completed by 31 December 1992. Consequently, the obligation to implement the measures required to complete the internal market programme cannot be enforced at the instance of private individuals: see *INPS* v *Baglieri* Case C–297/92 [1993] ECR 5211.

Council Regulation 2679/98 was adopted to further remove obstacles to free movement within the internal market, particularly in respect of goods. Under the system established by this Regulation, when an obstacle occurs or a threat thereof emerges, any Member State which has relevant information can transmit this to the Commission. The Commission will then immediately transmit to the Member States that information and any information from any other source which it may consider relevant. If the Commission considers that the obstacle exists, it will notify the

Member State concerned and request it to take all necessary and proportionate measures. The Member States shall, within five working days of receipt of the text, either inform the Commission of the steps which it has taken or intends to take, or communicate a reasoned submission as to why there is no obstacle constituting a breach of Articles 28–30 of the EC Treaty.

The Council also adopted a Resolution concerning the free movement of goods. Member States undertook to do all within their power to maintain the free movement of goods and to deal rapidly with actions which seriously disrupt the free movement of goods. They also agreed to ensure that effective review procedures are available for any person who has been harmed as a result of a breach of the free movement of goods rules.

9.8 The right of free circulation of non-Community goods

Goods entering the Community from non-Community countries are subject to the Common Customs Tariff (CCT), which is a comprehensive Community-wide regime for assessing customs duties on non-EC goods: see section 13.4, below. The CCT supersedes the individual tariff schedules and customs laws of the Member State, although the Community continues to rely on national customs officials to enforce its provisions.

Once goods have passed through the CCT, according to Article 24(1) of the EC Treaty they shall be considered to be in 'free circulation' in the Community if:

1. the relevant import formalities have been completed;
2. any customs duties having an equivalent effect have been levied; and
3. the goods have not benefited from a total or partial drawback of such duties or charges.

Article 23(2) of the Treaty requires that once foreign goods are in free circulation they may not be subject to customs duties, quantitative restrictions or measures having an equivalent effect if they cross the border of one Member State into the territory of another: see *Grandes Distilleries Paureux* v *Directeur des Services Fiscaux* Case 86/78 [1979] ECR 975.

10

Free Movement of Persons

10.1 Introduction

10.2 Definition of workers

10.3 Basic rights of workers and their families

10.4 Right to remain: Regulation 1251/70

10.5 Residence permit: Directive 68/360

10.6 Right of Member States to restrict the free movement of persons

10.7 Safeguards for individuals exercising the right of free movement

10.8 The exception for employees in the public sector

10.1 Introduction

Article 39, which is directly effective, provides that discrimination between workers of the Member States regarding employment, remuneration and other conditions of work and employment shall be abolished. Article 39(2) is still extensively relied on to challenge national laws and practices which discriminate in the employment of workers on the grounds of nationals, notwithstanding the considerable secondary legislation which operates in this area of the law: see, for example, *Allue* v *Universita degli Studi di Venezia* Cases C–259/91, C–331/91 and C–332/91 [1993] ECR 4309; and *Spotti* v *Freistaat Bayern* Case 272/92 [1993] ECR 5185.

The Article itself contains its own provision for derogation in 39(3) which allows limitations on grounds of public policy, security and health. Additionally the Article does not apply to employment in the public service: 39(4).

Article 40 provides that Article 39 will be supplemented by secondary legislation, as indeed it has been by the following means:

Regulation	1612/68	–	Workers' rights
Directive	68/360	–	Residence permits
Regulation	1251/70	–	Remaining after employment
Directive	64/221	–	Justifying exclusions

139

10.2 Definition of workers

Not surprisingly the treaty fails to define workers. Attempts at definition are to be found in *Levin* v *Staatsecretaris van Justitie* Case 53/81 [1982] ECR 1035, where a part-time worker was held to be a worker within the article. There are certain tests to be applied: the workers must be pursuing an effective and genuine activity which is not marginal or ancillary, and the activity must be economic. Whether the tests are satisfied is a matter for the national court.

Levin was followed by *Kempf* v *Staatsecretaris van Justitie* Case 139/85 [1987] CMLR 764. A German national, Kempf, had been earning a living in the Netherlands by giving music lessons, some 12 hours weekly, for which he received very little money. He required social security payments to bring his income up to subsistence level. He had also drawn sickness benefits from the state. Dutch law provided that these benefits were only available to workers. On his application for a residence permit a reference was made to the European Court. Advocate-General Slynn reiterated the *Levin* tests, and, in discussing the drawing of state benefit in order to reach subsistence level, he suggested that this would no more than raise a question as to whether a genuine and effective activity was being pursued. It was held that Kempf was a worker and as such was entitled to a residence permit. It is evident therefore that the hours spent working and the wages received are simply factors to be taken into consideration in determining whether a person falls within the article. They are not conclusive.

The call for a broad interpretation of the word 'worker' was taken up in *Lawrie-Blum* v *Land Baden-Württenberg* Case 66/85 [1987] 3 CMLR 767. This case concerned a trainee teacher, a British national, who as part of her training took classes for which she was paid. The remuneration received was below that of a qualified teacher. She subsequently applied for a post as a secondary school teacher but was refused because of her nationality. The reference by the national court elicited from the European Court of Justice the proposition, echoing *Kempf*, that the term worker 'should receive as wide a meaning as possible'. The Court pointed out that Article 39 provided a fundamental right and cited the following as requirements to be met to achieve the status of worker: providing services for another over a given period, which were under the direction of that other and which were in return for payment. The Court was satisfied that Lawrie-Blum met all requirements and was further satisfied that she was pursuing an economic activity.

Although not strictly workers in the true sense of that term, students enjoy special rights due to the vocational nature of their studies. Therefore, a special regime has been introduced to regulate their right to exercise this freedom. In particular, Council Directive 93/96/EEC (1993) confers on students the right of residence when pursuing their studies in Member States other than their own.

10.3 Basic rights of workers and their families

Regulation 1612/68 specifies exactly what a worker is entitled to do in a Member State. He or she has the right to:

1. Take employment with the same priority as nationals of that state: Article 1(1) and (2).
2. Seek employment and receive the same assistance as nationals from the employment offices: Article 5.
3. Enjoy the same treatment regarding remuneration, dismissal and if he or she becomes unemployed, reinstatement or re-employment: Article 7(1).
4. Enjoy the same social and tax advantages: Article 7(2). Another regulation which complements and expands this article is Regulation 1408/71 which concerns the application of social security schemes to employed persons, to self-employed persons and to members of their families moving within the Community. The Regulation is designed to ensure that in the social security areas of sickness and maternity benefit, invalidity benefit, old-age benefit, survivors' benefit, benefits in respect of accidents at work and occupational diseases, unemployment benefits and family benefits, there will be no discrimination on grounds of nationality, and that benefit will be paid notwithstanding that the recipient resides in another Member State.
5. Enjoy the same right as a national regarding training: Article 7(3).
6. Membership of trade unions: Article 8.
7. Enjoy the same rights as nationals regarding housing: Article 9.

In addition the Regulation allows the worker to be joined by his or her family who are his or her spouse and descendants under 21 years, and dependent relatives in the ascendant line of worker and spouse: Article 10.

Article 11 allows those embraced by Article 10 to take up employment in the state and Article 12 allows the children equal access to education.

It can be seen that a worker within Article 39 has the right to equal treatment as a national, and such rights as he/she enjoys will be accorded to spouses and dependent relatives.

The Court's view of the rights is robust. In *Mr and Mrs F v Belgian State* Case 7/75 [1975] ECR 679 Advocate-General Trabucchi stated that a migrant worker is not a mere source of labour but a human being, and Community law should serve to remove obstacles to the mobility of workers and especially obstacles to 'the integration of his family in the host country'.

The case of *Emir Gül v Regierungspräsident Düsseldorf* Case 131/85 [1987] 1 CMLR 501 gives a further illustration of the court's attitude. Gül, a Cypriot, was a doctor who in 1971 married a British national. His spouse worked as a hairdresser in Germany. Dr Gül was given temporary leave to practise medicine in Germany provided that he returned to Cyprus on completion of that period. He eventually applied for permanent permission to practise.

The only limitation on a spouse's right to work envisaged in *Mr and Mrs F* was that the host nation's qualification requirements had to be satisfied. In *Gül*, the point was raised as to whether the right granted by Article 11 of the Regulation extended to the practising of medicine. The Court followed Advocate-General Trabucchi's line and decided that lack of appropriate qualifications was the only limitation under Article 11. Accordingly Gül was entitled to practise.

The principle of non-discrimination was further tested in the case of *Netherlands* v *Reed* Case 59/85 [1986] ECR 1283 through its examination of Article 10 and especially the word 'spouse'. Reed, a British national who was unmarried, sought work there but found Mr W, another British national working in the Netherlands. She moved in with him but remained unemployed. She subsequently applied for a residence permit which was refused. Dutch law allowed non-nationals to extend their rights to residence permits to cohabitees if the relationship had been formed prior to entry into the country. Dutch nationals, on the other hand, suffered no such restraint: their cohabitees of Dutch nationals could be admitted. In the Article 234 referral, the Court refused to extend the word spouse to include a cohabitee. The Court allowed the admission of Reed on other grounds, namely Article 6 (Regulation 1612/68, above). W had the right to enjoy the same social advantages as a Dutch national and should not be discriminated against.

In *Diatta* v *Berlin* Case 267/83 [1986] 2 CMLR, on an Article 234 reference, it was held that separated spouses who were non-nationals of a Member State could still enjoy the status of spouse notwithstanding the fact that they no longer cohabited.

A similar decision was rendered in *R* v *Immigration Appeal Tribunal and Singh, ex parte Secretary of State for the Home Department* Case C–370/90 [1992] 3 CMLR 358. In this case Mr Singh, an Indian national, married a British citizen in the UK in 1982. The couple then left the UK to work in Germany where both obtained employment. They subsequently returned to the UK to start a private business. However, at no time during this period did Mr Singh acquire British nationality.

In 1987 a decree nisi of divorce was pronounced against Mr Singh, and the date of the expiry of his temporary leave to remain in the UK was brought forward to September of that year. After the expiry of this period Mr Singh remained in the UK without permission, and eventually a deportation order was made out against him.

The question of whether Mr Singh was entitled to exercise the right of free movement of workers to continue to reside in the UK, after initiating this right by travelling to Germany as the spouse of a Community worker, was brought before the Immigration Appeal Tribunal. The tribunal ruled in Mr Singh's favour. According to the decision of the tribunal, the right of free movement included the right to return to and reside in the country from which the party left to exercise the right of free movement in another Member State.

The matter was referred to the European Court, which upheld the ruling of the tribunal. Once an individual travels from one Community country to another for the purpose of obtaining employment, the whole gambit of Community rights under the principle of the free movement of workers is activated. This includes the right of the spouse of a Community worker to return with his or her spouse to their original Member State. Inside the home country, the individual and his or her spouse are entitled to exercise the right of free movement and cannot be prevented from doing so on the grounds of nationality.

The European Court has also considered the application of Article 39 to the rules of private organisations and bodies which have the effect of restricting the movement of workers. In *Union des Associations Européennes de Football* v *Jean-Marc Bosman* Case C–415/93 [1995] ECR I–4921, the Court ruled on the legality of the rules of football organisations and their compatibility with Article 39 and the prohibition of discrimination on the grounds of nationality. The body in question, UEFA, is the organisation which regulates the national football associations of some 50 countries, including those of the 15 Member States. It enacts rules which are implemented at national level by the individual national football associations. In this case two of these rules were reviewed by the European Court.

The first concerned the imposition of transfer fees which allowed national football clubs to impose a transfer fee when a player moved from one club to another. In the absence of such a fee, which was set by the transferring club, a player could not move from one club to another. These requirements were written into individual players contracts. If a club refused to accept the fee offered by another club, it could prevent the player moving, in which case the player in question would be unable to break his contractual link with his club.

The second regulation concerned restrictions on the number of non-national players that could be fielded by a club. The number of non-national players which could be fielded at any one time during a game was restricted to three. UEFA justified this rule on the basis that it preserved the national element in football clubs.

Bosman was a Belgian football player who had been prevented from transferring from a Belgian team to a French team because the fee offered by the French team was inadequate. As a result he was unable to transfer and his football career was destroyed. He sued the Belgian football team, the Belgian national football association and UEFA claiming that these rules violated Community law. Both questions were referred to the European Court for a preliminary ruling.

The Court ruled first that the transfer fees contravened Article 39 of the EC Treaty because they interfered with the right of free movement for football players. The Court accepted that the same rules applied inside Member States but held that the nature of these rules was too excessive and constituted a barrier to the cross-border movement of players inside the Community.

The Court also found that the nationality restrictions contravened Article 39 and, in particular, the prohibition on discrimination on the grounds of nationality. The rules could not be justified as preserving the national identity of teams and violated one of the fundamental freedoms of Community law.

10.4 Right to remain: Regulation 1251/70

This Regulation provides that having been employed in a Member State the worker
has the right to remain if:

1. He or she has been employed and has reached pensionable age having worked for
   the previous 12 months and resided there continuously for more than three
   years.
2. After continuous residence for more than two years he or she becomes
   permanently incapable of work: Article 2(b).

These rights are extended by Article 3 to the worker's family, subject to the
conditions laid down in that article. Article 3(2) provides:

> 'If, however, the worker dies during his working life and before having acquired the right
> to remain in the territory of the state concerned, members of his family shall be entitled
> to remain there permanently on condition that:
> a) the worker, on the date of his decease, had resided continuously in the territory of that
> Member State for at least two years; or
> b) his death resulted from an accident at work or an occupational disease; or
> c) the surviving spouse is a national of the state of residence or lost the nationality of that
> state by marriage to that worker.'

The right to remain after ceasing employment also extends to employees and
self-employed persons who have decided to retire. Council Directive 90/365/EEC,
which came into effect in July 1994, requires Member States to grant the right of
residence to nationals of other Member States who have been employed or self-
employed and are recipients of an invalidity or early retirement pension, an old age
pension or a pension in respect of industrial accident or disease. Entitlement to this
right requires the individual to prove to the national authorities that he or she
receives sufficient income from these sources as not to be a burden on the social
security system of the host state.

10.5 Residence permit: Directive 68/360

To gain entry to a Member State a person covered by Regulation 1612/68 need only
produce a passport or an identity card: Article 3, Directive 68/360. Article 4 of the
Directive states that the Member State shall then grant right of residence to those
satisfying Article 3. Article 4(2) provides that a document entitled 'Residence Permit
for a National of a Member State of the EEC' *shall* be issued. It is simply proof of
right of residence. The worker can be employed prior to completion of the
formalities for obtaining a permit: Article 5.

The permit itself must be valid for at least five years, throughout the Member
State: Article 6. Article 8 extends the right of residence to those employed for less
than three months, frontier workers – that is, those who return to their own

Member State every day or week – and seasonal workers. They need not be required to apply for residence permits.

The question as to whether a worker's rights were conditional upon the issue of a residence permit by a national authority, or whether the rights were granted directly by Article 39 of the EC Treaty, was decided in *Procureur du Roi* v *Jean Noël Royer* Case 48/75 [1976] ECR 497. It was held that:

1. The right of nationals of a Member State to enter and reside in the territory of another Member State is conferred directly by the treaty.
2. Article 4 of Directive 68/360 entails an obligation for the Member States to issue a residence permit to anyone providing proof required by the Directive.
3. The mere failure by a national to comply with formalities concerning entry is not behaviour threatening to public policy and by itself cannot justify a measure ordering expulsion or imprisonment.

In addition to the protection afforded by *Royer* the worker may not be required to seek other permits: see *Sagulo* v *The State* Case 8/77 [1977] ECR 1495 and *Pieck* Case 157/79 [1980] ECR 2171.

10.6 Right of Member States to restrict the free movement of persons

Article 39(3) provides that it shall entail the right, subject to limitations justified on grounds of public policy, public security or public health, to:

1. Accept offers of employment actually made.
2. Move freely within the territory of Member States for this purpose.
3. Stay in a Member State for the purpose of employment in accordance with the provisions governing the employment of nationals of that state laid down by law, regulation or administrative action.
4. Remain in the territory of a Member State after having been employed in that state, subject to conditions which shall be embodied in implementing regulations to be drawn up by the Commission.

This provision is somewhat amplified by Directive 64/221, which provides, inter alia, that refusal of entry or expulsion from territory will not be allowed on permitted grounds simply to achieve economic ends: Article 2. Article 3 provides that measures taken on grounds of public policy or public security shall be based exclusively on the personal conduct of the individual concerned – previous criminal convictions are not sufficient grounds, nor is expiry of passport nor failure to apply for a residence permit.

Diseases or disabilities justifying refusal of entry or issue of a residence permit are only those listed in the annex to the Directive: Article 4 (TB, syphilis, diseases subject to quarantine – endangering public health policy or public security).

Article 4(3) prohibits the introduction of new provisions or practices which are more restrictive than those already in force.

It is instructive to examine the Court's attitude to the derogations afforded under the treaty and the directive. *Van Duyn* v *Home Office* Case 41/74 [1975] CMLR 1 gives a line on the court's thinking specifically in reference to Article 3(1) of Directive 64/221. Ms Yvonne Van Duyn, a Dutch national, was returned to the Netherlands by immigration officials at Gatwick Airport. She had stated that she was going to work for the Church of Scientology, in East Grinstead. The United Kingdom government considered the activities of the church to be socially harmful. Ms Van Duyn appealed, and a reference to the European Court was made. In answer to the three questions posed, the ECJ handed down the following rulings:

1. Article 39 of the EC Treaty is directly effective.
2. Article 3(1) of Directive 64/221 confers rights on an individual which must be upheld by the national courts.
3. Article 39 and Article 3(1) of Directive 64/221 must be interpreted as meaning that a Member State, in imposing restrictions justified on grounds of public policy, is entitled to take into account, as a matter of personal conduct of the individual concerned, the fact that the individual is associated with some body or organisation whose activities the Member State considers socially harmful, though not unlawful within the state, and despite the fact that no restriction is placed upon nationals of the Member State who wish to take employment with the organisation.

Article 3(1) of the Directive fell to be discussed again soon after in *Bonsignore* v *Oberstadtdirektor Köln* Case 67/74 [1975] ECR 297. In this case an Italian national, Carmelo Bonsignore, resident in Germany, shot his brother by accident. The weapon he used was a pistol he had illegally acquired. He was ordered to be deported, having been fined for unlawful possession of a pistol. A reference to the European Court was made, seeking a ruling on Articles 3(1) and 3(2) of the Directive, in particular whether nationals of Member States be deported to deter other foreign nationals. The Court responded clearly. It indicated that any departure from the rules concerning free movement had to be construed strictly, so a Member State could not deport to deter, and any deportation had to be made on the basis of the behaviour of the individual concerned. Future behaviour was only relevant in so far as there were clear indications that the individual would commit further offences.

Despite this ruling, however, the Court has conceded that cases do arise occasionally where the behaviour of the individual, while not giving any indication as to future behaviour, does nevertheless give rise to such public concern as to justify deportation: *R* v *Bouchereau* Case 30/77 [1977] ECR 1999. The Court acknowledged that a propensity to act in a certain way could be evinced by past behaviour, and, if that behaviour constituted a threat to public policy, then, on those narrow grounds, deportation would be justified.

The word 'justified' was discussed in *Rutili* v *French Minister of the Interior* Case 36/75 [1975] ECR 1219. Rutili was an Italian resident in France. He had been involved in certain political movements in 1968. He applied for and was issued with a residence permit which had strict limitations placed on it. He could only live in certain parts of France.

A reference to the European Court was made. The first question was whether Article 39(3) referred only to legislative decisions of Member States or also to individual decisions taken in application of legislative decisions. The Court indicated that it was up to the national courts to comply with Community law.

The second question concerned the word 'justified'. Here the Court said that the word must be construed strictly, and free movement must be allowed unless an individual's conduct constituted a genuine and sufficiently serious threat to public policy. In other words, restrictions are only justifiable if they are necessary for the protection of public safety and national security in a democratic society. The threat to public safety and national security must be genuine and sufficiently serious: *R v Bouchereau*.

Equally, Member States are not permitted to impose residence requirements based on nationality to prevent Community nationals from taking up employment in their territory. In other words, attempts by Member States to impose nationality requirements under the guise of residency will be frowned upon by the European Court. An example of this type of discrimination occurred in *Clean Car Auto Service GmbH and Landeshauptmann von Wien* Case C–350/96 [1998] 2 CMLR 637. This case involved an Austrian company which applied for registration to trade, but was rejected on the grounds that the company had appointed as manager a person not resident in Austria. The Austrian government claimed this requirement was necessary to ensure the effective management of a company.

The Court found that the residence requirement contained in the Austrian laws constituted unjustified indirect discrimination contrary to the EC Treaty rules on freedom of movement. The ECJ observed that, whilst it is true that the Austrian rules apply regardless of the nationality of the person to be appointed as manager, national rules under which a distinction is drawn on the basis of residence are likely to operate mainly to the detriment of nationals of other Member States, as non-residents are, in the majority of cases, non-nationals. See Chapter 16, section 16.3, for further details.

10.7 Safeguards for individuals exercising the right of free movement

The Directive contains the following safeguards: Article 5 provides that a decision to grant or refuse a first residence permit should be taken as soon as possible but certainly no later than six months after application. The applicant may remain in the Member State during that time; Article 5(2) inquiries may be made of the home Member State about police records. The decision to refuse must give its grounds (Article 6) unless state security is involved. After refusal the applicant may remain for at least 15 days, if the matter is urgent, and at least a month otherwise: Article 7.

The remedies available to the applicant are those that are available to nationals in respect of administrative decisions: Article 8. If there is no right of appeal to a court of law then the decision to expel can only be taken by the administrative authorities after an opinion has been sought from a body where the applicant may be able to defend him or herself in person: Article 9. These latter provisions do not apply in cases of urgency. *Santillo* Case 131/79 [1980] ECR 1585, which held Articles 8 and 9 directly effective, provides a gloss on the question of giving an opinion. Here the opinion was given on Santillo's conviction for indecency offences in 1974. The deportation order was made in 1979. The ECJ held that the opinion and order for deportation must be proximate. In this case it was not, but the Divisional Court did not comply with the Court's ruling.

The Directive also does not prevent Member States from adopting measures to monitor population movements. For example, in *Lynne Watson and Alessandro Belmann* Case 118/75 [1976] ECR 1185, the European Court held that the Italian government did not act illegally in requiring foreign nationals staying in hotels within the country to register with the police authorities within 24 hours.

The defendants in the case claimed that this requirement infringed their right to freedom of movement under Article 39. The Court rejected this argument on the grounds that Member States were entitled to maintain records of foreign nationals entering, residing in and leaving their territory.

10.8 The exception for employees in the public sector

Article 39(4) states that the provisions of Article 39 do not apply to employment in the public service. The proviso raises the rather thorny question of what precisely is the public service. In *EC Commission v Belgium (Re State Employees)* Case 149/79 [1980] ECR 3881 the Court declared it was posts which involve direct or indirect involvement in exercising powers 'conferred by public law and duties designed to safeguard the general interests of the state and other public authorities'. The Court went on to point out that such posts usually involve 'allegiance to the state.' A range of posts was cited as falling within Article 39(4), such as works supervisor or office supervisor employed by a city council, whereas train drivers, plumbers, nurses employed by the same authority fell outside.

EC Commission v France Case 307/84 [1986] ECR 1725 involved proceedings brought by the European Commission against France, which insisted that only French nationals could be appointed as nurses in a public hospital. The Court held that such a provision was contrary to Article 39, saying that public service implied an occupation which involved the safeguarding of the public interest of the state. It is also evident from *Lawrie-Blum* (above) that teaching in a state school is not employment in the public service.

It must be noted that once a national of a Member State is in employment in the public service, Article 39(4) does not justify discrimination against that individual: *Sotgiu v Deutsches Bundespost* Case 152/73 [1974] ECR 153.

11

Right of Establishment and the Freedom to Provide Services

11.1 Introduction

11.2 The right of establishment: Article 43

11.3 Qualifications

11.4 Companies

11.5 Right to supply services: Article 49

11.6 Right to receive services

11.1 Introduction

The articles providing the right of establishment and the freedom to provide services are Articles 43 and 49 of the EC Treaty respectively. These Articles are reinforced by Article 12 of the EC Treaty. Taken together they ensure that restrictions on the right and the freedom to provide professional and commercial services are to be progressively abolished. The European Court has, on a number of occasions, held Member States in violation of Community law for discriminating in favour of their own nationals when regulating professional activities within their territories: see, for example, *EC Commission* v *Luxembourg (Re Access to the Medical Profession)* Case C–351/90 [1992] 3 CMLR 124.

Article 43 has been supplemented by Directive 73/148, and the general programme for the abolition of restrictions on freedom of establishment is further supplemented by directives relating to qualifications. Article 49 may also be regulated by the above directives.

Articles 43 and 49 may seem to overlap, but in separating their application a rule of thumb may be employed: Article 43 applies in a situation where a person may wish to pursue an activity wholly within another Member State, whereas Article 49 applies where a person simply conducts professional forays into another Member State without establishing a business presence there.

11.2 Right of establishment: Article 43

This Article is directly effective (*Reyners* v *Belgian State* Case 2/74 [1974] ECR 631) but derogations are provided for in Article 46. The grounds in Article 46 are the same as in Article 39(3): public policy, public security and public health. The rights afforded by Article 43 and the Directive are almost identical to those provided under Article 39 and its attendant regulations and directives: see *Procureur du Roi* v *Jean Noël Royer* Case 48/75 [1976] ECR 497. The same may be said of Article 49. They all revolve around the Article 12 axis and apply to all discrimination on the grounds of nationality, whether the discrimination is by public or private bodies. The stumbling block, however, is qualifications.

Prior to considering this problem it should be pointed out that none of the provisions relating to the freedom of establishment may be relied on by nationals to evade requirements imposed for the purposes of regulating a profession. The EC Treaty provisions concerning the right of establishment do not apply to activities conducted wholly within a single Member State by its own nationals. It is necessary to establish a nexus between the facts and a Community measure, such as a Directive harmonising standards, in order to achieve such an effect. For example, in *Ministerio Fiscal* v *Lopez Brea* Cases C–330 and 331/90 [1992] 2 CMLR 397 the European Court held that two Spanish nationals holding themselves out as estate agents in Spain, who did not in fact possess the necessary professional qualifications, could not rely on the protection of the right of establishment or Article 43 as a defence to their prosecution.

11.3 Qualifications

There is no doubt that mutual recognition of qualifications would facilitate the operation of these Articles, and indeed the EC Treaty provides in Article 47 that directives will be issued providing for such an end. There would appear to be no problem in the areas where a qualification can be standardised, such as medicine. It is in this professional area that there has been most movement. Directives 75/362 and 75/363 ensure the mutual recognition of medical diplomas and certain medical qualifications.

Where a profession has been the subject of harmonising legislation, Member States are prohibited from implementing such measures in a manner likely to prevent its proper functioning. Thus, in *EC Commission* v *Germany (Re Restrictions on the Legal Profession)* Case C–427/85 [1989] 2 CMLR 677, the European Court held that Germany was not entitled to require foreign lawyers practising in Germany to be supervised at all times by German lawyers in order to ensure that the foreign lawyers received proper experience. This rule was held to be disproportionate to the object sought to be achieved, which was the protection of the public from inappropriately qualified legal advisers.

The position as regards professional qualifications that have not been the subject of harmonising legislation appears to be that Member States are entitled to specify the conditions required for appointment to such positions to ensure that appointees possess sufficient knowledge and qualifications. Nevertheless, such restrictions impede the effective exercise of the freedom of establishments and should be construed narrowly: see *UNECTEF* v *George Heylens* Case C–222/86 [1989] 1 CMLR 901.

Directive 89/48 EEC, which concerns the system for the recognition of higher-education diplomas awarded on completion of professional education and training of at least three years' duration, may provide many of the solutions for settling disagreements in this controversial area. The Directive briefly lays down that any diploma, certificate or other evidence of formal qualification awarded by a competent authority in a Member State which is the fruit of at least three years' study (Article 1) will be recognised by any other Member State, and the holder cannot be refused permission to take up the profession on the same conditions as apply to a national of that other Member State: Article 3. The host Member State may require the applicant to provide evidence of professional experience not exceeding four years, and to complete an adaptation period not exceeding three years, or take an aptitude test: Article 4. Once recognised, the applicant may use the 'professional title of the host Member State corresponding to that profession': Article 7.

Even where a profession has been subject to harmonising measures to equate different professional qualifications from institutions and professional bodies in Member States, a state is still required to ensure that the right of individuals under Article 43 are not infringed. For example, in *Haim* v *Kassenzahnartzliche Vereinigung Nordrhein* Case C–319/92 [1994] 2 CMLR 169, the European Court found against the German authorities for failing to take into account the experience of a dentist who had worked in Belgium as well as Turkey when assessing his application for admission to that profession. Instead, the German authorities had denied his application on the grounds that he had not completed a preparatory training period when in fact he had practised as a qualified dentist in these countries for a considerable number of years.

This decision is significant because, even though legislation harmonising professional qualifications was in place, violations of Article 43 may still occur if Member States fail to take account of practical professional experience. In other words, the Court has gone one step further than the legislation in imposing an obligation on Member States to ensure effective application of the terms of Article 43 notwithstanding harmonising legislation.

11.4 Companies

Article 48 provides for the establishment of companies thus:

> 'Companies or firms formed in accordance with the law of a Member State and having their registered office, central administration or principal place of business within the Community shall, for the purposes of this Chapter, be treated in the same way as natural persons who are nationals of Member States.
>
>   "Companies or firms" means companies or firms constituted under civil or commercial law, including co-operative societies, and other legal persons governed by public or private law, save for those which are non-profit making.'

In the second paragraph of the article non-profit making organisations are excluded. This presumably means that charities and trade unions, inter alia, will not be covered by this very widely drawn article.

11.5 Right to supply services: Article 49

This Article, which is directly effective (*Van Binsbergen* v *Bestuur van de Bedrijfvereniging Voor de Metaalnijverheid* Case 33/74 [1975] 1 CMLR 298), states that an individual may provide services in a Member State other than the one in which he or she is established. 'Services' fall to be defined in Article 50 as those which are normally provided for remuneration and in particular include activities of an industrial character, of a commercial character, and of craftsmen and the professions. Such services may be pursued under the same conditions as those imposed by a Member State on its own nationals.

The scope of the term 'services' is broad, and in *Society for the Protection of Unborn Children (Ireland)* v *Grogan* Case C–159/90 [1991] 3 CMLR 849 the European Court held that medical services, including abortion clinics, were services within the meaning of Article 50. In arriving at its conclusion in this case, the Court dismissed the moral arguments surrounding abortion which were a matter for the legislature of individual Member States. This implies that if an activity is unlawful according to the law of a Member State, the Court will respect the laws of that state and will not try to compel a state to decriminalise the provision of a service.

There is generally no difficulty in indentifying what economic activity amounts to a service under the Article. The cases are few and far between but include the unusual *Dona* v *Mantero* Case 13/76 [1976] ECR 133, where playing professional football was covered by the Article, and the esoteric *Walrave and Koch* v *Association Union Cycliste Internationale* Case 36/74 [1974] ECR 1405, where a professional pace-setter was held to be covered by the Article.

11.6 Right to receive services

Although not obviously within the strict wording of Article 49, it has been held that the converse of the Article also applies, that is, that a person may go into another Member State to receive a service. Article 12 of the Treaty ensures that in the exercise of this right there is to be no discrimination: see *Luisi* Case 26/83 [1984] ECR 377. The matter was raised again in *Gravier* v *City of Liège* Case 293/83 [1985] 3 CMLR 1. The Court in this case determined that conditions relating to access to vocational training fell within the Treaty. The Court formulated a test whereby it could be determined whether a course of studies amounted to vocational training.

If a form of education prepared for qualification for a profession trade or employment, or gave the requisite training for the profession, trade or employment, then it was vocational training. In *Gravier* the study of cartoons was held to be vocational training. The test was approved in *Blaizot et al* v *University of Liège* Case 24/86 [1989] 1 CMLR 57 where it was held that a registration fee payable only by Belgian nationals was discriminatory; it was contrary to Article 12. However, realising that the judgment might cause hardship, the Court held that, although the fee was returnable in the present case, the judgment was not retroactive. The above judgment has limitations, however, in that although the payment of fees falls within the scope of the Treaty, the payment of maintenance grants does not, as it is a matter of national educational and social policy. This ruling applies whether or not a condition of acceptance into the university is that the student works, thereby making him or her a worker under Article 39 and Regulation 1612/68. The work would only be ancillary to his or her studies: see *Brown* v *Secretary of State for Scotland* Case 197/86 [1988] ECR 3205.

In fact, the Court has not limited the right to receive services to education, training and vocational programmes, but has extended the scope of this doctrine to include the right to travel to other Member States for the purpose of obtaining any form of services, even the general services afforded to tourists. Once an individual has travelled to another Member State, he or she is entitled to the protection of the prohibition on discrimination on the grounds of nationality when exercising this right: *Luisi and Carbone* v *Ministero del Tesoro* Cases 286/82 and 26/83 [1984] ECR 377.

For example, a British citizen who was violently assaulted outside a Metro station in Paris was entitled to compensation from the French equivalent of the Criminal Injuries Compensation Board on the ground that laws and regulations which prevent the proper exercise of the right to receive services through discrimination are contrary to Community law: *Cowan* v *Trésor Public* Case 186/87 [1990] 2 CMLR 613. Persons exercising the right to receive services are entitled to be protected from harm on the same basis as nationals and residents and must be free from all forms of discrimination on the grounds of nationality.

12

European Competition Law

12.1 Introduction

12.2 Procedure

12.3 Article 81 EC Treaty

12.4 Article 82 EC Treaty

12.5 Merger control

12.1 Introduction

As one of the key elements in the creation of an internal market among the twelve Member States of the Community, the EC Treaty envisaged the adoption of a Community-wide competition policy to 'ensure that competition within the common market is not distorted': Article 3(g) of the EC Treaty. This policy has been established by the Council, but the European Commission has extensive delegated powers to administer it. In fact, through its mandate to administer, the Commission has effectively shaped the present form of competition policy.

The aim of the policy is to support progress towards the elimination of barriers to trade between Member States. They are required to eliminate all quantitative restrictions on imports and exports, together with all measures having an equivalent effect to such restrictions, in accordance with Articles 28 and 29 of the Treaty. But the effect of reducing national barriers to trade such as these would be severely diminished if private individuals or companies were allowed to erect private obstructions to trade through their commercial activities. To prevent such an occurrence, Community competition policy attacks certain types of private commercial agreements and anti-competitive practices by companies in dominant positions within a particular market. The aim is to reduce unfair competition through the intervention of the Community agencies.

The Commission has been given substantial authority to investigate complaints alleging violations of Community competition rules. It also has authority to review agreements submitted by private parties to ensure that any potentially anti-competitive terms are acceptable in the light of the policy objectives of Community competition law. In both these capacities the Commission has powers to require the production of materials, to conduct inspections at private premises and to demand explanations from persons subject to investigation.

As a corollary to its investigative function, the Commission also has authority to grant clearance to agreements submitted to it for review, to exempt agreements and, ultimately, to fine parties found to have engaged in anti-competitive behaviour. The relationship between the European Commission and private parties as regards these matters can broadly be described as the procedural laws of Community competition policy.

The substantive rules of competition law are contained in Articles 81 and 82 of the EC Treaty. Briefly, Article 81 prohibits all agreements, decisions and concerted practices between private parties which affect trade between Member States and which have as either their object or effect the prevention, restriction or distortion of competition within the Community. Article 82, on the other hand, prohibits any abuses by one or more parties of a dominant position within a particular market, again in so far as such behaviour affects trade between Member States.

Both Articles are intended to counter different forms of commercial behaviour. The major distinction between the Articles is that Article 81 deals with agreements between two or more parties while Article 82 essentially concerns abusive behaviour, normally by a single party, but conceivably by a small number of parties. However, these two provisions should not be compartmentalised. It is perfectly possible that a particular activity might contravene both provisions although, certainly in the past, this has been more the exception than the rule.

Another aspect of competition dealt with at Community level is that of merger control. Although there is no specific provision of the Treaty dealing with this subject, the Commission has historically considered that mergers and acquisitions of a sufficient size can product effects contrary to Articles 81 and 82. Eventually, a Council Regulation was enacted in 1989 to allow the Commission to review the compatibility of mergers and acquisitions within the Community for anti-competitive effects contrary to these Articles. This measure will be considered in more detail later in this chapter.

To allow a comprehensive description of Community competition policy, the procedural law of the subject will be discussed first before proceeding to the substantive rules. After this, Community competition will be considered in more detail, firstly as regards the application of Articles 81 and 82 and secondly in relation to the Merger Control Regulation.

12.2 Procedure

The procedural rules of Community competition policy have become exceptionally complex and, as we shall see, have been the basis for a considerable volume of appeals to the European Court, and now to the Court of First Instance, against findings by the Commission. The source of these procedural rules is not any express provision of the EC Treaty but regulations enacted by the Council and the Commission.

The basic regulation concerning procedure in competition matters is Council Regulation 17/62 (1962) which governs matters such as notifications of agreements, clearance, powers to terminate infringements and powers to fine. This Regulation is considered the basic Regulation because it is the primary measure conferring authority on the Commission to act in Community competition matters.

In addition, these procedural rules have often been supplemented by safeguards developed by the European Court and the Court of First Instance in the name of general principles of law. In fact, procedural safeguards derived from this latter source have been established mainly to fill omissions in the legislative framework for conducting investigations. One illustration of the European Court protecting the procedural rights of parties involved in an investigation is *SA Asia Motors France* v *EC Commission* Case T–28/90 [1992] 5 CMLR 431, where the Commission was found to have committed violations of procedural law and the decision of the Commission on the matter was annulled. The Court found that the Commission had failed to exercise the proper standards of appraisal and respect for procedural guarantees. In particular, the Commission had made a number of factual errors in conducting its investigation which could not be justified and which, in the circumstances, vitiated the Commission's decision.

Anti-competitive agreements and behaviour come to the attention of the Commission through two main avenues. First, agreements that contain provisions infringing Article 81 must, according to the terms of the basic Regulation, be notified to the Commission for its attention. Parties notify agreements to the Commission to obtain negative clearance from the Commission or exemption under Article 81(3). In the event that the terms of an agreement notified to the Commission through this procedure are considered to be anti-competitive, the parties to the agreement will be required to alter its terms before it comes into effect.

Alternatively, anti-competitive agreements or behaviour may come to the attention of the Commission through a complaint lodged by a private party, usually a commercial competitor. It should also be noted that the Commission may investigate allegations of anti-competitive behaviour, without prior notification or a complaint, when such matters come to its attention, eg through the media.

Private parties cannot, however, compel the Commission to conduct an investigation and the Commission exercises considerable discretion as to whether a complaint should be investigated or rejected. As a general principle, the European Commission now concentrates its investigative activities to matters which are of 'sufficient Community interest'. Where such an interest is not present, a party injured by anti-competitive activities must seek relief through national courts as opposed to making complaints to the European Commission: see *Automec* v *EC Commission* Case T–24/90 [1992] 5 CMLR 431. This is also made clear in the

Commission's Notice on Co-operation between Community Institutions and National Courts 1993.

The enforcement of Community competition law is also partly the responsibility of national competition authorities. Moreover, the Commission has, for some time, been examining possible ways to decentralise the application of EC competition rules. To this end, it published in 1997 a Notice setting out the ways in which the European Commission and the national competition authorities of the Member States can co-operate in handling cases which fall within Articles 81 and 82 of the EC Treaty. This Notice is the counterpart to the 1993 Co-operation Notice on Relations between National Courts and the Commission on Competition Matters.

Under the framework of Community competition law, both the national authorities and the Commission are jointly responsible for applying Articles 81 and 82, although it is only the Commission who can grant an individual exemption under Article 81(3). The Commission's aim in adopting the Notice is to encourage the wider application of the competition rules by national authorities who can use their more detailed knowledge of local markets and businesses. The intention of the Commission is that businesses will start to approach national competition authorities more frequently and therefore indirectly reduce the Commission's workload. This would leave the Commission free to handle cases with a truly Community dimension.

The 1997 Notice sets down rules which, generally, allow national authorities to deal with cases having a mainly local impact and which, prima facie, are unlikely to be exempted under Article 81(3). However, the Commission reserves the right to handle cases involving a 'particular Community interest' even if they could be dealt with by a national authority. These include cases which: (i) raise a new point of law; or (ii) involve alleged anti-competitive behaviour by a public undertaking or an undertaking interested with the operation of services of general economic interest.

At the Community level, the principal sanction against anti-competitive behaviour is the power to fine conferred on the Commission. In general, this power is exercised sparingly and only used in cases where the anti-competitive behaviour is serious, detrimentally affects the interests of consumers or has continued unchecked for a considerable number of years.

The final matter to be considered as a matter of procedural law is the judicial review of Commission decisions sanctioning private parties for anti-competitive behaviour. Review is generally conducted on the basis of Article 230(4) of the EC Treaty on the four grounds established for that purpose in this provision. The Court of First Instance now has jurisdiction to hear such applications at first instance, subject to appeal to the European Court itself.

Notifications, negative clearance and exemptions

Article 81(1) of the EC Treaty, as we shall see later, prohibits certain types of anti-competitive agreements where these affect trade between Member States.

Agreements which fall within Article 81(1) are therefore illegal unless they benefit from the exception provisions contained in Article 81(3). But there is no black-and-white line between agreements that fall inside Article 81(1) and those that do not.

Regulation 17/62 establishes a procedure whereby agreements can be notified to the Commission for clarification as regards their potentially anti-competitive effects. However, it should be noted that this procedure is only available to parties contemplating entering into an agreement which falls under Article 81(1). It does not apply to parties engaged in behaviour contrary to Article 82.

Notification of agreements to the Commission

If an agreement is considered to fall within the scope of Article 81(1), it should be notified to the Commission unless:

1. notification is not necessary due to the existence of a dispensation; or
2. the agreement or contract falls within a group exemption.

In other words, if an agreement between two or more parties affects trade between Member States and has as its object or effect the prevention, restriction or distortion of competition, there is a presumption in favour of notification.

Dispensations. A number of categories of dispensation have been established by both the Commission and the Court. Arguably the three most important dispensations are the de minimus rule, the commercial agents rule and the parent/subsidiary rule.

Agreements of minor importance are covered by the de minimus rule, as codified in the *Commission Notice Concerning Agreements, Decisions and Concerted Practices of Minor Importance*: see section 12.3, below.

The Community competition rules are considered not to apply to agreements between agents and principals and transactions between parent and subsidiaries, on the basis that such agreement relate only to the exercise of authority of one party. The parent/subsidiary rule applies to the commercial relationships between a parent company and its subsidiaries which, for the purposes of applying competition law, are to be treated as a single entity. Agreements or practices between companies belonging to a group forming a single economic unit do not violate the terms of Article 81(1) if the subsidiary has no real freedom to determine its own market behaviour: *Viho* v *EC Commission* Case T–102/92 [1995] ECR II–17.

Group exemptions. Article 81(3) of the Treaty establishes a number of criteria for exempting agreements from the rigours of Article 81(1). These will be considered in more detail later. At this point, it is sufficient to note that this provision gives authority to the Commission to create block exemptions.

Block exemptions are regulations declaring the inapplicability of Community competition rules to certain types of agreement. If an agreement benefits under the terms of such an exemption, notification is not required.

Negative clearance

The primary purpose of notification is to ensure that no provision of an agreement falls foul of the anti-competitive restrictions contained in Article 81(1). Certification that this is in fact the case is known as 'negative clearance'. If, after an investigation, the Commission decides that the terms of an agreement notified do not infringe Community competition law, it is empowered to grant negative clearance, or approval, in the form of a formal decision or a comfort letter. Both of these devices allow the Commission to certify to the parties involved that, as the agreement stands, there are no offending provisions.

Notification for negative clearance means that the applicants wish the Commission to certify that the agreement is not prohibited under Article 81(1) for any one of the following reasons:

1. The agreement falls within the scope of the de minimus rule;
2. The agreement is the subject of a dispensation, such as the one for agent/principal agreements;
3. The agreement does not affect trade between Member States or does not meet one of the other conditions established under Article 81(1);
4. The agreement is covered by an express exemption such as Article 2 of Regulation 26/62 on the application of Community competition policy to the agricultural sector; or
5. Confirmation that the agreement is in fact covered by the terms of a block exemption.

Therefore, in the case of doubt as to the competitive implications of an agreement, the matter can be clarified by means of an application for negative clearance.

Applications for individual exemption

Applications for exemption should be distinguished from notifications for negative clearance. Individual exemption applications should be made where it is clear that an agreement falls within Article 81(1) and is not covered by either a dispensation or a block exemption: see *VAG France SA* v *Etablissements Magne SA* Case 10/86 [1988] 4 CMLR 98. The conditions for individual exemption are prescribed in Article 81(3) of the EC Treaty.

From previous decisions of the Commission it is clear that the two most relevant factors in deciding whether or not an agreement may qualify for individual exemption are the nature of the agreement and the position of the parties to the agreement in the market for the relevant product or service.

The Commission hardly ever exempts price-fixing cartels or market-sharing agreements on the basis that the consumer rarely benefits from such arrangements. But, equally, agreements which increase efficiency or which promote consumer choice, such as licensing, distribution and joint venture agreements, are infrequently denied the benefit of individual exemption.

Similarly, small and medium-sized companies are often granted individual exemptions whereas larger companies may find the Commission less tolerant towards their commercial activities.

Post-notification procedure
Notification of an agreement will result in one of four possible post-notification outcomes:

1. A provisional decision indicating that the Commission believes that Article 81(1) is applicable to the agreement and that Article 81(3) does not apply.
2. The commencement of an investigation into the commercial activities of the parties involved in the notification. Although notification of an agreement protects the parties involved against the possible imposition of fines, Article 15(6) of the basic Regulation allows the Commission to terminate this immunity if 'after preliminary examination it is of the opinion that Article 81(1) applies' and Article 81(3) cannot be raised as a defence.
3. The publication of a formal decision granting either negative clearance or exemption. Formal decisions may be rendered by the Commission to grant both negative clearance and individual exemption, but one cannot be rendered unless the formal procedural steps have been complied with and in particular notification of the investigation has been published in the *Official Journal*.
4. The grant of a 'comfort letter' by which the Commission closes the file without any formal decision having been adopted. In order to expedite the conclusion of investigations, the Commission has engaged in a policy of issuing administrative letters, or comfort letters, which are merely letters signed by an official of the Commission indicating the grounds on which the Commission believes that no action is necessary.

Investigations

The Commission's powers to investigate are contained in Council Regulation 17/62 and can be broadly classified as follows:

1. power to obtain information from the parties involved in the investigation;
2. power to conduct inspections;
3. power to convene hearings; and
4. power to grant interim relief.

Power to obtain information
Under Article 11(1) of the Regulation, in carrying out its duties the Commission may obtain 'all information necessary' for the purposes of the investigation from interested private parties and the governments and competent authorities of the Member States. In exercising this power to obtain information from private parties, it acts in two stages.

First, the Commission makes an informal request to the parties to produce the relevant information. If no response is received in response to the request, it proceeds to the second stage. This involves the adoption of a formal decision requiring the production of the relevant materials, and failure to comply with the terms of the decision may itself lead to the imposition of fines.

The scope of information 'necessary' for the purposes of conducting the investigation falls broadly within the discretion of the Commission to decide. It appears that all information relating to the business activities of the companies under investigation is necessary unless it can be shown to be very irrelevant. In the judgment of the Court of First Instance in *Samenwerkende Elektriciteits Produktiebedrijven NV (SEP) v EC Commission* Case T–39/90 [1992] 5 CMLR 33, the broad scope of this discretion was confirmed. This case involved an investigation into the commercial relationship between a Dutch electricity production company and its state-controlled gas supplier. The relationship between the parties was governed by a code of conduct which provided, inter alia, that the state-controlled company had a monopoly on the supply of gas in the Netherlands. During the course of the investigation it was revealed that the electricity company had entered into a contract for the supply of gas with a Norwegian company. This arrangement was possibly contrary to Dutch law.

The Commission requested production of the contract between the Dutch electricity supplier and the Norwegian gas supplier. The company refused to provide a copy of the contract on the grounds, first, that it was not relevant to the investigation and, second, that the national authorities might obtain a copy and commence proceedings for the infringement of the national monopoly. The Commission passed a decision to compel the disclosure of the contract, and the applicant appealed to the Court against this decision.

The Court upheld the discretion of the Commission in selecting which material was relevant to its investigation. The Commission was entitled to have sight of the contract in order to assess the legality of related agreements under investigation. More specifically, it was required to identify the pattern of business conduct being pursued by the Dutch company. The content of the category of information which is 'necessary' extends to all material which the Commission reasonably believes has a connection with the practices being investigated.

A request for confidentiality may be submitted along with any information provided to the Commission by a private party. Article 20 of Regulation 17/62 requires that information obtained by request or inspection can only be used for the purposes of satisfying the relevant request. In general the onus is on the party subject to an investigation to claim confidentiality, but in at least one case the Commission was reprimanded by the Court for supplying a document to a third party without allowing the party under investigation an opportunity to object to its disclosure: see *AKZO v EC Commission* Case 53/85 [1986] ECR 1965.

Private parties subject to investigation have limited rights to refuse to supply information. The most significant safeguard is that correspondence between the parties and external legal advisers may benefit from the right of client/lawyer confidentiality, a right established through the decisions of the European Court: see *AM & S Europe* v *EC Commission* Case 155/79 [1982] ECR 1575.

Other rights which private parties are entitled to exercise include the right to legal representation: *Hoechst AG* v *EC Commission* Cases 46/87 and 227/88 [1991] 4 CMLR 410. However, the right not to incriminate oneself during the course of investigation has been rejected by the Court: see *Solvay & Cie* v *EC Commission* Case 27/88 [1991] 4 CMLR 502.

Conduct of inspections

Again the Commission's powers to conduct on-the-spot investigations are extensive. Article 14(1) of the Regulation allows Commission officials to:

1. examine the books and business records of the company;
2. take copies of books and business records;
3. ask for oral explanations on the spot; and
4. enter any premises, land or means of transport of parties under investigation.

The Commission also exercises these powers in two stages. First, Commission officials visit premises with a simple mandate from the Commission authorising inspection. If these officials are refused access to premises or records, the Commission may adopt a decision under Article 14(3) requiring companies to submit to investigations authorised by the decision. The subject-matter and purpose of the investigation must be specified in the decision, and fines may be imposed for non-compliance.

The officials of the competent authorities may be requested to assist the Commission officials in their investigation. This assistance is required when the Commission wishes to search premises. The Commission has no express authority to conduct searches of premises despite the terms of Article 14(1)(d) of the Regulation. In practice, the Commission seeks the co-operation of the national authorities for conducting searches, which extends to obtaining the necessary warrants and orders to authorise searches of premises.

The rights of the Commission and its agents to enter premises were considered fully by the European Court in *Hoechst AG* v *EC Commission* (above). The European Commission adopted decisions authorising the search and seizure of documents at the headquarters of a company believed to be indulging in anti-competitive practices. These decisions were adopted after the company had refused to supply the Commission with certain information which it believed was confidential.

Regulation 17/62 specifies the powers of the Commission to conduct investigations, but it is silent on the right of the Commission to search premises in Member States and the right of individuals to privacy and to object to such searches. Nevertheless, the Commission proceeded with the search after obtaining the necessary permission from the national authorities and imposed fines on the company for failing to comply with the Commission's requests in the first place.

The plaintiffs applied to the Court for a declaration that these fines were unlawful. In their arguments, the plaintiffs claimed that the Commission had infringed their basic human rights. These rights were imputed into European Community law by virtue of international conventions signed by the Member States and through the general constitutional provisions of the Member States protecting the privacy of the individual.

The Court expressed a certain degree of sympathy with these arguments and declared that a number of fundamental human rights existed in European Community law, including the rights to lawyer/client confidentiality, privileged correspondence and legal representation. All of these can now be relied upon against the intrusion of the Commission into the business activities of companies.

As regards the main issue of the right of the Commission to search the premises, the Court upheld its right to search premises subject to certain safeguards. First, it must identify the documents required in advance of its search. Second, it must respect the rules of national law, which may require the production of a search warrant. Thus the Court concluded:

> 'If the Commission intends, with the assistance of the national authorities, to carry out an investigation other than with the co-operation of the undertakings concerned, it is required to respect the relevant procedural guarantees laid down by national law.'

However, in the circumstances of this particular case, the Court ultimately held that the Commission had not exceeded its powers because it had sought and obtained the co-operation of the relevant national authorities and had fulfilled the necessary national procedural requirements.

Power to convene hearings

The Commission is required to allow interested parties an opportunity to present their arguments and views directly to its officials. The procedures for the convening of hearings to discharge this obligation are regulated by Commission Regulation 99/63 (1963). The main purpose of holding such meetings is to allow parties to make representations in their favour at various stages in the proceedings. These rules were recently augmented by Commission Regulation 2842/98 which applies to the conduct of hearings for interested parties. Different rules are applied in such hearings depending on whether the relevant parties are: (i) parties to which the Commission has addressed objections; (ii) applicants and complainants; or (iii) other interested parties.

Power to grant interim relief

Although no such powers are expressly conferred in Regulation 17/62, the Commission has been deemed to possess an inherent power to issue decisions providing interim relief to complaining parties to prevent injury caused by the anti-competitive practices of business competitors. The European Court upheld the right to provide relief to a complaining party where there is an immediate danger of irreparable harm to the business activities of the complainer: *Camera Care* v *EC Commission* Case 792/79R [1980] ECR 119. Since this decision, the conditions necessary for the provision of interim relief have been more fully discussed by the Court.

In *La Cinq* v *EC Commission* Case T–44/90 [1992] 4 CMLR 449 the applicants raised an action against the Commission's refusal to grant interim relief against the activities of competitors. The applicant was a French broadcasting company which had been refused membership of the European Broadcasting Union (EBU). Membership of the organisation would have allowed the applicant to transmit sports events on more competitive terms than the sub-licensing arrangements which were required in the absence of membership. The applicants requested the Commission to adopt a decision compelling the EBU to accept its applicant, but the Commission refused to do so.

The Court of First Instance stated that the Commission could only adopt interim measures of protection if the following three conditions were satisfied:

1. the practices against which a complaint was lodged were prima facie likely to infringe Community law;
2. proven urgency existed; and
3. there was a need to avoid serious and irreparable damage to the party seeking relief.

In the particular circumstances of this case, the Court held that the Commission was correct in refusing to provide relief because not all of these conditions were satisfied.

Power to fine

According to Article 15 of Regulation 17/62, the Commission may impose fines ranging from ECU 1,000 to ECU 1,000,000, or a sum in excess of this limit but not exceeding 10 per cent of the turnover of the undertakings found to have violated Articles 81(1) or 82. In addition, fines may be imposed for the supply of false or misleading information, for the submission of incomplete books or other documents or for refusal to submit to an investigation.

The policy of the Commission towards fining is a matter that is influenced by many factors. The following three are considered relevant to such a determination:

1. The size of the companies engaged in the anti-competitive behaviour: see *Belasco* v *EC Commission* Case T–124/89 [1991] 4 CMLR 96.
2. The steps taken by the party to mitigate the infringement prior to the decision imposing fines has been rendered: see *National Panasonic (UK) Ltd* v *EC Commission* Case 136/79 [1980] 3 CMLR 169; [1980] ECR 2033.
3. The nature of the infringement. For example, the Commission considers certain practices, such as predatory pricing, to be particularly repugnant to Community

competition policy: see *Tetra Pak Rausing SA* v *EC Commission* Case T–51/89 [1991] 4 CMLR 334.

The application of these principles can been seen by reference to two recent cases. In 1998, the European Commission adopted a decision imposing fines on the parties to the Trans-Atlantic Conference Agreement (TACA). The members of TACA had a joint market share in excess of 60 per cent and included 15 of the world's largest shipping lines which dominated container trade across the North Atlantic. In 1994 the members of the TACA had applied for exemption of the agreements pursuant to Article 81(3) of the EC Treaty. However, the Commission found that only price-fixing arrangements on transport between Northern Europe and the USA could be exempted. Three other types of price-fixing – inland transport services, prices paid to freight forwarders and agreements on the terms of service contracts – all breached the EU's anti-cartel law. Accordingly, the Commission found that the TACA members had collectively abused their dominant position. The total fines imposed amounted to ECU 273 million.

In the same year, the Commission also fined the German car maker, Volkswagen, ECU 102 million for persistent infringement of EC competition rules. The fine is the largest ever financial penalty inflicted by the Commission on an individual company: see *EC Commission* v *Volkswagen* [1998] 5 CMLR 33. In this case the Commission's investigation revealed that Volkswagen sought to partition the single market, contrary to EC competition rules. The company prevented its Italian dealerships supplying its cars for export to German and Austrian final customers. The company penalised dealers who sold models outside their territory, for example by threatening termination of the dealer's contracts, actual termination of such contracts, reduction of profit margins and bonuses for dealers, and rationing deliveries to Italian dealers. All sales by Italian dealerships were monitored and the company advised their dealers in Italy not to give the real reason for the refusal to sell to foreign customers

The Commission has also adopted a Notice in 1997 on reduced fines for cartel informers designed to encourage participants in cartels to offer evidence of such activities to the Commission. The Notice gives much greater discretion to the Commission as to how it will treat cartel informers. The two main guidelines set down are as follows:

1. Total immunity from fines for companies reporting cartels is subject to the broad discretion of the Commission. However, as a general rule, such companies will benefit from a minimum reduction of 75 per cent of the fine which would have been imposed had the company not come forward.
2. Companies first reporting cartelistic behaviour immediately after an investigation has been opened by the Commission may obtain a reduction of between 50 per cent and 75 per cent of the final fine, again subject to the discretion of the Commission.

In both cases, reporting companies must satisfy a number of pre-conditions before being granted immunity. First, the informing company must not have been a ringleader in setting up the cartel. Second, the company must be the first to come forward to the Commission with substantial evidence of the cartel. Third, the company must pull out of the cartel no later than the time disclosure is made to the Commission. Fourth, it must provide the Commission with all information it possesses in relation to the activities of the cartel and must maintain continuous and complete co-operation with the Commission throughout the investigation. Failure to meet these requirements may mean the withdrawal of exemption.

The Notice also apply to anti-competitive practices other than cartels. There is therefore substantial uncertainty in this area, especially since the Notice is not a codification of previous practice.

The Commission also has authority to require undertakings to follow particular courses of action such as discontinuing the infringements.

While the Commission has authority to fix the amount of the fine, the national authorities concerned are obliged to enforce the decision, by virtue of Article 256 EC Treaty, in accordance with their national rules of procedure.

Judicial review

Judicial review of Commission decisions in the area of Community competition law is generally conducted under Article 230(4) of the EC Treaty. Originally judicial review of competition decisions was conducted by the European Court of Justice. Jurisdiction to hear such cases was transferred in September 1989 to the Court of First Instance which now has jurisdiction to hear:

> '... actions brought against an institution of the Communities by natural or legal persons pursuant to Article 230(4) (action of annulment) and Article 232(3) (action for failure to act) of the EC Treaty and in relation to the implementation of the competition rules applicable to undertakings'.

The Court also has concurrent jurisdiction to consider claims for damages brought against Community institutions in relation to the above matters.

It will be recalled from section 5.3, above, that Article 230 specifies four separate grounds for review. Most appeals are brought on the basis of an infringement of an essential procedural requirement or of the terms of the Community Treaties and laws enacted under the authority of such Treaties.

The most dramatic illustration of a Commission decision annulled on the basis of an infringement of an essential procedural requirement was the *PVC Cartel Case* Cases T–79, 84–86, 89 and 91–92/89 [1992] 4 CMLR 357. The Commission investigated the commercial activities of a number of plastic companies alleged to have operated a cartel to fix the price of certain chemical products. Eventually the Commission imposed fines totalling ECU 23,500,000 and issued an order requiring the companies to desist from the practices found to have infringed Article 81(1).

The decision imposing the fines was adopted in Dutch and Italian by the Commissioner responsible at the time for competition matters before it had been finalised or had been altered after his mandate had expired. The companies against which the fines were imposed challenged the decision on a number of procedural grounds. First, they claimed that a single Commissioner was not permitted to adopt a decision of this nature by himself or after his mandate had expired. Second, it was argued that the decision should have been adopted in the languages of all the companies under investigation. Third, it was asserted that the Commission had no power to amend the decision after the measure had been adopted.

The Court of First Instance upheld the applicants on all of these grounds. The Commission had failed to observe its own rules of internal procedure and the decision was annulled. In particular, the Court criticised the Commission for not properly authenticating its decision in accordance with Article 12 of its rules of procedure and because the exact date of adoption could not be identified from the text of the decision. The Court also rejected the contention that the Commission was entitled to amend its decision retroactively.

The European Court of Justice subsequently set aside the Court of First Instance judgment in the *PVC Cartel Case* on the ground that the tribunal had erred in deciding that the Commission's decision was non-existent because of the procedural irregularities contained in the decision. Nevertheless, the Court did annul the Commission's decision on the grounds of infringement of an essential procedural requirement confirming the CFI's findings if not its conclusions: *EC Commission* v *BASF and Others* Case C–137/92P [1994] ECR I–2555.

Decisions can also be reviewed on the basis that the Commission has acted contrary to the terms of the Community Treaty or of a measure derived from their authority: see for example, *Suiker Unie* v *EC Commission* Cases 40–48, 50, 54–56, 111, 113, 114/73 [1975] ECR 1663.

12.3 Article 81 EC Treaty

Article 81 provides as follows:

'1. The following shall be prohibited as incompatible with the Common Market: all agreements between undertakings, decisions by associations of undertakings and concerted practices which may affect trade between Member States and which have as their object or effect the prevention, restriction or distortion of competition within the Common Market, and in particular those which:
a) directly or indirectly fix purchase or selling prices or any other trading conditions;
b) limit or control production, markets, technical development, or investment;
c) share markets or sources of supply;
d) apply dissimilar conditions to equivalent transactions with other trading parties, thereby placing them at a competitive disadvantage;
e) make the conclusion of contracts subject to acceptance by the other parties of supplementary obligations which, by their nature or according to commercial usage, have no connection with the subject of such contracts.

2. Any agreements or decisions prohibited pursuant to this article shall be automatically void.

3. The provisions of paragraph 1 may, however, be declared inapplicable in the case of:
– any agreement or category of agreements between undertakings;
– any decision or category of decisions by associations of undertakings;
– any concerted practice or category of concerted practices;

which contributes to improving the production or distribution of goods or to promoting technical or economic progress, while allowing consumers a fair share of the resulting benefit, and which does not:

a) impose on the undertakings concerned restrictions which are not indispensable to the attainment of these objectives;

b) afford such undertakings the possibility of eliminating competition in respect of a substantial part of the products in question.'

Preliminary matters

Article 81(1) prohibits agreements, decisions and concerted practices between undertakings which affect trade between Member States and which have, as their object or effect, the prevention, restriction or distortion of competition within the Community. Before proceeding to consider more closely the types of agreement prohibited under Article 81, it is therefore necessary to consider the following questions:

1. What is the definition of 'an undertaking' for this purpose?
2. What types of arrangement constitute agreements, decisions and concerted practices?
3. What is the effect of the requirement that the arrangement must affect trade between Member States?

The concept of undertaking

Both Articles 81 and 82 refer to the concept of 'undertakings' but do not expressly define the term itself. The European Court has, however, had an opportunity to consider this point and has stated that an undertaking is:

> '... a single organisation of personal, tangible and intangible elements, attached to an autonomous legal entity and pursuing a long-term economic aim': *Mannesmann* v *High Authority* Case 8/61 [1962] ECR 357.

This definition embraces all natural and legal persons engaged in commercial activities whether profit-making or otherwise. The fact that an entity is a non-profit-making organisation is irrelevant for the purpose of identifying an undertaking: *Heintz van Landewyck Sarl* v *EC Commission* Case 108/78 [1980] ECR 3125. The critical characteristic is whether or not the entity is engaged in economic or commercial activities.

Agreements, decisions and concerted practices

Agreements. The term 'agreements' includes all contracts in the sense of binding contractual obligations, whether written, verbal, or partly written and partly verbal. Further, an arrangement between two or more parties may constitute an agreement for the purpose of Article 81(1) even although the arrangement in question has no binding legal effect: see *Atka A/S* v *BP Kemi A/S* [1979] CMLR 684.

Unrecorded understandings, the mutual adoption of common rules and so-called gentlemen's agreements are also agreements for the purposes of competition law: see *Boehringer* v *EC Commission* Case 45/69 [1970] ECR 769.

Agreements which prevent, distort or restrict competition are classified as either horizontal agreements or vertical agreements. Horizontal agreements are arrangements made between competitors, or potential competitors, while vertical agreements concern arrangements between undertakings at different stages of the process through which a product or service passes from the manufacturer or supplier to the final consumer.

Illustrations of horizontal agreements include contracts dividing markets among competitors, price fixing, export and import bans, cartels and boycotts. Examples of vertical agreements include those for exclusive distribution, patent licensing, and exclusive purchasing.

Decisions by associations of undertakings. The category of decisions by associations of undertakings generally covers the situation where a trade association makes recommendations to its members, eg about profit margins, even if those recommendations are not binding: *Cementhandelaren* v *EC Commission* Case 8/72 [1972] ECR 977. The legal form of the association does not matter: *Milchforderungsfonds Decision* (1985).

Concerted practices. Concerted practices relate to types of informal co-operation between undertakings. In *Imperial Chemical Industries Ltd* v *EC Commission* Case 48/69 [1972] CMLR 557 the Court defined a concerted practice as one where there is no formal agreement, but the undertakings involved 'knowingly substitute co-operation between themselves for the risks of competition'. A coherent plan need not be worked out, and there need not be direct contact between the undertakings, but the aim is to remove in advance 'any uncertainty as to the future conduct of their competitors': see *Suiker Unie* v *EC Commission* Cases 40–48, 50, 54–56, 111, 113, 114/73 [1975] ECR 1663. The *ICI* case gives an illustration of a concerted practice. There were price rises by uniform percentages within days of each other in different markets. The Commission dismissed the idea of coincidence. Was there an oligopolistic market (that is, one where there is a leader who dictates in effect the conditions of the market and in relation to whose marketing strategy the others have to act)? The Commission decided that there was not.

The same definition of concerted practice was applied by the European Court in the *Wood Pulp Cartel Case (No 2)* Cases C–114/85 and C–125–129/85 [1993] 4 CMLR 435, but the Court held that a 'firm, precise and consistent body of evidence' is necessary to prove the existence of a concerted practice. In its investigation, the European Commission had found that parallel price announcements provided sufficient evidence of a concerted practice. The Court rejected this test and held that parallel price announcements only constituted a concerted practice when this was the only plausible explanation for the behaviour. Instead the Commission must rely on more concrete attempts on the part of producers to reduce uncertainty as to the future conduct of competitors.

Effect on trade between Member States

It is only when agreements 'may affect trade' between two or more Member States of the Community that they are subject to the prohibitions of Article 81(1). In the absence of such an effect, an agreement will not fall within the scope of the prohibition. As the European Court expressly stated in one of its early cases:

> 'It is only to the extent to which agreements may affect trade between Member States that the deterioration in competition falls under the prohibition of European Union law contained in Article [81]; otherwise it escapes the prohibition': *Consten and Grundig* v *EC Commission* Cases 56 and 58/64 [1966] ECR 299.

The question of effect on patterns of trade between Member States is therefore critical to the application of Article 81 (and of 82 for that matter). How this issue is approached by the Commission and the Court may be illustrated by considering a few cases.

Consten and Grundig v *EC Commission* concerned an agreement between Grundig, a German company, and Consten, a French wholesale company. The French company agreed to act as sole distributors of Grundig's products in France. The agreement provided, inter alia, that Grundig would not sell to any other French firm or let dealers in other states export to France. Consten agreed not to sell other products or export to other countries. Consten would, in addition, register Grundig's trademark in France.

Another French firm bought Grundig's goods from a German distributor and imported them into France.

The Commission investigated and gave a decision which was upheld by the Court. They stated that the aim of the agreement between Consten and Grundig was to isolate the French market with the object of preventing parallel imports. Its overall effect was to affect trade between Member States.

Does the effect have to be detrimental? The Court said that if the pattern of trade is altered then trade is 'affected.'

In a more recent case, the Court turned its attention to the effect of exclusive beer supply agreements between breweries and their tenants. In *Delimitis* v *Henninger Brau AG* Case C–234/89 [1992] 5 CMLR 210, the facts were that a German brewery provided financial assistance to a tenant who, in return, accepted an obligation to purchase a certain volume of beer from the brewery. The tenant failed to meet this minimum purchasing requirement, and the brewery deducted penalties for this failure from his deposit. He raised an action for recovery of the sums in the national court and the court, referred the question of the compatibility of this type of agreement with Community competition law to the European Court for interpretation.

In its decision, the Court provided a clear illustration of the methodology involved in determining whether an agreement has an effect on trade between Member States. The first step in this process is to identify the relevant market. This is done by determining, first, the relevant product market and, second, the relevant geographical market.

The relevant product market is primarily defined on the basis of the nature of the economic activity in question. In this circumstances of this particular case, the Court identified the relevant product as beer. The sale of beer products takes place in two main forms: through direct retail channels such as off-licences and through premises for the sale and consumption of drinks such as bars and cafés.

From a consumer point of view, these two economic activities can be distinguished. The first is the mere purchase of a product while the latter is the purchase of a product linked to the supply of a service. Thus, the relevant product market was held to be the sale of beer products in premises.

The other aspect of the relevant market is the relevant geographical market. In this case, the Court noted that most agreements of this nature are still entered into at national levels. In the circumstances, the relevant geographical market was considered to be the German national market for beer distributed for sale in premises.

The second step is to consider whether the existence of the agreement under consideration affects the relevant market. The assessment of the effect on markets is made primarily in relation to the sealing-off or closing-off of the relevant market to non-national Community producers of similar or competing products. In *Delimitis* v *Henninger Brau AG* the Court made the assessment of the sealing-off effect in relation to: (a) the number of outlets tied by similar agreements; (b) the duration of the contracts entered into; (c) the quantity of the product subject to such restrictions; and (d) the proportion between those quantities and the quantities sold to unrelated independent producers.

Ultimately the Court found that the agreement under examination in this case, when considered in the context of all the other similar arrangements maintained by the particular brewery, affected trade between Member States. Hence the particular conditions for the application of Article 81 were found by the Court to have been satisfied.

The word 'may' presents some difficulty which was not wholly solved by the Court in *Technique Minière* v *Maschinenbau Ulm GmbH* Case 56/65 [1966] ECR 235, which stated that the requirements of Article 81 would be satisfied if the agreement, decision or practice had a direct, indirect actual or potential influence on the pattern of trade between Member States.

What if the agreement affects only one state? The Court is of the opinion that such an agreement may be in breach of Article 81 if it is either part of a larger agreement or if it prevents imports from other Member States: *Brasserie de Haecht* v *Wilkin* Case 48/72 [1973] ECR 77. According to *Consten*: 'It is not necessary to take into consideration the actual effects of an agreement where its purpose is to prevent, restrict or distort competition.' It seems that agreements should be subjected to consideration in an economic context to see if their effect on competition would not be simply minimal.

Minor agreements therefore escape the prohibition contained in Article 81 because their effect relative to trade between Member States is not of a sufficient impact to raise concern. This decision has given rise to the de minimus rule which provides that agreements having an insignificant effect on trade are not subject to the application of Article 81(1).

In 1986 the Commission published its first *Notice Concerning Agreements, Decisions and Concerted Practices of Minor Importance*, to allow guidance to the application of this test. This Notice was revoked by a new De Minimis Notice in 1998. Now, agreements which potentially infringe Article 81 must be notified to the Commission unless they benefit either from block exemption or are within the de minimis rules. Agreements which are considered de minimis are now:

1. in the case of vertical agreements (ie agreements operating between different levels in the market), agreements concerning less than a 10 per cent market share;
2. in the case of horizontal agreements (ie agreements between companies at the same level in the market), agreements concerning less than a 5 per cent market share.

However, the Notice introduces a black list of restrictive clauses which will not be tolerated (even where the agreement is within the threshold limits), including:

1. horizontal agreements intended to fix prices, limit production or sales or divide up supply sources; and
2. vertical agreements for fixing resale prices or giving territorial protection for contracting companies or third parties.

Anti-competitive agreements

Article 81(1) itself identifies five categories of agreement which may have the object or effect of preventing, restricting or distorting competition within the Community. These are:

1. agreements directly or indirectly fixing purchase or selling prices or any other trading conditions;
2. agreements limiting or controlling production, markets, technical developments or investment;
3. agreements sharing markets or sources of supply;

4. agreements applying dissimilar conditions to equivalent transactions with other trading parties and thereby placing them at a competitive disadvantage; and
5. agreements making the conclusion of contracts subject to acceptance by the other parties of supplementary obligations which, by their nature, have no connection with the subject-matter of such contracts.

This list is intended to be non-exhaustive. It does not identify all the types of agreement that may be subject to the rigours of Article 81(1), but where an agreement contains one of these restrictions there is a strong presumption that a distortion of competition will result.

The agreement need not take the form of a written agreement such as those described above. Often an anti-competitive arrangement takes the form of an unwritten agreement or a consensus among the parties. This is particularly true in the case of cartels. Those established to regulate supply or prices are condemned under Article 81(1) and, to date at least, there have been no circumstances justifying such arrangements.

A number of investigations have been conducted by the Commission into the existence of cartels, and the following arrangements have been held as contrary to Community competition policy:

1. Arrangements between producers to set target prices for the sale of a product even although it applied in only one Member State: *Cementhandelaren v EC Commission* (above).
2. Agreements to fix prices and to apportion markets: *In Re Italian Flat Glass Suppliers* Cases T–68 and 77–78/79 [1992] 5 CMLR 502.
3. The setting of volume targets for production: *Polypropylene* [1988] 4 CMLR 86.

An equally repugnant practice is that of market sharing. This is where two or more competing producers agree to refraining from competing in the markets of other producers in return for their refraining to compete in the others' market. This practice is condemned whether the apportionment is made on the basis of geography or product ranges: see *Siemens-Fanne* [1988] 4 CMLR 945 and *ACF Chemiefarma NV v EC Commission* Case 41/69 [1970] ECR 661.

Increasingly, applications have been made to the European Court by companies trying to challenge fines by alleging that the European Commission has failed to apply proper evidential standards in arriving at findings of anti-competitive behaviour. One example of this type of case is *Sarrio v EC Commission* Case T–334/94 [1998] 5 CMLR 195. In this case the applicant was found by the European Commission to have participated in a cartel prohibited under Article 81 of the EC Treaty. The company in question was found to have engaged in a number of concerted practices, with its competitors, consisting of:

1. agreeing regular price increases for products;
2. planning and implementing simultaneous and uniform price increases with its competitors;

3. reaching understandings on maintaining the market shares of the major producers at constant levels; and
4. taking concerted measures to control the supply of the product to ensure the implementation of the concerted price rises.

As a result it was fined ECU 15.5 million. However, in its defence, the applicant claimed that it was only engaged to a limited extent in these practices. It requested the Court to annul the Commission's decision on a number of procedural grounds, including infringement of the rights of defence, lack of evidence of active participation and lack of proof anti-competitive practices. In addition, the applicant asked the Court to reduce the fine imposed on the grounds that it was excessive in relation to its behaviour.

The Court found that the Commission had sufficient evidence of the applicant's participation in the cartel and therefore refused to annul the Commission's decision as far as the evidential findings were concerned. The rights of the defence had not been infringed and the evidence adduced by the Commission was sufficient to support its findings. As regards the level of fines imposed, the Court allowed some minor modifications. It adjusted the level of fine due from ECU 15.5 million to ECU 14 million. This was based on a miscalculation of the period of time that one of the applicant's subsidiaries had participated in the cartel. The remaining claims for reductions in the levels of fine were rejected by the Court.

Exemptions under Article 81(3)

Article 81(3) specifically establishes criteria for exempting agreements, decisions and concerted practices from Article 81(1). Agreements which satisfy the requirements of Article 81(3) are neither void under Article 81(2) nor subject to the imposition of fines.

Two positive tests and two negative tests must be satisfied before an agreement can benefit under the exemption. The agreement must:

1. contribute to improving the production or distribution of goods or promoting technical or economic progress; and
2. allow a fair share of the resulting benefits under the agreement to accrue to the consumer.

The agreement must *not*:

1. impose any restrictions which go beyond the positive aims of the agreement or practice; nor
2. create the possibility of eliminating competition in respect of a substantial part of the products in question.

Two types of exemption have been created on the basis of the authority of this provision. First, individual exemptions may be issued by the Commission after the formal notification of an agreement has been brought to its attention. Second, block (or group) exemptions which are applicable to certain categories of agreement have been established by the Commission.

The procedure for obtaining an individual exemption is specified in Regulation 17/62. Individual exemptions are granted in the form of Commission decisions. These decisions are issued for a limited period and may be made conditional on the fulfilment of certain obligations. A decision may be renewed if the relevant conditions continue to be satisfied.

Naturally, an individual exemption will only be granted if the Commission considers that the four conditions in Article 81(3) are satisfied.

To reduce the bureaucratic burdens that would otherwise be imposed by applications for individual exemption, the Commission is empowered to establish group exemption categories: Council Regulations 19/65 and 1215/99. The Commission has enacted a number of Regulations to grant group exemption to certain types of agreement including: (a) exclusive distribution agreements – Commission Regulation 1983/83; (b) exclusive purchasing – Commission Regulation 1984/83; (c) motor vehicle distribution agreements – Commission Regulation 123/86; (d) specialisation agreements – Commission Regulation 417/85; (e) research and development agreements – Commission Regulation 518/85; (f) franchising agreements – Commission Regulation 4087/88; and (g) technology transfer agreements – Commission Regulation 240/96.

If an agreement falls within the scope of a group exemption established under a regulation, the parties to the agreement are not required to notify the Commission of the existence of the agreement, and the parties cannot be fined by the Commission for violating competition law.

Revision of the application of competition law to vertical restraints

The Commission has recently adopted a Communication on the application of competition rules to vertical restraints which proposes a number of significant changes to the block exemption system in the case of vertical restraints. The proposal is to introduce a single, but wider, block exemption regulation that will exempt all vertical agreements except for a limited number of hardcore restraints from the application of Article 81(1) of the EC Treaty. In order to limit the exemption to companies which do not have significant market power, the Regulation will establish one or two market thresholds, beyond which companies cannot benefit from the safe harbour. For companies with market shares above the thresholds there will be no presumption of illegality and they will be examined under Article 81(3).

The Council has now adopted Council Regulation 1215/99 amending Council Regulation 19/65, which gives the Commission authority to adopt block exemption regulations. Under the new system there will be a wider category of agreements that may be subject to block exemptions. The Commission has the power to issue a block exemption covering all kinds of vertical restraints in the following circumstances:

1. two or more undertakings have entered into the agreement;
2. the agreements concern: the supply or purchase, or both, of goods for resale or processing, or the marketing of services, including exclusive distribution agreements, exclusive purchasing agreements, franchising agreements and selective distribution agreements, or any combination of the above.

Complaints and remedies

A private party who believes that a competitor is engaging in anti-competitive practices to its detriment has two primary course of action through which measures may be adopted to secure a remedy:

1. a complaint may be lodged with the European Commission as a preliminary step towards an investigation; or
2. legal proceedings may be initiated in a national court to establish an infringement. Proceedings against another private individual cannot be brought directly before the European Court.

Complaints to the European Commission

Private parties who believe that their competitors have infringed a rule of Community competition law may lodge complaints with DG IV of the European Commission, the department responsible for the administration of competition matters. A complaint should set out the following facts and law: (a) a description of the parties to the agreement and their business activities; (b) the nature of the arrangement or agreement claimed to be anti-competitive; (c) a description of the market for the goods or services affected by the practice; and (d) a statement of the law believed to be applicable to the facts set out in the complaint.

Once the Commission has received a complaint, it may initiate an investigation if it believes that there are sufficient facts alleged to amount to an infringement of competition law.

There are a number of advantages to proceeding through the complaint procedure. First, a party lodging a complaint incurs nominal legal expenses – the Commission will assume responsibility for the investigation and any ultimate court proceedings. Second, parties lodging complaints may be able to secure a greater degree of anonymity than would be the case in court proceedings.

There are two main disadvantages to making a complaint in contrast to litigation. First, the Commission cannot be compelled to institute an investigation. This is a matter that remains within the discretion of the Commission: see *Star Fruit Co SA v EC Commission* Case 247/87 [1990] 1 CMLR 733. Second, in the event that an infringement is established after an investigation by the Commission, the complainer is not automatically awarded damages in respect of injury caused by the anti-competitive practice.

Remedies through the national courts

As an alternative to a complaint to the Commission, a private party affected by the anti-competitive effects of a competitor's business practices may raise proceedings in the national courts of the party alleged to have been engaging in the infringement.

Both Articles 81(1) and 82 have direct effect and are capable of creating rights which may be relied on by private individuals; see *BRT* v *SABAM* Case 127/73 [1974] ECR 313 and *Garden Cottage Foods Ltd* v *Milk Marketing Board* [1984] AC 130. In other words, these provisions may form the basis for an action for damages against the party engaged in the violation for injury caused to the business activities of the plaintiff.

In addition, Article 81(2) also declares that any agreement contrary to Article 81(1) is automatically void. However, the European Court has applied the doctrine of severability to this provision. Only those terms of an agreement which are contrary to the Article are void; the rest remain in force. The agreement itself is void only if those parts of it which are anti-competitive cannot be severed from the agreement itself: *Technique Minière* v *Maschinenbau Ulm GmbH* (above).

An infringement of Article 81(1) may also form the basis of an action of injunction to prevent the party allegedly infringing competition law from continuing to do so.

Co-ordination between the Commission and the national courts in the enforcement of Community competition law is extremely important. Thus, if the Commission has granted an individual exemption to the terms of an agreement, it is important that a national court takes cognisance of this fact. Similarly, a number of matters remain within the exclusive competence of the Commission, and the courts have no authority to rule on matters concerning these issues: see *Delimitis* v *Henninger Brau AG* (above).

In order to develop this co-ordination, the Commission published a *Notice to National Courts on the Application of Articles 81 and 82* (1993). This Notice sets out in detail the procedure which national courts should follow if an allegation of an infringement of Community competition law arises before them. It also establishes a mechanism to allow a national court to seek guidance from the Commission in the interpretation and application of the points of competition law which arise before it.

The main drawback of litigation in national courts is that such a procedure is both expensive and protracted. Furthermore, the plaintiff assumes responsibility for conducting the action itself, whereas if a complaint is made to the Commission it is that body which prosecutes the matter. Difficulties also arise where the infringement is of a transnational nature involving multiple jurisdictions.

The main redeeming feature of litigation is that the plaintiff can recover damages to compensate for injury sustained as a consequence of the anti-competitive behaviour.

12.4 Article 82 EC Treaty

Article 82 states that:

> 'Any abuse by one or more undertakings of a dominant position within the Common Market or in a substantial part of it shall be prohibited as incompatible with the common market in so far as it may affect trade between Member States. Such abuse may, in particular, consist in:
> 1. directly or indirectly imposing unfair purchase or selling prices or unfair trading conditions;
> 2. limiting production, markets or technical development to the prejudice of consumers;
> 3. applying dissimilar conditions to equivalent transactions with other trading parties, thereby placing them at a competitive disadvantage;
> 4. making the conclusion of contracts subject to acceptance by the other parties of supplementary obligations which, by their nature or according to commercial usage, have no connection with the subject of such contracts.'

Preliminary matters

The practices prohibited under Article 82 are broadly similar in nature to those addressed in Article 81(1) but the primary difference is that Article 82 is intended to regulate the activities of generally one, or at most a few, parties, whereas the essence of Article 81(1) is the existence of an agreement, decision or concerted practice among a number of parties.

This is not to say, however, that Article 82 only applies to the activities of single companies. For example, in *In Re Italian Flat Glass Suppliers* (above), the European Court held that the provision could be applied to three Italian glass producers. The number of parties is not the critical factor, although in investigations under Article 82 this number does tend to be small. The important element is the position of the parties in the relevant market and their behaviour.

Article 82 does share a number of common features with Article 81(1). For example, the concept of 'undertaking' referred to in Article 81(1) also applies to investigations under Article 82. Similarly, both Articles require that the practices being carried on affect trade between Member States, and the analysis given to this requirement under Article 81 is equally applicable to investigations under Article 82.

The Court of First Instance has held that Articles 81 and 82 may be applied to the same behaviour by the same parties, but the Commission is not entitled simply to reiterate the same facts allowing action under Article 81(1) to justify a simultaneous investigation under Article 81: *In Re Flat Glass*, above. But this safeguard does not prevent companies with no economic ties, other than parallel commercial behaviour, from being subject to investigation under both provisions if it can be shown that, in addition to engaging in practices prohibited under Article 81, the parties possess a collective dominant position in the relevant market and are engaging in abusive behaviour.

Article 82 essentially concerns the issue of market dominance, ie monopolies, duopolies, oligopolies etc, but it should be made clear that market dominance per se is not prohibited under this Article. Rather, it is the abuse of a dominant position that is attacked.

To establish a breach of Article 82, it is first necessary to identify the relevant market to which the alleged violation relates. In common with Article 81, this requires identification of both a product market and a geographical market. Once the relevant market has been identified, the next stage is to assess the degree of dominance exercised by the parties under investigation. Only after such an assessment has been made is it possible to confirm whether an undertaking maintains a dominant position.

In the event that a dominant position is confirmed, it is then necessary to proceed to examine the existence of any abusive behaviour that can be attributed to the party. It is the existence of abuse that is the sine qua non for the application of Article 82. In the absence of such behaviour there can never be a violation of Article 82.

The relevant market

The Commission's 1998 Notice on Relevant Markets explains the application of the concept of relevant product and geographic markets for the purposes of EC competition law. It is first necessary to identify what the relevant market is in order to decide whether there is or might be a restriction of competition or the abuse of a dominant position. The Notice sets out basic principles for market definition, recognising that firms are subject to three main elements, namely: demand substitutability; supply substitutability; and potential competition.

In defining the relevant product market, the Commission first analyses the product's characteristics and its intended use. As for whether two products are demand substitutes, the Commission looks at: evidence of substitution in the recent past; the views of customers and competitors; consumer preferences; barriers and costs associated with switching demand to potential substitutes; and the different categories of customers and price discrimination.

To define geographic markets, the Commission looks at the distribution of the parties' and their competitors' market shares and will usually conduct a preliminary analysis of pricing and price differences at national and Community level. It also checks supply factors to ensure that companies located in distinct areas are not prevented from developing their sales in competitive terms throughout the whole geographic market. Finally, the Commission takes into account the continuing process of market integration, particularly in areas of concentrations and structural joint ventures.

The relevant product market

The Commission must identify the relevant product market because competition can only be judged between like products. The delineation is important also because boundaries have to be set in which the market power of the undertaking in question may be considered. The following are loose guidelines which have been developed through the decisions and cases.

Interchangeability or substitutability. If products are not interchangeable then they are not part of the same product market. They may be so if they are reasonably interchangeable. To determine interchangeability, the use, nature and price of the goods must be considered as well as the customers. In *Michelin* v *EC Commission* Case 322/81 [1983] ECR 3461, the relevant market was new replacement tyres; the Commission thereby excluded original equipment tyres which are ordered by the car makers. The 'market' excluded retreads and industrial tyres for heavy machinery which would presumably form their own relevant market.

In another case, the issue of the relevant product was considered from the perspective of interchangeability. In *Hilti* v *EC Commission* Case T–30/89 [1992] 4 CMLR 16, the Court of First Instance was asked to decide the number of separate product markets for nail guns, nail cartridge strips for such apparatus and the nails themselves. The Commission considered that each of these three products constituted a separate and independent product market, while the applicants asserted that there was only one single indivisible market for all of these products because each of them could not be used by consumers without the others.

The Court upheld the argument of the Commission. All the products could be manufactured separately and could be purchased without having to purchase the others. Their interchangeability was therefore restricted. Similarly, other products could be substituted for each of the products. For example, nails and cartridges could be purchased from other suppliers to fit the equipment. The finding of three separate product markets was therefore confirmed. The findings of the Court of First Instance in the *Hilti* case were upheld by the European Court on appeal: see *Hilti AG* v *EC Commission (No 2)* Case C–53/92P [1994] 4 CMLR 614.

The Commission has also recently had to consider the relevant product market for chemical products where there is often a wide range of interchangeable or substitutable products. In *AKZO Chemie BV* v *EC Commission* Case C–62/82 [1993] 5 CMLR 197, the Commission identified the relevant product as organic peroxides even though such products had a wide range of uses. In order to isolate the relevant product market, the Commission considered the uses for which such products could be applied and decided that abusive behaviour had only been perpetrated in relation to one type of application of the products, namely bleaching agents, as opposed to other applications for the products in the plastics sector. The relevant product was therefore defined as organic peroxides used as bleaching agents and this finding was upheld by the European Court.

Cross-elasticity of demand and supply. The simple question to be answered here is whether, if there was an increase in the price of a product, the consumer would choose another. If so, those two products are in the same market – probably. In *United Brands* v *EC Commission* Case 27/76 [1978] ECR 1391 it was held that bananas were the relevant market. The Court had toyed with the idea that there might be cross-elasticity of demand between bananas and other fresh fruits, but if there was it did not amount to very much. There were other factors to be considered, like the end use of the product and whether certain users can switch readily. In *United Brands* it was noted that certain users, the sick, the elderly and babies, could not switch to other fresh fruits.

Continental Can v *EC Commission* Case 6/72 [1972] ECR 157 concerned supply. Where a product could be manufactured by other undertakings without too much time and expense being involved, then that undertaking could be considered part of the relevant market.

The relevant geographical market

The relevant geographical market is the area within the Community in which the practice produces its effects. This is presumed to be the whole of the Community if the products that are the subject of the investigation are regularly bought and sold in all Member States. Therefore, the relevant geographical market will be smaller than the Community in three main instances:

1. If the nature and characteristics of the product, ie high transportation costs, short shelf life, etc, restrict distribution.
2. Where the movement of the product within the Community is hinder by barriers to entry into another national market caused by state intervention, ie quotas, non-tariff barriers, technical requirements, etc.
3. Where the marketing and sales efforts by the company under investigation are intentionally restricted to a particular part of the Community.

A single Member State may be the relevant geographical market. In *Michelin, Suiker Unie* above, the European Court considered that Belgium and Luxembourg formed a substantial part of the common market. *Continental Can* and *Hugin* v *EC Commission* Case 22/78 [1979] ECR 1869 decided that part of a Member State could be considered substantial. In *BP* v *EC Commission* Case 77/77 [1978] ECR 1513 the Advocate-General expressed the opinion that Luxembourg should be considered a substantial part of the market. It had about two per cent of the Community population at the time.

The concept of dominance

A dominant position is defined as being one which gives an undertaking an ability to prevent effective competition and to behave to an appreciable extent independently of its competitors: see *United Brands* (above).

The court will look at several factors to determine dominance, but market shares are important. 'Very large shares are, in themselves, evidence of the existence of a dominant position.': see *Hoffman-La Roche* v *Commission* Case 85/76 [1979] ECR 1869.

The magic figure of 50 per cent is not conclusive, however, as such a market share would need to be held for some time and should also give the undertaking involved 'freedom of action'. United Brands held between 41 per cent and 45 per cent of the market. Their dominance was judged in the light of the holding of their nearest competitors, which was several times less.

Other indicators of dominance include the so-called structural factors which provide the following indicators:

1. Strict quality control – *United Brands*.
2. Technological lead – *Michelin*.
3. Well developed sales networks – *Hoffman-La Roche*.
4. Negligible potential competition – *United Brands*.

The concept of abuse

Abuse is not defined in the treaty, but the Court in *Hoffman-La Roche* said that an abuse will influence the structure of the market and weaken and hinder competition. The 'abuse' must therefore be discerned by its effects. Among those effects are the following:

1. Unfairness imposed by the dominant undertaking. Obviously this would mean that the price of the product is excessive. It would be excessive if the price bore no relation to the economic value of the product supplied: *General Motors v EC Commission* Case 26/75 [1975] ECR 1367. It could also include discriminatory prices, where an undertaking simply charged as much as a market could bear, as in *United Brands*, especially when coupled with measures designed to keep the markets separate, like the imposition of the so-called 'green banana clauses' – a prohibition on the sale of green bananas to prevent re-exportation.
2. Giving rebates. The giving of rebates affects competition by putting pressure on a distributor or retailer to favour a particular supplier's products in order to earn the rebate. *Michelin, Suiker Unie* and *Hoffman-La Roche* all provide examples of this particular evidence of abuse. Hoffman-La Roche compounded their abuse by including the so-called 'English clause' in their agreements; this provided that their customers could still earn their 'loyalty rebates' even if they obtained supplies at a lower price from a competitor. It was thought that thereby Hoffman-La Roche would obtain useful information about the marketing strategy of rival undertakings: see also *Sanpellegrino v Coca Cola* [1989] 4 CMLR 137.
3. Refusal to supply. The leading case is *Commercial Solvents Corporation v EC Commission* Cases 6–7/74 [1974] ECR 223 where it was stated:

   'However, an undertaking being in a dominant position as regards the production of raw materials and therefore able to control the supply to manufacturers of derivatives cannot, just because it decides to start manufacturing those derivatives (in competition with its former customers), act in such a way as to eliminate their competition which, in the case in question, would amount to eliminating one of the principal manufacturers of ethambutol in the common market. Since such conduct is contrary to the objectives expressed in Article 3(g) of the Treaty and set out in greater detail in Articles [81] and

[82], it follows that an undertaking which has a dominant position in the market in raw materials and which, with the object of reserving such raw material for manufacturing its own derivatives, and therefore risks eliminating all competition on the part of this customer, is abusing its dominant position within the meaning of Article [82].'

But not all refusal to supply is abusive: *BP v EC Commission* (above), where BP only supplied contractual and regular customers during an oil shortage. This was not abusive.

A more obvious example of an abusive refusal to supply was the action taken by three television companies – BBC, ITV and RTE, an Irish television company – to retain their monopolies in the publication of television advance weekly publishings. A company, Magill TV Guide Limited, had been set up for the purposes of publishing advance television listings for all three stations in one product. Injunctions were brought out to prevent publication by the company of the listings by the stations concerned.

The publishing company sought to have these injunctions removed on the ground that such a prohibition infringed Article 82 in so far as it amounted to a refusal to supply. This perpetuated the monopolies of the various companies as regards their weekly publications, including the *TV Times* and the *Radio Times*. However, the company went out of business and the Commission took up the matter.

The Commission decided that these practices amounted to an abuse of a dominant position and ordered the television companies to supply the information. The companies appealed this decision to the Court of First Instance. In three virtually identical decisions, the Court of First Instance upheld the findings of the Commission: see *Independent Television Publications Limited v EC Commission* Case T–76/89 [1991] 4 CMLR 745. The decision is interesting because it shows that not only positive actions may be found anti-competitive. Failures to act or omissions can be just as anti-competitive and equally as liable to be found in violation of Article 82.

4. Refusal to give access to essential facilities. The concept of essential facilities and the abusive refusal to grant access to these facilities was considered by the Court in *Oscar Bronner v Mediaprint* Case C–7/97, Judgment of 26 November 1998, not yet reported. The ECJ ruled that, for an abuse of dominant position to exist under the essential facilities doctrine, it is necessary that: (i) the refusal of the service is likely to eliminate all competition in the market on the part of the person requesting the service; (ii) such refusal is incapable of being objectively justified; and (iii) the service in itself is indispensable to carrying on that person's business, inasmuch as there is no actual or potential substitute.

5. Acquisitions and mergers. A dominant position in the manufacturing or distribution of a product or service may also lead to abuse where one producer or supplier is able to absorb competitors. Such a market dominance would, however, only amount to abuse if the acquisition or merger was undertaken with an anti-competitive motive in mind: *Tetra Pak Rausing SA v EC Commission* (above).

The period of investigation into dominance and abuse

The European Commission must conduct its investigation into dominance and abuse of a dominant position over an appropriate period. The overriding criterion is that the period selected for the investigation of the market conditions, the abusive practices and the existence of a dominant position must be adequate to facilitate proper appraisal: see *BPB Industries & British Gypsum* v *EC Commission* Case T–65/89 [1993] ECR 389. A choice of an inadequate period which is either too short on the one hand or too extensive on the other may lead to the final findings of the Commission being annulled.

The period over which abuse has been perpetrated is also a relevant factor in assessing the levels of fines which may be imposed by the European Commission against a guilty party.

12.5 Merger control

Background to merger control

The Community competition provisions make no express reference to the control of mergers or acquisitions in the Community. But notwithstanding this omission, the Commission has been prepared to apply both Articles 81 and 82 to mergers and takeovers. The following are illustrations of this practice:

1. The acquisition of a competitor by a company which maintains a dominant position in a market may amount to an abuse of that position contrary to Article 82: see *Continental Can* v *EC Commission* and *Tetra Pak Rausing SA* v *EC Commission* (both above).
2. Article 81(1) may be applied to acquisitions of shareholdings where a company acquires a minority stake in a competitor as leverage for the co-ordination of marketing strategy between two undertakings: *British–American Tobacco (BAT) & RJ Reynolds Industries Inc* v *EC Commission* Cases 142 and 156/84 [1986] ECR 1899.
3. Article 81(1) may be infringed if a company enters into a joint venture or acquires an interest in a third company if the other principal shareholder is in a related field of business.
4. Consortium bids may also violate Article 81(1) if the consortium involves competitors seeking to acquire a competitor or attempting to influence its behaviour.

After a series of controversial decisions in the 1980s, the Council agreed to adopt Community legislation setting out the powers of the Commission to investigate mergers and takeovers. This power was restricted to levels above a certain threshold. Council Regulation 4064/89 (1989) was enacted for this purpose and came into force in September 1990. This Regulation, known as the Merger Control Regulation, has since been amended by Council Regulation 1310/97.

EC Merger Control rules apply to 'concentrations'. A concentration arises where either:

1. two or more previously independent undertakings merge into one; or
2. one or more persons already controlling at least one undertaking acquire, whether by purchase of securities or assets, direct or indirect control of the whole or part of one or more other undertakings.

Article 1 of the Merger Control Regulation, as amended, confers jurisdiction on the Commission over all mergers involving a 'Community dimension'. A concentration has a Community dimension where:

1. the aggregate worldwide turnover of all the undertakings concerned is more than ECU 5,000 million; and
2. the aggregate Community-wide turnover of each of the undertakings concerned is more than ECU 250 million.

The Community dimension is, however, excluded where each of the undertakings concerned has more than two-thirds of its aggregate Community-wide turnover in one and the same Member State.

On the basis of the amending Regulation, concentrations which do not meet the above thresholds are still caught where:

1. the combined aggregate worldwide turnover of all the undertakings involved in the merger is more than ECU 2,500 million; and
2. in each of at least three Member States, the combined aggregate turnover of all the undertakings concerned is more than ECU 100 million; and
3. in each of at least these three Member States, the aggregate turnover of each of at least two of the undertakings concerned is more than ECU 25 million; and
4. the aggregate Community-wide turnover of each of at least two of the undertakings concerned is more than ECU 100 million.

However, where the undertakings concerned achieve more than two-thirds of their Community-wide turnover within the same Member State, the merger will still not have a Community dimension.

Merging companies have to go through two tiers of threshold in order to assess whether a merger has a Community dimension. First, they must assess whether they meet the thresholds under the original Regulation. Second, if these thresholds are not met, they must determine whether they fulfil the additional cumulative criteria in the new Regulation. The new rules mean that the Commission's jurisdiction will be extended to transactions which, under Council Regulation 4064/89, may be assessed under several national merger control procedures.

The amending Regulation removes the requirement that concentrative joint ventures must not involve co-ordination between the parents, or between one of them and the joint venture, in order to come within the Regulation. Joint ventures falling within the Regulation are those which perform on a lasting basis all the functions of an autonomous economic entity. Their possible co-ordinative aspects, however, will be assessed under the Article 81 criteria.

Aggregate turnover is calculated on the basis of amounts derived by the undertakings concerned in the preceding financial year from the sale of goods or the supply of services during the course of ordinary trading activities. Deductions are permitted for sales rebates, value added tax and other taxes directly related to turnover.

Even if a merger is approved by the Commission, Member States retain a veto over mergers in particularly sensitive sectors of their national economies. Member States may take appropriate measures to protect legitimate national interests such as public security, the plurality of the media and the maintenance of prudent rules for the conduct of commerce. However, such measures are subject to the requirement that they must be compatible with the general principles and rules of European Union law.

The Commission is empowered to impose fines on persons, undertakings or associations of undertakings if they intentionally or negligently fail to notify the Commission of a concentration with a Community dimension. These fines range from ECU 1,000 to ECU 50,000.

Once a concentration with a Community dimension has been notified, the Commission has two options available. First, it can conclude that the concentration does not fall within the scope of the Regulation and must record such a finding by means of a decision.

Alternatively, the Commission may determine that the concentration falls within the Regulation, in which event it may take one of two courses of action:

1. The Commission may decide that the concentration, while within the scope of the Regulation, is not incompatible with the common market and will not therefore be opposed; or
2. The Commission may find that the concentration falls within the Regulation and is incompatible with the common market, in which case it is obliged to initiate an investigation.

In each of these cases, the Commission must make its decision within one month of the notification.

To appraise the compatibility of a concentration with the common market, the Commission must evaluate the implications of the concentration in the light of the need to preserve and develop efficient competition within the Community, taking into account, inter alia, the structure of all the relevant markets concerned and the actual or potential competition from other undertakings both within and outside the Community: see *Re the Concentration between Espn Inc and Others* [1993] 4 CMLR M1.

In making this assessment, the Commission must consider the market position of the undertakings concerned, their economic and financial power, the opportunities available to both suppliers and consumers, access to supplies and markets, the existence of legal or other barriers to entry of the product into particular markets and the interests of intermediate and ultimate consumers, as well as technical and economic development and progress: see generally *Re the Concentration between Elf Acquitaine and Occidental Petroleum* [1993] 4 CMLR M9 and *Re the Concentration between Nestlé SA and Source Perrier SA* [1993] 4 CMLR M17.

The Commission has the power to impose fines on parties for failing to properly notify concentrations. For example, in a recent case concerning a company called Moller, the Commission imposed a fine of Euro 219,000 on the Danish company for failing to notify and for putting into effect three concentrations. The three transactions in question were in fact subsequently cleared by the Commission. They were, however, put into effect several months before they were notified. Nevertheless, the Commission concluded that the company clearly breached its obligation to notify the transactions in due time and its obligation not to implement them without the Commission's authorisation. Furthermore, the infringements lasted for a significant period of time.

The relatively low amount of the fine was justified by four factors:

1. the company recognised its breach;
2. the failure to notify did not damage competition;
3. the company voluntarily informed the Commission of its failure to notify the transactions in question before the Commission discovered the infringement itself; and
4. the company infringed the law at a time when the Commission had not yet adopted its first decision imposing fines under the Merger Regulation.

It is, however, unlikely that the Commission would be so lenient in the future.

Matters such as notifications, time limits, hearings and other procedural issues under the Merger Control Regulation are dealt with under Commission Regulation 3384/94 (1994).

13

External Relations of the European Community

13.1 Introduction

The subject of the external relations of the Community concerns the ability of the European Community to enter into international relationships with individual states, groups of states and international organisations. The European Community conducts these relationships through normal diplomatic channels such as maintaining diplomatic ties and participating in international conferences, negotiations and discussions. More formal means of conducting these relationships involve the negotiation and conclusion of international treaties and declarations.

The power of the European Community to engage in such activities is not unlimited but is restricted to those subjects regulated at the international level which fall within its competence by virtue of the Community Treaties. Where the Member States have transferred authority to act on their behalf to the Community, it is authorised to act at the international level. Conversely, where such authority has not been conferred, the Member States remain free to regulate their relationships with non-Community states as they see fit.

The Community has been expressly conferred with limited international personality to conduct its external affairs with non-Community states. This permits the Community to negotiate directly with third states and international organisations. In addition, the Community also administers the various trade protection mechanisms – known as trade protection laws – to protect Community industries from unfair foreign competition.

From a legal perspective, authority to exercise power to regulate external affairs is vested in the Community by virtue of two main instruments, the Common Commercial Policy and the Common Customs Tariff.

The Common Commercial Policy provisions of the EC Treaty define the scope of the Community's mandate to conduct trade policy. The Common Customs Tariff is a Community-wide tariff schedule which has replaced the individual national tariff schedules with a single harmonised and comprehensive system to levy duties on goods entering the Community. Together, both these instruments form the present basis of the Community's external trade policy.

While the external relations competence of the Community has traditionally been confined, in general, to economic and commercial matters, the position is no longer the same now the Treaty on European Union has been approved. This Agreement contains a number of provisions concerning a common foreign and security policy among the Member States. Strictly speaking, this co-operation remains outside the scope of the EC Treaty since the provisions concerning this subject take the form of a separate Title in the Treaty on European Union. However, brief consideration will be given to this matter at the end of the discussion on the traditional areas of the Community's external policy.

13.2 Capacity of the Community to enter into international agreements with third countries

The most important element of the Community's external policy is its ability to enter into international agreements with third states and international organisations which bind both the Community and the Member States. These agreements form the legal framework through which the Community regulates its relationships with non-Community states.

The Community does not enjoy unlimited capacity to enter into the negotiation or conclusion of all types of international agreements on behalf of the Member States. Where the subject-matter of an international agreement is related to the objectives and purpose of the Community, the Community has competence to act, but in the absence of such a connection it does not have such authority. These are the two polar extremes. Unfortunately, the distinction between those subjects which concern the Community under the Community Treaties and those which do not is not always clear cut.

This problem has given rise to the practice of negotiating different forms of treaty between the Community and the Member States on the one hand and third countries on the other hand. There are basically three forms of treaty which involve the Community:

1. Community agreements: these are treaties entered into by the Community in its own right. The Member States are not involved in the negotiation or conclusion of this type of agreement except through the medium of the Council of Ministers. Community agreements are used when the subject-matter of the agreement falls exclusively within the competence of the Community.
2. Mixed agreements: these are treaties involving both the Community and the Member States in the negotiation and conclusion of their terms. Such agreements are required when the subject-matter of an agreement concerns matters within the competencies of both the Community and the Member States.
3. International agreements entered into by the Member States: these are treaties which all the individual Member States have entered into either before or after the Community came into being. They concern matters outside the jurisdiction of the Community. Even although all the Member States participate in such agreements, the obligations are assumed by the Member States as individual countries.

The form of treaty used by the Community and the Member States to conclude international negotiations with third states depends essentially on the subject-matter of the agreement. If the subject matter fall within the exclusive competence of either the Community or the Member States, Community agreements or agreements by the Member States respectively are the appropriate types of agreements. Where competence over the subject is divided between the Community and the Member States, a mixed agreement is required.

Community agreements

The Community has express authority to enter into two forms of international agreement without the participation of the Member States:

1. Article 133 of the EC Treaty, as amended, authorises the Community to enter into commercial agreements relating to tariff and trade matters for the purpose of achieving the objectives of the Common Commercial Policy. This authority expressly extends to export aids, credit and finance and subsidies.
2. Article 310 of the Treaty, as amended, authorises the Community to negotiate, with third states, unions of states and international organisations, association agreements creating reciprocal rights and obligations and to facilitate common action through special procedures.

In order to define the scope of the Community's powers under these provisions, the European Commission has sought a number of opinions from the European Court. In the most significant decision, in *EC Commission* v *EC Council (Re ERTA)* Case 22/70 [1971] ECR 263, the Court held that the competence or capacity of the Community to enter into international agreements arose not only from these express provisions but also from the provisions of the Treaty which require the negotiation of international obligations for their achievement. As a result, the Court declared:

'The Community enjoys the capacity to establish contractual links with third countries over the whole field of objectives defined in Part One (Articles 1 to 7) of the Treaty.'

This decision has given rise to the 'doctrine of implied powers'. Where authority to achieve a particular aim is not expressly stated in the Community Treaties, but the Community has been given responsibility to achieve such an objective, power to accomplish such an objective is impliedly conferred on the Community, which also includes the power to regulate the matter relative to third states. This doctrine has been confirmed in a number of subsequent decisions of the European Court: see *Re Laying-Up Fund for Inland Waterway Vessels* Opinion 1/76 [1977] ECR 741 and *International Agreement on Rubber* Opinion 2/78 [1979] 3 CMLR 639.

These implied powers supplement the express powers of the Community. Whether an agreement with a third state is negotiated by the Community on the basis of an express power or an implied power does not alter its character or status as a Community agreement.

Mixed agreements

Since Member States have not transferred absolute sovereignty to the Community but only that part relative to the competence of the Community under the terms of the Treaties, conflicts may arise where an international agreement contains terms which fall within both the competence of the Community and that of individual Member States. Implementation of such agreements requires joint action on the part of the Community and the Member States.

In a mixed agreement, each of these parties acts in its own name and undertake to perform the obligations which fall within its competence. An example of a mixed agreement is the Final Act of the UN Convention on the Law of the Sea 1982, which related to issues within the jurisdiction of the Community, ie fishing rights, as well as those of the Member States, ie territorial sea, nationality of ships, etc. The Montreal Protocol on Substances that Deplete the Ozone Layer 1989 is another illustration of an agreement which required execution by both the Community and its Member States.

A similar arrangement was also required for approval and ratification of the ILO Convention on Safety in the Use of Chemicals. This agreement was negotiated by the Community and the Member States. The European Commission sought clarification from the European Court as to the relative competencies of each of the parties in this process. In *Re ILO Convention 170 on Chemicals at Work* Opinion 2/91 [1993] 3 CMLR 800 the Court found that the Community had internal legislative competence over this matter but had not exercised it. Therefore Community competence was not exclusive, and Member States were permitted to participate in the process.

Often the question of whether an international agreement is a Community agreement or a mixed agreement is a matter of dispute between the Community authorities and the Member States. For example, during the Tokyo Round of GATT negotiations, a number of Member States challenged the Community's exclusive authority to negotiate the 1979 multilateral agreements. Eventually, a number of these agreements were ratified through both Community processes and the national constitutional processes of some of the Member States.

Limited clarification of the European Community's competence to conclude international agreements has come in the Court's opinion in *Re Uruguay Round Final Act* Opinion 1/94 [1995] 1 CMLR 205. The European Commission requested the European court to confirm the competence of the Community to approve international agreements relating to trade in goods and services as well as intellectual property rights. The Court confirmed that the Community had exclusive competence to conclude agreements concerning trade in goods but shared competence with Member States in the other two sectors. Since the Community did not have exclusive competence over all the matters contained in the agreement, a mixed agreement was required and the Member States also ratified the terms of the agreement. It should be noted that the Treaty of Amsterdam modified Article 133 so that it now covers international negotiations on services and intellectual property rights.

International agreements entered into by the Member States

The Member States of the Community were parties to a number of international agreements prior to the formation of the Community, including both the GATT and the European Convention on Human Rights 1950. The Community is deemed to have succeeded to treaties concluded before 1957 only if they contain matters within its competence. In one case relating to the status of the GATT in European Community law, the European Court declared:

> 'In so far as under the EEC Treaty the Community has assumed the powers previously exercised by the Member States in the area governed by the GATT, the provisions of that agreement have the effect of binding the Community': *International Fruit Company* v *Produktschap voor Groenten en Fruit* Cases 51 and 54/71 [1972] ECR 1219.

The quality of direct effect of such treaties is, however, governed by a rigorous set of principles which effectively deny the creation of rights for private individuals: see section 7.3, above.

There is also no restriction on the Member States, after 1957, entering into international agreements which do not fall within the scope of the Community Treaties either among themselves or with non-Community states. Although such agreements are becoming increasingly rare, they do not form part of European Community law if they concern matters outside the scope of the Community Treaties.

13.3 The European Community as an international actor

The European Community is a participant at the international level by virtue of two powers: authority to conduct external relations and authority to participate in certain international organisations. For this purpose the Community has limited international legal personality by virtue of Article 281 of the EC Treaty.

On this basis the Community has entered into a substantial number of bilateral and multilateral treaties on a wide range of mainly commercial matters with third states, in its own capacity. As we have seen in the earlier section, such agreements are known as Community agreements. The procedure for the negotiation and adoption of such agreements is specified in Article 300 of the Treaty.

Procedure for the negotiation of Community agreements

The Commission has authority to open discussions with third states and international organisations under Article 300(1) but generally only does so after having been authorised by the Council of Ministers. Its mandate to negotiate is normally contained in negotiating directives issued by the Council. After the mandate has been granted, the Commission conducts exploratory discussions before the start of formal negotiations.

The actual conduct of negotiations is also the responsibility of the Commission. In the performance of this task the Commission is assisted by the 133 Committee, which is a committee of representatives from the Member States which 'advises' the Commission during its negotiations. This committee monitors the progress of discussions and clarifies the Council's negotiating mandate as the negotiations progress.

Subject to the powers vested in the Commission to negotiate, the Council has the final authority to conclude such agreements. Conclusion of an agreement technically requires the adoption of measures inside the Community legal order to give effect to the agreement and also completion of the necessary formalities, such as ratification, at the international level.

The Treaty on European Union has made a number of minor changes to this procedure. These alterations are, on the whole, intended to confer greater responsibility on the Commission in the negotiation stages while reserving the powers of the Council in relation to the conclusion of such agreements.

The Commission now has authority to make recommendations to the Council in relation to the manner in which negotiations should proceed. The Council will authorise the Commission to negotiate on the basis of these recommendations but subject to consultation with special committees appointed by the Council.

Now the Treaty has come into force, the majority required in the Council for the approval of such agreements will, in most cases, be a qualified majority, the exception being in the case of agreements covering fields for which unanimity is required for the adoption of internal measures.

The European Parliament's right to be consulted prior to the adoption of such agreements is also considerably enhanced under the amendments to be made by the Treaty on European Union. However, the European Parliament will be subject to time-limits for delivering its opinion, and if an opinion is not rendered within this period the Council will be able to act without further delay.

Subjects covered by the various types of Community agreements

Agreements between the Community and non-Community countries may be classified according to subject-matter and content into five groups: (a) multilateral trade agreements; (b) bilateral free trade agreements; (c) association agreements; (d) co-operation agreements; and (e) development and assistance agreements. These agreements vary, in both content and legal structure, according to the relationship which is to be regulated by the particular agreement.

Multilateral trade agreements are negotiated primarily in the forum of the WTO which is the international organisation responsible for the conduct of world trade. Periodic discussions – known as multilateral trade negotiations – are held in the WTO, where European Commission officials represent the Community. In the past, such discussions have produced a series of multilateral treaties. For example, in 1979, a number of such treaties were concluded to regulate subsidies, government procurement, technical barriers to trade and anti-dumping measures.

Bilateral free trade agreements have been negotiated with both individual states and international organisations. In 1992 the Community and the European Free Trade Area (EFTA), which consists of nine European countries, agreed on the terms of the Agreement on the European Economic Area. This establishes a free trade area between the Community and the EFTA countries based on the four freedoms of Community law supported by the Community rules of competition policy. In some respects the EEA Agreement goes far beyond the tradition concept of a free trade agreement because of the types of commercial activity covered and the comprehensive nature of the agreement.

The Community's policy towards Eastern Europe has also involved the extensive use of free trade agreements. For example, free trade agreements known as 'Interim Agreements' were concluded by the Community with Hungary, Poland and Czechoslovakia in 1992. Similar types of agreement are also at present being negotiated with other Eastern European states such as Romania. A free trade agreement has also been negotiated between the Community and Israel.

As a preliminary stage towards full membership of the Community, non-Community states have traditionally entered into association agreements to regulate their relationship with the Community. This type of agreement is generally more comprehensive than a free trade agreement, regulating issues such as the movement of goods, persons, services and capital as well as aid and economic co-operation. Prior to membership, Spain, Portugal and Greece each had association accords with the Community. At present, this type of agreement also regulates the relationship of the Community with Turkey, Cyprus and Malta.

Co-operation agreements are the most flexible form of Community agreement. The Community has an elaborate network of such agreements with many countries dealing with different subjects. Co-operation agreements are in force with many of the countries of Northern Africa, Asia and the Pacific Rim. These treaties often deal with economic, technical and financial co-operation and assistance. Also, such agreements frequently regulate the provision of aid by the Community.

Agreements have also been negotiated to regulate co-operation in particular subject areas with specific states. For example, in 1998, the Community approved an agreement with the United States on the application of positive comity principles in the enforcement of their competition laws. The agreement covers situations in which: anti-competitive activities are occurring in the whole or in a substantial part of the territory of one of the parties; such activities are adversely affecting the interests of the other party; and the activities in question are not permissible under the competition laws of the party in the territory in which they are occurring. The agreement sets out the procedure whereby the competition authorities of the EC can ask the competition authorities of the US to take action against anti-competitive activities which affect European companies in the US and vice-versa. It also allows competition authorities to request dawn raids by their counterparts across the Atlantic on companies suspected of breaking the law.

The final category of Community agreement is development and assistance agreements which regulate the Community's relationships with developing countries. The most elaborate example of this type are the Lome agreements which regulate aid and imports from the former colonies of Member States in Africa, the Caribbean and the Pacific. This system is regularly reviewed, the last one being negotiated in 1989.

The participation of the Community in international organisations

The Community also participates in a number of international organisations including the Organisation for Economic Co-operation and Development (OECD) and the World Trade Organisation (WTO), already mentioned above.

The OECD consists of many of the industrialised Western countries and is primarily concerned with economic policy co-operation.

The WTO is the principal international organisation dealing with world trade regulation. Issues such as tariff levels, quantitative restrictions, subsidies, technical restrictions on trade, customs procedures and anti-dumping and anti-subsidy measures are all dealt with in this organisation. Since these subjects all fall within the scope of the Community's competence, the representatives of the Member States in this organisation have been substantially replaced by Commission officials.

13.4 The Common Customs Tariff

Goods entering the Community from non-Community states are subject to the Common Customs Tariff (CCT) which is a comprehensive Community regime to regulate the levying of duties on non-EC goods. The CCT supersedes the individual tariff schedules and customs law of the Member States, although national customs officials enforce its provisions. The Community has exclusive competence to regulate the CCT, and measures enacted by Member States which conflict with its provisions are void: see *Sociaal Fonds voor der Diamantarbeiders* v *NV Indiamex* Cases 2 and 3/69 [1973] ECR 1609.

The CCT specifies a particular tariff for each product imported into the Community according to its description. These take three forms. Ad valorem tariffs are calculated as a percentage of the value of the goods imported. Fixed tariffs apply a duty rate according to the quantity or volume of the products imported regardless of their value. Mixed tariffs are applied by a formula which combine both fixed and ad valorem elements. The most common form of tariff is the ad valorem tariff.

The tariff nomenclature for each product is set out in Council Regulation 2658/87 (1987) as amended by Commission Regulation 2261/98 (1998). The rules setting out the actual procedure, determination of origin and valuation are contained in the Community's Customs Code which is Council Regulation 2913/92 (1992) as supplemented by Commission Regulation 2454/93 (1993).

Tariff classifications

Rates of duty are assessed according to the origin of the imported product. Where the country of origin is a member of the WTO, the Most-Favoured-Nation (MFN) rate is applicable unless the country benefits from a preferred rate specified for developing countries under the Lome Convention scheme or the General System of Preferences (GSP). If the country of origin is not a member of the WTO or entitled to preferred treatment, the standard rate of duty applies. Rates of duty may be amended on a country-by-country basis by the negotiation of a free trade or association agreement.

Description of the goods

Liability to duties depends on the classification of the goods in the scheme of the CCT which in turn depends on the description given to the goods. The nomenclatures stated in the CCT do not invariably correspond to all types of imported goods. In such cases, products which are not covered by any tariff heading must be classified under the heading for the products for which they are most analogous: see, eg, *Re Imports of Compact Disc Players* Case 2/91 [1993] 1 CMLR 780. This assessment is made on not only the physical characteristics of the goods but also their intended purpose and commercial value: see *Huber* v *Hauptzollamt Frankfurt-am-Main-Flughafen* Case 291/87 [1990] 2 CMLR 159.

Valuation

Where customs duties are calculated on an ad valorem basis, the value attributed to the goods is important to determine liability. The fundamental principle is that goods should be given their actual commercial value at the port of entry into the Community. This is known as the 'arm's length sales price'. Where an export sale is made to a Community purchaser and the parties are commercially unrelated, the invoice price represents the value of the goods as long as: (a) the purchaser remains free to dispose of the goods at his discretion without restrictions other than those imposed by law, (b) no additional payment is required under the transaction, and (c) no part of the consideration involved remains unquantifiable: see *Brown Boveri & Cie AG* v *Hauptzollamt Mannheim* Case C–79/89 [1993] 1 CMLR 814.

Rules of origin

As noted earlier, determination of the origin of goods is essential for the proper application of the CCT since rates vary according to the country from which the goods came. For this purpose, the country of origin is the state which produced the goods and not the country from which the goods were shipped to the Community.

Council Regulation 2913/92 (1992), as amended, specifies the general rules for establishing the origin of goods. Goods originate in the country in which they were wholly obtained or produced or, alternatively, where the last economically justified and substantial processing occurred. Goods wholly produced in a territory include minerals and agricultural commodities. Manufactured goods present greater problems in this respect.

In general, the country of origin of manufactured goods is either where the last substantial economic process occurred to them, resulting in a transformation of the component parts, or where a major stage of manufacturing occurred. The Community Regulation specifically prohibits the assessment of origin based on economic processes undertaken simply for the purposes of obtaining a lower duty rate. The Commission has enacted a number of regulations to clarify this distinction. Further, the European Court has subjected these regulations to a test of objectivity and in at least one case has held that a stricter concept of origin was applied than was necessary in the circumstances: see *SR Industries* v *Administration des Douanes* Case 91/86 [1988] ECR 378.

Principle of free circulation

Article 24(1) of the EC Treaty provides that products from a third country shall be considered to be in free circulation in the Community if the import formalities connected with the CCT have been satisfied. According to Article 23(2), once non-EC goods are in free circulation they may not be subject to quantitative restrictions or measures having an equivalent effect for the purposes of intra-Community trade.

This has significant consequences. Most importantly, no additional import requirements may be imposed on goods originating from third states if they are in free circulation in another Member State.

13.5 The Common Commercial Policy

The Common Commercial Policy (CCP) is the Community's commercial instrument for regulating its trade relations with other states. Article 133 of the EC Treaty is the constitutional basis for this instrument and provides:

> 'The Common Commercial Policy shall be based on uniform principles, particularly in regard to changes in tariff rates, the conclusion of tariff and trade agreements, the achievement of uniformity in measures of liberalisation, export policy and measures to protect trade such as those to be taken in the case of dumping or subsidies.'

This list of relevant subjects is not exhaustive as the European Court's decision in the *ERTA* case, above, demonstrates. The competence of the Community in matters covered by the CCP extends to all matters within the purposes and aims of the Community.

The procedure for the formulation of the CCP is similar to the normal decision-making processes within the Community, with the principal exception that the European Commission is responsible for conducting negotiations with third states. While the Commission almost invariably has its negotiating mandate set by the Member States, on occasions there have been splits between the Commission and the Member States in the conduct of negotiations.

The creation of the CCP among the original six Member States was a primary goal of the EC Treaty: see Article 3(b) EC Treaty. The Treaty transfers exclusive authority to formulate trade policy to the Community institutions. Individual Member States no longer retain authority to act in matters in which the Community has adopted measures in pursuit of the CCP: see *Donkerwolcke* v *Procureur de la République* Case 41/76 [1976] ECR 1921. This means that Member States cannot legislate in fields covered by Community measures nor can they enter into international obligations which would restrict the powers of the Community.

But, despite the expiry of the transition period for the completion of the CCP, Member States have continued to express reluctance to transfer complete authority to the Community to formulate a comprehensive and coherent commercial policy. This reluctance may be attributed to two factors: first, the institutional structure for the formulation and administration of the policy is inadequate; second, the actual objectives of the policy are fragmented and not stated with a sufficient degree of precision in the Treaty to encourage a transfer of competence to the Community.

The consequence is that, at present, the CCP is not a continuous unbroken superstructure. It consists of a complex framework of international agreements and Community measures, and in those areas of policy not yet covered by Community measures Member States may continue to act: see *Bulk Oil* v *Sun International* [1986] 2 All ER 744. The failure to enact Community measures to cover all aspects of the policy has left loopholes for Member States to restrict, prohibit or limit imports from non-EC countries, a practice which has been considered lawful by the European Court in a number of cases: see *Tezi Textiel* v *EC Commission* Case 59/84 [1986] ECR 887.

Neither the Single European Act nor the Treaty on European Union significantly amended the CCP provisions of the Treaty, and therefore this possibility of gaps in the policy remains.

13.6 Trade protection laws

The Community has a number of powers to impose measures on imports from non-EC countries in order to protect industry and commerce within the Community from unfair foreign trade practices. These measures may be classified into four categories:

1. anti-dumping measures;
2. anti-subsidy measures;
3. safeguard measures; and
4. measures under the New Commercial Policy Instrument.

Anti-dumping measures

The Community authorities are authorised to impose anti-dumping duties on foreign products which have been deemed to have been dumped within the Community and which have caused injury to a Community industry: Council Regulation 384/96 (1996). A foreign product has been dumped inside the Community if it has been introduced into the internal market at a price less than the comparable price for the product in the country of origin.

A dumping complaint may be lodged by any legal person (an individual, firm or company), or by an association not having legal personality acting on behalf of a Community industry. Investigations of such complaints must normally be concluded within one year from the initiation of the complaint.

The basic substantive elements of an anti-dumping investigation are the existence of dumping, injury and 'Community interests' requiring intervention.

The procedure for determining the existence of dumping in the Community is deceptively simple. It involves four basic steps:

1. the determination of the normal value of the goods on the market of their country of origin;
2. the determination of the price at which the goods are sold in the Community, after adjustments;
3. comparison of the normal value with the Community price; and
4. the calculation of the 'margin of dumping' (the normal price minus the export price.

Normal value is the price of the goods in the country of origin, while the export price is the price of the goods inside the Community. The margin of dumping is the difference between these two figures and is also the measure of the anti-dumping duty which will be levied to neutralise the unfair competitive advantage enjoyed by the foreign product.

In addition to establishing the existence of dumped products, it is also necessary to prove that these products have caused material injury to an industry within the Community. In other words, the efficiency, productivity or profitability of the Community industry must be damaged by the imports.

Finally, before anti-dumping duties may be imposed, it must be established that the interests of the Community call for such intervention. No list of Community interests is provided in the basic regulation. The concept will cover a wide range of factors, the most important being the protection of the consumer, protection of foreign investment, employment and the interests of Community users of the imported products in production of other goods.

If all these elements are established after the Commission's investigation, the imported products may be subject to anti-dumping duties which are assessed on each product according to their country of origin.

Protection against dumped products is the most prevalent form of trade protection measure employed by the European Community.

Anti-subsidy measures

Anti-subsidy duties are imposed on foreign products which have benefited from subsidies from foreign governments during their manufacture, distribution or export, but again only if these products cause injury to Community industries producing similar goods. The authority under which the Community imposes such duties is Council Regulation 2026/97 (1997).

Again, anti-subsidy measures are imposed only after a Commission investigation. The investigation must establish that:

1. a subsidy has been paid by a foreign government to the producers of the goods;
2. material injury is being caused by these imported goods to a Community industry; and
3. Community interests call for intervention.

Anti-subsidy investigations and anti-dumping investigations are very similar in their nature, with the exception that in an anti-subsidy investigation the illegitimate practice being countered is subsidisation, whereas in anti-dumping investigations the unfair practice is dumping.

Safeguard measures

Imports into the Community may also be subject to safeguard measures under the relevant provisions of Council Regulation 3285/94 (1994). If foreign products are being imported into the Community in such increased quantities as to cause, or threaten to cause, serious injury to a Community industry, safeguard measures may be imposed to protect that industry, regardless of the cause or source of the increase in the volume of imports. The standard is that of serious injury, not material injury or merely injury. This is a higher threshold than that in the case for anti-dumping and anti-subsidy investigations.

If the existence of increased imports and serious injury are both established, the Community may impose additional duties, tariffs or quotas on the importation of such products to protect the Community industry.

Measures under the Trade Barrier Regulation (TBR)

The European Commission is empowered to investigate allegations of obstacles to trade erected by non-EC countries under the Trade Barrier Regulation (TBR), Council Regulation 3286/94 (1994). EC companies or industries may lodge a complaint with the Commission requesting the examination of foreign trade practices which impede EC exports. If these allegations are found to be true, and if the complainant can show injury, the Commission is required to enter into discussions with the third state with a view to removing the obstacle to trade. If a negotiated settlement proves ineffective, the matter may be brought to the attention of the WTO dispute settlement body for resolution.

13.7 New competencies in external relations added by the Treaty on European Union

The Treaty on European Union introduces a new field of competence in external relations, namely co-operation between the Member States in common foreign and security policy. This objective is contained in Title V of the Treaty which, unlike the provisions relating to economic and monetary union, stands outside the EC Treaty. Neither Title V nor Title VI of the Treaty (co-operation in the areas of justice and home affairs) involve amendments to the Community Treaties. They are separate and independent provisions which, together with the Community Treaties, form the basis of the new European Union which is established by the Treaty on

European Union. Therefore, strictly speaking, these provisions exist independently alongside the external relations provisions of the EC Treaty and do not add to the Community's competencies in this area. But, since this Title impinges on matters relating to the external relations of the Community, it should at least briefly be considered at this point.

The European Union and its Member States are to define and implement the terms of the common foreign and security policy. The objectives of this policy are stated to be:

1. to safeguard the common values, fundamental interests and independence of the Union;
2. to strengthen the security of the Union and its Member States in all ways;
3. to preserve peace and strengthen international security, in accordance with the UN Charter and the principles of the Helsinki Final Act;
4. to promote international co-operation; and
5. to promote and consolidate democracy and the rule of law and respect for human rights and fundamental freedoms.

These aims are, while laudable in theory, vaguely stated. In fact, only the intention to achieve common foreign policy objectives is stated with any degree of certainty.

Detailed provisions have been established to facilitate co-ordination and co-operation in this area, based essentially on the exchange of views and consultations. Where necessary, the Council of Ministers will define a common position on particular matters. Each Member State is obliged to ensure that its national policies conform to any such common position.

The relationship between the present terms of the EC Treaty concerning external relations and the relevant terms of the Treaty on European Union concerning foreign policy is that the latter will supplement the former, leading to a broader Community competence at the international level. Trade policy will no longer form the main element of the Community's relations with third states. Instead, the European Union will have competence in a broad spectrum of international affairs in so far as such matters relate to foreign policy.

Law of the European Convention on Human Rights

14

The Institutions and System Established by the European Convention on Human Rights

14.1 Introduction

14.2 Institutional structure

14.3 Applications by state contracting parties

14.4 Applications by private individuals

14.5 The relationship between the European Convention and the law of the European Community and the law of the United Kingdom

14.1 Introduction

The legal system established under the European Convention for the Protection of Human Rights and Fundamental Freedoms exists independently of the European Union legal order and it should always be borne in mind that the two legal systems function quite separately. Again, while the institutions created under the Convention have similar names to those of the European Union – such as the European Commission and the European Court – there is no institutional connection between agencies established under each of these agreements.

The European Convention on Human Rights was also signed in Rome, in 1950, but is an instrument administered by another European organisation, the Council of Europe. All the states that are members of the Council of Europe have ratified the European Convention on Human Rights, which now has 40 contracting parties.

In essence, the Convention establishes a procedure to allow complaints from both states and private individuals to be lodged claiming violations of the human rights contained in the Convention. The Convention does not attempt to change the national laws of those states that are parties to it, although a number of countries have chosen to incorporate its terms into their national legal systems. Rather, it sets up a system to facilitate the making of complaints concerning inconsistencies between national laws and the terms of the Convention.

The Convention itself is divided into three sections. The first identifies the substantive rights guaranteed by the Convention to individuals within the jurisdiction of a state which is a party to the Convention. These rights concern fundamental human rights such as the right to life, to freedom from torture, to due process of law and to freedom of expression.

The second section sets up the institutional organs of the system for the protection of these rights. The third section concerns miscellaneous matters such as the financial operation of the system, reservations and dispute settlement.

This part of the textbook is divided into two chapters. This chapter deals with the institutional structure established under the Convention to ensure respect for the rights contained in the agreement. In addition, it considers the important subject of the procedure established under the Convention for making inter-state and private party complaints. The procedural law of the Convention determines the admissibility of applications and the conditions which must be satisfied before an application is accepted. Finally, a section is included which discusses the relationship between the law established under the Convention on the one hand and the law of the European Union and the law of the United Kingdom on the other.

The second chapter discusses the nature and content of the substantive rights and freedoms guaranteed under the Convention. This requires an examination not only of the nature of the rights conferred but also the exceptions and derogations to these rights and freedoms permitted under the Convention.

14.2 Institutional structure

The Committee of Ministers

The Council of Europe, which was established in 1949, has as its principal organ a Committee of Ministers. When the European Convention on Human Rights was agreed, the contracting parties decided that certain functions should be entrusted to the Committee of Ministers of the Council of Europe. The Committee of Ministers is the executive organ within the system. Authority has been conferred for carrying out a number of responsibilities under the Convention which can generally be classified as: (a) administrative functions; (b) judicial and quasi-judicial functions; and (c) supervisory functions.

Administrative functions
The most important administrative functions of the Committee of Ministers relate to the appointment of personnel to the Court of Human Rights.

Judicial functions
The Committee is in reality a political body, composed of national representatives, and it is therefore surprising that it should have any role to play in a process which

is essentially legal in nature. This participation came about as a result of the inability of the draughtsmen of the Convention to decide whether the system should revolve around procedures for the exercise of compulsory jurisdiction by the Court. This inability to reach a compromise between one or the other option eventually resulted in the Committee having a limited judicial function in the procedures established under the Convention.

Supervisory functions

The main supervisory power of the Committee of Ministers is conferred by Article 54 of the Convention which provides that the Committee shall supervise the execution of decisions by the Court which find against contracting states. It appears that the duty of supervision relates both to judgments on the merits of a case and to the enforcement of awards of damages against contracting states.

This mechanism works well when states are willing to change their national laws to comply with the rulings of the European Court which is, in fact, the situation in the vast majority of cases. In such circumstances, the Committee merely notes that the necessary measures or steps have been taken to comply with the decision of the Court. However, where a state demonstrates a reluctance to comply with the terms of a Court decision, no additional compunction can be placed on that state by the Committee of Ministers other than the pressures of adverse international public opinion.

The European Commission of Human Rights

The European Commission of Human Rights was set up in 1954 to protect the rights granted to individuals under the Convention. Its main function was to investigate complaints and to decide whether violations of the Convention had been committed by contracting parties. The Commission consisted of the same number of members as contracting parties and, since no two members of the Commission might be the same nationality, each contracting party was entitled to nominate a member.

The most important function of the Commission was to investigate alleged breaches of the Convention brought either by other state contracting parties or by private individuals in those cases where contracting parties had consented to such procedures. The European Court of Human Rights had jurisdiction for all cases concerning the interpretation and application of the Convention which were referred to it by the contracting parties or by the Commission. The vast majority of cases were brought to the attention of the Court after a reference from the Commission. Private parties had no direct access to the Court. Private complaints had to be lodged with the Commission which had the option to decide whether or not a case should have been referred to the Court for a decision.

The increasing work-load showed that the original structure was badly in need of reform. On average, a complaint could take as long as five years from initiation of a complaint to a ruling from the European Court of Human Rights. Equally, the number of complaints rejected for failing to meet the rigorous standards required for admissibility demonstrated the inability of the institutional structure to provide proper relief to aggrieved individuals.

On 11 May 1994, Protocol No 11 opened for signature in Strasbourg: see (1994) 17 EHRR 501. The last ratification of Protocol No 11 was deposited in October 1997. This Protocol completely revamped the institutional structure of the system and, most importantly, compelled the abolition of the European Commission and the creation of a single full-time court. On 1 November 1998 Protocol No 11 entered into force and these changes came into effect

Private parties are therefore now able to go directly to the European Court for redress and complaints are no longer filtered through the Commission. The Protocol, however, provides that the Commission remains active for one year, until 31 October 1999, in order to deal with cases which were declared admissible before the reform entered into force.

The Court of Human Rights

The composition of the Court

The European Court of Human Rights consists of the same number of judges as the number of the contracting parties. These judges are elected by the Parliamentary Assembly of the Council of Europe by a majority of votes cast from a list of three candidates nominated by the High Contracting Party. All candidates for appointment must be of a high moral character and must either possess the qualifications required for appointment to high judicial office or must be juriconsults of recognised competence.

The judges of the Court are elected for a period of six years and are eligible thereafter for re-election. Elections are held every three years at which time one-half of the bench of the Court is subject to re-election. The Court itself elects the President and two Vice-Presidents.

Under rule 4 of the Court's rules of procedures which came into force as from 4 November 1998, the judges may not during their term of office engage in any activity which is incompatible with their independence or impartiality or with the demands of a full-time office. Judges sit on the Court in their individual capacity and do not act as representatives of their government. They often vote against the interests of their own country.

The Court is divided into four Sections. Each Section's members are geographically and gender balanced. Committees of three judges are formed within each Section for one year in order to handle the cases.

The jurisdiction of the Court

The jurisdiction of the Court extends to all cases concerning the interpretation and application of the Convention and the protocols thereto which are referred to it by the contracting parties, by private complainants and by the Committee of Ministers.

In particular, the Court may now receive applications from:

1. any contracting party alleging breach of the Convention and protocols by another contracting party;
2. any person, non–governmental organisation or group of individuals claiming to be the victim of a violation by one of the contracting parties of the rights laid down in the Convention and protocols;
3. The Committee of Ministers, when it requires the Court to give an advisory opinion on legal questions on the interpretation of the Convention and protocols.

The procedure of the Court

The Court hears application sitting either in Grand Chamber or in a Chamber. The Grand Chamber is composed of 17 judges. It includes the President and Vice-Presidents of the Court and the Section Presidents. Each Chamber is composed of seven judges, including the President of the Section and the Judge elected in respect of any contracting party concerned.

Hearings are public, unless the Chamber, in view of exceptional circumstances, decides otherwise. Documents deposited with the Registrar are accessible to the public unless the President of the Court decides otherwise. The Court's deliberations on the merits of the case are, however, secret.

Applications to the Court are assigned to a Section. Decisions on admissibility are taken either by a Chamber or by a Committee.

During the procedure on the merits, the Court may conduct negotiations to obtain a friendly settlement. Chambers decide by a majority vote. If the judgment does not represent, in whole or in part, the unanimous opinion, any judge is entitled to deliver a separate opinion.

Within three months from the Chamber's judgment, any party may request the case to be referred to the Grand Chamber if it raises a serious question of interpretation or application or a general issue of general importance. These requests are examined by a panel of five judges of the Grand Chamber.

According to Article 44, the judgment of a Chamber becomes final:

1. when the parties declare that they will not request reference of the case to the Grand Chamber;
2. three months after the date of the judgment, if no reference to the Grand Chamber has been requested; or
3. when the Grand Chamber rejects the request to refer.

The judgments of the Grand Chamber are final.

The contracting parties have each agreed in Article 46 of the Convention to abide by the decision of the Court in any case in which they are parties. Nonetheless, the Committee of Ministers is charged with ensuring that all final judgments are properly executed.

The function and powers of the Court

The function of the Court is to decide whether infractions of the Convention have occurred. This is clear from Article 41 of the Convention which states:

> 'If the Court finds that there has been a violation of the Convention or the protocols thereto, and if the internal law of the High Contracting Party concerned allows only partial reparation to be made, the Court shall, if necessary, afford just satisfaction to the injured party.'

This Article lies at the heart of the whole Convention regime. From its terms, it is clear that the system is designed to afford satisfaction against contracting parties found in violation of the terms of the Convention. The Court cannot therefore settle a dispute between two private individuals. The dispute must arise between one or more individuals and a state. Further, the powers of the Court are not merely declaratory; it is empowered to award sums in damages as compensation for violations of the Convention.

However, the Court cannot prescribe what remedial measures should be taken by a state to rectify an infringement. Article 46 merely states:

> 'The High Contracting Parties undertake to abide the final judgment of the Court in any case to which they are parties'

In normal circumstances, states amend their legislation to rectify violations of the Convention found to exist either in their laws or the judgments of their national courts. Judgments of the Court do not therefore automatically amend the law of contracting states.

14.3 Applications by state contracting parties

Article 33 sets out the right of a contracting party to bring an application to the attention of the Court. In particular, Article 33 states:

> 'Any High Contracting Party may refer to the Court any alleged breach of the provisions of the Convention and the protocols thereto by another High Contracting Party'

Two important points should be noted about the procedure established under Article 33 of the Convention. First, it is not necessary for a contracting party to claim that another contracting party has infringed the rights of nationals from the first state. Any violation of the rights guaranteed under the Convention constitutes a ground for an inter-state application even if the state accused of the violations is alleged to have deprived its own national of these rights.

Second, a different standard applies under this procedure to the requirement of exhausting all available local remedies, which is one of the most significant impediments faced by private parties initiating a claim. In *Austria v Italy* (1982) the Commission held that a state raising the defence of non-exhaustion has a duty to show that such remedies exist within the legal system and that they have not been exhausted. In other words, the onus is reversed from that which applies in private applications where the individual is required to demonstrate that all available remedies have been exhausted.

Of the cases brought under this procedure, most have been politically motivated. For example, in 1956 and 1957 Greece brought two applications against Cyprus concerning alleged mistreatment of prisoners in Cyprus. These applications were part of the broader political dispute between Greece, Turkey and Cyprus. Once Cyprus became independent, Cyprus itself brought a series of claims against Turkey complaining of violations of the Convention by Turkey during the Turkish intervention in the island's affairs.

Similarly, five applications were brought against Greece between 1967 and 1972 by Denmark, Norway, Sweden and The Netherlands against violations of the Convention allegedly committed by the government of Greece which at that time consisted of a military junta. The Commission carried out an extensive investigation on the matter but, as the report was being considered by the Committee of Ministers, the Greek government withdrew from the Council of Ministers and denounced the Convention. Greece subsequently rejoined the Council of Europe and the Convention after a democratic government had successfully supplanted the junta.

Ireland also has brought an inter-state application against the United Kingdom in 1971 and 1972 alleging violations of the Convention committed by British forces in Northern Ireland. While the principal allegation – that of torture – was not sustained, the Court of Human Rights found violations of Article 3 of the Convention for activities characterised as inhuman and degrading.

14.4 Application by private individuals

Before the institutional system was reformed, private complaints were allowed only to be made to the Commission and only in so far as the contracting state against which the complaint was lodged had declared that it recognised the competence of the Commission to receive the case.

Under the new system, the Court may receive applications from any private parties (Article 34). The contracting states undertake not to hinder in any way the effective exercise of this right by private parties.

There are, however, a number of important prerequisites which must be satisfied before an application is deemed admissible. The first is that the applicant must claim to be the victim of a violation. It is not enough that a violation of the terms of the Convention has occurred; the applicant must be directly affected by it or have a personal interest in it. Second, the applicant must have exhausted all domestic remedies available to him or her in the legal system of the state allegedly committing the violation. Third, an application may be considered inadmissible because it fails to meet the conditions set down in Article 35(2) of the Convention.

Exhaustion of domestic remedies

Article 35(1) of the Convention states that:

> 'The Court may only deal with the matter after all domestic remedies have been exhausted according to generally recognised rules of international law, and within a period of six months from the date on which the final decision was taken.'

The rationale for this principle is simply that a state accused of the violation should have an opportunity to redress the wrong through its own legal processes before being brought before the international procedure.

In the past, the Commission consistently held that it is for the applicant to prove that he or she has exhausted every remedy available to him or her in the legal system of the state which has allegedly committed the violation. This has been a major hurdle to the use of the procedure by private parties.

Three general principles underpin this doctrine, namely: the applicant must have exhausted all available remedies; the remedy must be effective; and certain circumstances can relieve the applicant from this obligation.

The applicant must have exhausted all available remedies

The requirement of exhausting all available remedies means that the applicant must have exhausted not only the remedies available in the ordinary courts but also the whole range of legal remedies available in that state to an individual in the particular circumstances. This includes special administrative procedures which exist in some countries to provide individuals with access to special prerogatives exercised by government officials.

Within the domestic legal system, this requirement also means that the applicant must have exhausted all appeal processes made available. Once the final decision is reached, the six months' time limit begins to run.

The remedy must be effective

An applicant must pursue those avenues of legal recourse available to him or her which are the most appropriate, bearing in mind the rights which have allegedly been infringed. At the same time, an applicant need not pursue remedies which do not provide effective relief. The question is therefore whether or not the remedy available offers the applicant the possibility of an effective and sufficient remedy. As a general principle, it is not necessary for an applicant to have recourse to domestic tribunals if the result will inevitably be a repetition of the original decision which gave rise to the claim.

The circumstances which can relieve the applicant from the obligation

In reality, these circumstances are relatively limited, the principal one being that where a decision is bound to be a repetition of an earlier one, the applicant is relieved of this obligation. So, for example, the well-established jurisprudence of municipal tribunals may provide such a ground, although it is difficult to see how such a position can be established for certain without legal proceedings. Certainly in the past the Commission has rejected opinions from local lawyers stating that action was not necessary.

Applications incompatible with the terms of the Convention

The Convention itself contains a host of conditions which can prevent an application from being admissible. In procedural terms, an application will be inadmissible if it is anonymous or if it is substantially the same as a matter which has already been examined by the Commission or has already been submitted to another procedure or international investigation or settlement: Article 35(2). Similarly, a petition will be inadmissible if the application appears manifestly ill-founded in terms of the Convention and if the complaint amounts to an abuse of the right of petition: Article 35(3).

The application appears manifestly ill-founded in terms of the Convention

The Commission rarely declared complaints to be manifestly unfounded. In particular, where the Commission could not decide whether a case was admissible without making an examination of the facts, it had often stated that the application could not be manifestly ill-founded. For example, in *Klass v Germany* (1978) 2 EHRR 214, the Commission stated:

> 'With regard to the question whether under Article [35(3)] the application is inadmissible as being manifestly unfounded, the Commission finds that it raises complex questions of law and fact, which are also of general interest for the application of the Convention. Having carried out a preliminary examination of the information and arguments submitted by the parties, the Commission considers that the determination of these questions must depend upon an examination of the merits. It follows that the application cannot be regarded as manifestly ill-founded within the meaning of Article [35(3)].'

The complaint amounts to an abuse of the right of petition

On the basis of the past Commission's practice, the Court will consider at least three situations to amount to an abuse of the right to petition. First, the Court will consider a persistent and negligent disregard for the rules laid down to enable the preparation of applications to be an abuse of the right of petition. Second, where the facts of an application so obviously do not indicate a violation, the petition will be considered abusive. Finally, defamatory remarks in a petition or before the Court during the course of an investigation may give grounds for the Court to consider the application to be abusive.

14.6 The relationship between the European Convention and the law of the European Community and the law of the United Kingdom

European Community law

The European Community is not a contracting party to the European Convention on Human Rights, although there has been periodic discussion of this possibility within the institutions of the Community: see, eg, *Joint Declaration by the European Parliament, the Council and the Commission on European Rights* 1977, OJ C103/1 (1977). Therefore, the Convention is not strictly a formal source of Community law in the same manner that an agreement entered into between the Community and third states can be when certain conditions are satisfied.

While the EC Treaty, at least at present, concerns matters of an essentially economic nature, and the Convention regulates mainly political rights, as opposed to economic rights, the European Court has been required on a number of occasions to consider human rights issues. In these decisions there has been considerable overlap between the two systems and, at the same time, a significant potential for conflict.

For its part, the European Court has made considerable efforts to avoid such conflicts. Thus, in *Internationale Handelsgesellschaft GmbH v EVGF* Case 11/70 [1970] CMLR 255, the Court declared that 'respect for fundamental human rights forms an integral part of general principles of law protected by the Court of Justice'. But, in this particular case, the fundamental rights referred to were those embodied in the national constitutions of Member States and not in international instruments such as the European Convention or the two UN Covenants.

It was not until later that the European Court of Justice recognised that, in addition to 'constitutional traditions' of Member States, 'international treaties for the protection of human rights' could be referred to as general principles of Community law: *Nold v EC Commission* Case 4/73 [1974] 2 CMLR 338.

Since this recognition the European Court has been more willing to interpret Community law in light of the principles contained in the Convention. The following are a few examples:

1. the right to privacy: *National Panasonic (UK) Ltd v EC Commission* Case 136/79 [1980] ECR 2033;
2. the principle of legal professional privilege for lawyer/client communications: *AM & S Europe Ltd v EC Commission* Case 155/79 [1982] ECR 1575;
3. the right of substantive and procedural due process of law: *Musique Diffusion Française SA v EC Commission* Cases 100–103/80 [1985] ECR 1825;
4. the right to refrain from self-incrimination: *Heylens* Case 35/85 [1987] ECR 4097;
5. the retroactive application of criminal law: *R v Kirk* Case 63/83 [1984] ECR 2689;
6. the issue of abortion: *Society for the Protection of Unborn Children (Ireland) v Grogan* Case C–159/90 [1991] 3 CMLR 849.

Instead of the wholesale incorporation of the European Convention on Human Rights into the Community legal order, there has been a gradual penetration of its principles into Community law at the behest of the Court of Justice.

This piecemeal approach, however, does itself create problems. First, what course of action will the Court of Justice follow if the European Court of Human Rights, or the European Commission of Human Rights for that matter, renders a decision on a point of law which later arises in the Community context for resolution? Will the Court of Justice defer to the earlier ruling or will it pursue its own course even if the conclusions of the ECJ are inconsistent with the findings of the European Court of Human Rights? In fact the case of *Funke* v *France* [1993] 1 CMLR 897 raised just such concerns.

United Kingdom law

A number of states that are parties to the Convention, including the United Kingdom, were initially reluctant to incorporate the Convention within their domestic law. One reason for this is that successive governments have maintained that human rights are already adequately protected by law; another reason is that our constitutional traditions are opposed to allowing the courts any power to review the content of statutes. Accordingly the Convention was not originally part of the law applied and enforced by the British courts. In fact, judges did occasionally rely on provisions of the Convention in construing statutes, since the courts may presume that Parliament in legislation does not intend to contravene the treaty obligations of the United Kingdom.

For example, in *Waddington* v *Miah* [1974] 2 All ER 377 the House of Lords, in holding that the penal provisions of the Immigration Act 1971 were not retrospective, referred, inter alia, to Article 7 of the Convention which reads:

> '1. No one shall be held guilty of any criminal offence on account of any act or omission which did not constitute a criminal offence under national or international law at the time when it was committed. Nor shall a heavier penalty be imposed than the one that was applicable at the time the criminal offence was committed.
> 2. This article shall not prejudice the trial and punishment of any person for any act or omission which, at the time when it was committed, was criminal according to the general principles of law recognised by civilised nations.'

Lord Reid, in giving his speech, went on: 'So it is hardly credible that any government department would promote or that Parliament would pass retrospective criminal legislation.'

These words were cited with approval by Lord Denning MR in the case of *R* v *Home Secretary, ex parte Bhajan Singh* [1976] QB 198, where it was held that the 'right to marry and found a family' under Article 12 of the Convention must be read subject to Article 5(i)(f) which made it clear that where a person was imprisoned (as here) as an illegal immigrant he could not as of right require facilities for a marriage.

The Master of the Rolls went on to explain the Convention's relationship to English law:

'There are many cases in which it has been said, as plainly as can be, that a treaty does not become part of our English law except and insofar as it is made so by Parliament. If an Act of Parliament contained any provisions contrary to the Convention, the Act of Parliament must prevail. But I hope that no Act ever will be contrary to the Convention. So the point should not arise.

I would repeat that when anyone is considering a problem concerning human rights, we should seek to solve it in the light of the Convention and in conformity with it.'

This case was used as authority by Scarman LJ (as he then was), in support of the maxim, first recorded in Magna Carta, that justice delayed is justice denied, in the case of *R* v *Home Secretary, ex parte Phansopkar* [1976] QB 606. He maintained that:

'This hallowed principle of our law is now reinforced by the European Convention on Human Rights to which it is now the duty of our public authorities in administering the law, including the Immigration Act 1971, and of our courts in interpreting and applying the law, including the Act, to have regard.'

Scarman LJ went on:

'It may, of course, happen under our law that the basic rights to justice undeterred and to respect for family and private life have to yield to the express requirements of a statute. But in my judgment it is the duty of the courts, so long as they do not defy or disregard clear unequivocal provision, to construe statutes in a manner which promotes, not endangers, those rights. Problems of ambiguity or omission, if they arise under the language of an Act, should be resolved so as to give effect to, or at the very least, so as not to derogate from the rights recognised by, Magna Carta and the European Convention.'

This position has, however, dramatically changed since the enactment of the Human Rights Act 1998 (1998 c 42).

Section 1 of the Act creates so-called 'Convention rights' These rights are the human rights contained in Articles 2–12 and Article 14 of the European Convention on Human Rights, together with those of Articles 1–3 of the First Protocol and Articles 1 and 2 of the Sixth Protocol. These Articles are set out in Sch 1 of the Act.

These provisions are not directly incorporated into the law of the UK. Instead, certain courts are given power to make a declaration of incompatibility in the event that they find that a provision of primary legislation is incompatible with the Convention rights. These courts are the House of Lords, the Judicial Committee of the Privy Council, the High Court, the Court of Appeal, the Scottish High Court of Judiciary and the Scottish Court of Session. Lower courts are therefore deprived of this power and an appeal must be made from these courts in the event that a declaration of incompatibility is sought.

If a court with power to do so is satisfied that a provision of primary legislation is incompatible with the Convention rights, it is empowered to make a declaration of incompatibility: s4(2). In the case of secondary legislation, this power can be exercised if the court is satisfied:

1. that the provision is incompatible with a Convention right; and
2. that (disregarding any possibility of revocation) the primary legislation concerned prevents removal of the incompatibility: s4(4).

It should be noted that a declaration of incompatibility does not render the statute or statutory instrument ipso facto null and void in the same way as the US Supreme Court can rule. On the contrary, a declaration of incompatibility is expressly stated not to affect the validity, continuing operation or enforcement of the provision in respect of which it has been given: s4(6). Moreover, it is not binding on the parties to the proceedings in which it has been made. The effect of such a declaration is to put into effect a procedure for remedying the incompatibility. This procedure is set down in s10 of the statute.

In essence, the remedial procedure contained in s10 revolves around the power of Ministers of the Crown to make orders to remove the incompatibility if he or she believes that there are compelling reasons for invoking such a course of action. Controversially, this power extends to amendments to both primary and secondary legislation. However, the exercise of this power is subject to three safeguards. First, it cannot be invoked unless a declaration of incompatibility has been issued by a superior court and, moreover, all appeal stages of the case have been exhausted or abandoned. Second, the mnister exercising the power must find 'compelling reasons' for invoking this power. Finally, Sch 2 of the Act requires that no remedial order can be made unless:

1. a draft of the order has been approved by a resolution of each House of Parliament made after the end of a period of 60 days beginning on the day the draft was laid before the Houses; or
2. in cases of urgency, the order expressly declares that it is necessary to make the order without the draft being so approved which clearly is envisaged only in exceptional cases.

In addition, under s3(1) of the Act, a UK court or tribunal must interpret and apply primary legislation and subordinate legislation 'so far as it is possible to do so', in a way which is compatible with the Convention rights. In effect, this is simply a restatement of the previous case law of the UK courts in which the courts interpreted and applied the European Convention in the construction of statutes: see *Phansopkar*, above, and *R* v *Secretary of State for the Home Department, ex parte Brind* [1990] 1 All ER 469.

As a final point, a courts and tribunals at all levels are instructed under s2(1) of the Act to take into account the following sources of law when dealing with a case involving the interpretation and application of a Convention right:

1. judgments, decisions, declarations and advisory opinions of the European Court of Human Rights;
2. opinions of the former European Commission of Human Rights; and
3. decisions of the Committee of Ministers.

While not a wholesale incorporation of the European Convention of Human Rights into UK law, the Human Rights Act 1998 goes a considerable way towards removing the difficulties faced by courts and litigants prior to its enactment. Previously courts faced with glaring incompatibilities between UK domestic law and the Convention were bound to apply the principle of parliamentary sovereignty and allow the statutory provisions to prevail. Now, an avenue of escape has been established to allow the superior courts to make a declaration of incompatibility and facilitate remedial action at ministerial level. Within the next year, we should see how effective this procedure is in practice.

15

The Substantive Rights Established under the European Convention

15.1 Introduction

15.2 The right to life

15.3 The right to freedom from torture and inhuman and degrading treatment

15.4 The right to liberty and security of the person

15.5 The right to a fair trial

15.6 The right to privacy

15.7 The right to freedom of expression

15.8 The right of peaceful assembly

15.9 The right to marriage

15.1 Introduction

The substantive scope of the Convention is mainly restricted to political, as opposed to social and economic, rights. As a result, not all rights generally accepted as basic human rights are included within the Convention. Its terms are confined to those rights and liberties which the draughtsmen of the Convention considered would be generally accepted in the liberal democracies of Western Europe following the end of the Second World War.

Article 1 of the Convention requires all states ratifying its terms to extend the rights contained in the instrument to all persons within their respective jurisdictions. In other words, there is no requirement that an individual must be a national of one of the contracting parties before he or she is eligible to make an application under the terms of the Convention. The relevant nexus is the jurisdiction of a state and not citizenship or even residence, although jurisdiction and residence are often linked: see *Cruz Varas* v *Sweden (No 2)* (1992) 14 EHRR 1.

A total of twelve separate rights and liberties are stated in the Convention. These may be listed as follows:

Article 2	The right to life.
Article 3	Freedom from torture or inhuman or degrading treatment or punishment.
Article 4	Freedom from slavery or forced labour.
Article 5	The right to liberty and security of the person.
Article 6	The right to a fair and impartial trial including the right to be presumed innocent until proved guilty.
Article 7	Freedom from the application of retroactive criminal law.
Article 8	The right to respect for private and family life, home and correspondence.
Article 9	Freedom of thought, conscience and religion.
Article 10	Freedom of expression.
Article 11	Freedom of assembly and association.
Article 12	The right to marry and found a family
Article 13	The right to an effective remedy before a national authority.

Each of the above rights is, by virtue of Article 14, to be enjoyed 'without discrimination on any ground such as sex, race, colour, language, religion, political or other opinion, national or social origin, association with a national minority, property, birth or other status'. But this prohibition on discrimination only extends to the enjoyment of the rights created under the Convention and is not a blanket prohibition on the practice of discrimination: see *Abdulaziz, Cabales and Balkandali* v *United Kingdom* (1985) 7 EHRR 471. Another illustration of Article 14 being used in tandem with another right was *Hoffmann* v *Austria* (1994) 17 EHRR 293, where the Court held that the right to respect for family life had been infringed because of discrimination based on religion.

The scope of the Convention has been expanded on a number of occasions by several protocols. The first of these, the First Protocol, was concluded in 1952 and has been ratified by the United Kingdom. This establishes three new rights, namely that of every person to peaceful enjoyment of his or her possessions (Article 1), to education (Article 2) and to participate in free elections by secret ballot (Article 3).

The next to add substantive rights was the Fourth Protocol, which was concluded in 1963. This creates four more: to freedom from imprisonment for civil debts (Article 1), to freedom of movement of persons (Article 2), to enter and remain in the country of which one is a national (Article 3), and to freedom from collective expulsion (Article 4). This protocol has not been ratified by the United Kingdom because under UK immigration law not all citizens have the right to enter the state.

The Sixth Protocol to the Convention, which was concluded in 1983 and entered into force in March 1985, abolishes the death penalty for criminal offences. The United Kingdom has not signed this and in fact has indicated on a number of occasions that it has no intention of doing so.

The last one dealing with substantive rights is the Seventh Protocol which took effect from November 1988. This deals with a number of civil rights, including the procedural rights of aliens (Article 1), rights of appeal (Article 2), compensation for miscarriages of justice (Article 3), the right not to be tried or punished on more than one occasion (Article 4) and the rights of equality between spouses (Article 5).

The structure of each of these rights as elaborated in the text of the Convention varies according to its particular nature, but, as a general rule, each is subject to the general exception for derogations contained in Article 15 and also to specific exceptions usually included within the terms of the Article establishing the particular right itself.

According to Article 15, Member States may derogate from their obligations under the Convention, except those contained in Articles 2, 3, 4(1) and 7, to the extent strictly required by the exigencies of a situation, provided that such measures are not inconsistent with the obligations of the state in question under international law. This is the general principle allowing for derogations in time of war or other public emergencies. Member States must inform the Secretary-General of the Council of Europe of the measures taken and the reasons for their adoption.

Few of the rights in the Convention are stated in absolute terms. The vast majority, as we shall see, are subject to specific exceptions, the terms of which vary according to the subject-matter of the right. These particular exceptions will be discussed more fully as we turn to consider each of the substantive rights in more detail.

As a final point it should be noted that, although the Convention is binding under international law on each contracting party, there is no obligation to incorporate its terms into national law. In practice, it is for each state to decide the appropriate course of action. Approximately half the states which are parties to the Convention – including Austria, Belgium, Germany, Italy, Luxembourg and the Netherlands – have incorporated its terms into their domestic laws, but the impact of the Convention within each of these legal systems is far from uniform.

15.2 The right to life

Article 2(1) of the Convention states:

> 'Everyone's right to life shall be protected by law. No one shall be deprived of his life intentionally save in the execution of a sentence of a court following his conviction of a crime for which this penalty is provided by law.'

There has only been one case dealing with the most obvious potential infringement of this right, namely the use of lethal force to protect the public. The case in question is *McCann and Others* v *United Kingdom* Case 17/545 (1995) 21 EHRR 97. The fact of this case are straightforward. In March 1986, three terrorists from the Irish Republican Army (IRA) were shot dead by British soldiers while executing a plan to conduct a terrorist attack on British Army personnel in Gibraltar. The parents of the terrorists brought an application under the Convention claiming that the killings of the terrorists contravened Article 2 of the Convention by unlawfully depriving them of the right to life.

The Court rejected the contention made by the applicants that the killings were premeditated. There was no evidence to support this allegation and no evidence of implicit encouragement by the authorities to execute the terrorists. Nor did the reactions of the soldiers forced to execute the terrorists amount to a breach of Article 2. Their actions could be justified in the circumstances in which they found themselves.

However, the Court held that the control and organisation of the operation made the use of lethal force almost unavoidable. The failure of the authorities to arrest the terrorists earlier and a number of subsequent misjudgments suggested a lack of appropriate care in the control and organisation of the arrest operation. Hence, according to the majority of the Court, the use of lethal force constituted a use of force which was more than absolutely necessary to protect persons from injury caused by unlawful violence.

Nine judges of the Court dissented from the findings of the majority. Further, the Court refused to award pecuniary and non-pecuniary damages, it being inappropriate in the circumstances having regard to the fact that the three terrorists were in the process of planting a bomb with the intention of murder.

The other main instances when the right has been invoked concern abortion and the application of the death penalty. The same article is also relevant to the issue of euthanasia, although no case has yet arisen on this point.

It is not explicit from the text whether the right to life extends to unborn children, but in at least one case an application has been brought on the basis of Article 2(1) to prevent the termination of pregnancy. In *Paton v United Kingdom* (1980) 6 EHRR 408, an application was brought against the United Kingdom alleging that the Abortion Act 1967 was contrary to Article 2(1). The application was lodged by the father against his wife to prevent the carrying out of an abortion permitted under the terms of the 1967 Act.

In its decision the Commission found that Article 2(1) was not absolute in its coverage and that, in particular, there were implied limitations to its application where the life or health of a mother was jeopardised. The application was therefore rejected, with the explanation that the 1967 Act was consistent with the Convention because the right to life of a mother took precedence over the right to life of a foetus.

The carrying out of a death sentence is impliedly recognised by Article 2(1) by the qualification that an individual may be deprived of life in the execution of a sentence of a court where such a penalty is prescribed in law. In practice, in most of the contracting states the application of the death penalty has been considerably curtailed, even though in some states, including the United Kingdom, this penalty has been retained for certain offences.

The abolition of the death penalty is provided for in a separate Protocol to the Convention, the Sixth, Article 1 of which provides:

'The death penalty shall be abolished. No one shall be condemned to such penalty or executed.'

The only exception to this rule is provided in Article 2 of the Protocol, which retains the right of states to carry out executions in time of war or of imminent threat of war, but even in these circumstances the sentence may only be carried out in accordance with the provisions of the law. In other words, there must be no arbitrary use of the death penalty even in times of war.

Not all contracting states are parties to the Sixth Protocol. In the absence of the application of the Protocol it is unlikely that the carrying out of a sentence of death could be prevented if the crime for which it was to be applied was of sufficient gravity. In fact, the Court has recognised that capital punishment is still permitted under certain conditions even although the majority of contracting parties have acceded to the Protocol: *Soering* v *United Kingdom* (1989) 11 EHRR 439. The Protocol does not appear to alter the express right of states to carry out such sentences if they have not become parties to its terms.

That the right to life is not absolute is further confirmed by the existence of a number of grounds, other than capital punishment, under which the taking of life can be justified. The three grounds recognised in Article 2(2) of the Convention are:

1. in defence of any person from unlawful violence;
2. to effect a lawful arrest or to prevent the escape of a person lawfully detained; and
3. in action lawfully taken for the purpose of quelling a riot or insurrection.

These grounds have been included for the purpose of clarification rather than as exceptions to the general rule. However, it should be noted that these circumstances justify the taking of life only when it results from the use of force which is not more than absolutely necessary.

15.3 The right to freedom from torture and inhuman and degrading treatment

One of the few rights which is not subject to specific exceptions or to the general right of derogation contained in Article 15 of the Convention is Article 3, which simply declares:

'No one shall be subjected to torture or to inhuman or degrading treatment or punishment.'

This strongly suggests that torture, inhuman and degrading treatment will not be tolerated in any circumstances under the Convention.

In fact this provision forbids three distinct forms of abuse, namely torture, inhuman treatment or punishment and degrading treatment or punishment. The Court and the Commission have, in practice, tended to view the three separate practices as varying degrees of the same type of conduct. Certainly, in a large number of applications, each of these three practices are alleged as alternative grounds for violation of the Convention.

The concept of torture is not defined in the Convention, but the UN Declaration on the Protection of all Persons from Torture and Other Cruel, Inhuman or Degrading Treatment or Punishment 1975 defines it as 'an aggravated and deliberate form of cruel, inhuman and degrading treatment or punishment'. The European Court referred to this definition in its decision in *Ireland* v *United Kingdom* (1978) 2 EHRR 25 but declined to elaborate on the concept in its judgment.

The Commission has found the existence of acts of torture in at least one case. In the *Greek Case*, 12 Yb ECHR 194 (1969), the Commission examined certain practices of the Greek authorities in connection with the treatment of prisoners. It found that the beating of victims' feet, causing excruciating pain and suffering with the intention of breaking the spirit of the victims, amounted to torture. This finding was substantiated by the fact that the beatings were repetitious and conducted with the sanction of official tolerance. The national authorities took no measures to prevent the practice and refused to investigate allegations of such treatment. In the circumstances, the Greek authorities were found to have engaged in acts of torture contrary to Article 3.

In *Ireland* v *United Kingdom*, above, the Court provided some guidelines as to which types of behaviour would constitute torture. The Irish government alleged that a number of practices by the security forces in Northern Ireland were within the definition provided in Article 3. Specifically, the so-called 'five techniques', of hooding detainees, subjecting them to continuous noise, depriving them of sleep, withholding nourishment and forcing them to stand for prolonged periods against walls, were alleged to constitute torture.

The Court examined these measures but rejected the contention that they amounted to torture. By a vote of thirteen votes to four, it held that they did not constitute torture because they had not occasioned suffering of a sufficient intensity or cruelty. This implies that torture is an aggravated form of inhuman treatment inflicted with a particular intensity and degree of cruelty. Other factors also relevant to such a finding are the element of repetition, the duration of the application of the measures and the systematic application of different methods to achieve a particular aim.

Inhuman treatment or punishment appears to lie in the twilight between torture and degrading treatment. It does not imply the same degree of physical pain as torture and yet is more severe than the concept of degrading treatment.

The forms of inhuman treatment denounced by the Commission and Court have included the so-called 'five techniques' described above in *Ireland* v *United Kingdom*, above, which, while not amounting to torture, were held to be both inhuman and degrading treatment. Similarly, in *Soering* v *United Kingdom*, above, the Court held that the 'death row phenomenon', or more explicitly the length of time spent by a prisoner awaiting execution combined with the exceptional intensity of the mental anguish suffered by a person awaiting the carrying out of such a sentence, amounted to inhuman treatment.

Degrading treatment or punishment is the least severe form of physical injury to an individual which is condemned by the Convention. Again there is no definition of the concept, and its limits can only be deduced from the decisions and judgments of the human rights institutions.

One of the most frequently raised allegations of degrading treatment or punishment has been corporal punishment. In *Tyrer* v *United Kingdom* (1978) 2 EHRR 1 the Court considered the question of whether the birching of juveniles by the authorities on the Isle of Man as the punishment for certain offences amounted to inhuman treatment or degrading punishment.

The Court, at the outset, rejected the argument that the punishment amounted to either torture or inhuman treatment since there was not present a sufficient degree of suffering associated with these notions. Whether the treatment amounted to degrading punishment depended on the nature and context of the punishment itself, as well as the manner and method of its execution. In its judgment, the Court found that the degree of suffering inflicted constituted an assault on the victims' dignity and physical integrity of such a degree as amounted to degrading punishment. This finding was also supported by the fact that the punishment was of a public nature and was conducted in a particularly degrading manner.

Yet, in a similar case, the Court rejected the argument that corporal punishment in schools amounted to degrading punishment. In *Campbell and Cosans* v *United Kingdom* (1982) 4 EHRR 293 the issue was whether striking a pupil's hand with a leather strap as a form of punishment was degrading. The Court rejected the argument on the basis that the measure did not constitute degrading treatment because the applicants had not undergone, in the eyes or others or themselves, humiliation or debasement of a minimum degree of severity. However, the Court did find in favour of the applicants on another ground, namely a violation of the rights of individuals to religious convictions in the educational process under Article 2 of the First Protocol.

In the same context, Article 4 of the Convention prohibits slavery and servitude as well as most forms of forced or compulsory labour which are, in effect, varieties of torture. While Article 4 stands as a separate provision, in fact there have been few applications to the Commission based on violations of its terms.

15.4 The right to liberty and security of the person

Article 5 of the Convention elaborates a number of rights relating to arrest and detention. Article 5(1) states the general rule:

'Everyone has the right to liberty and security of person.'

This general principle is subject to six recognised exceptions, namely:

1. The lawful detention of a person after conviction by a competent court. Detention after conviction may, however, be inconsistent with the terms of the Convention if it is indefinite and without the right to periodic review of the sentence: see *Thynne* v *United Kingdom* (1990) 13 EHRR 309.
2. The lawful arrest or detention of a person for failure to comply with the lawful order of a court or in order to secure the fulfilment of any obligation prescribed by law.
3. The lawful arrest or detention of a person effected for the purpose of bringing him before the competent legal authority on reasonable suspicion of having committed an offence, or when it is reasonably considered necessary to prevent his committing an offence or fleeing after having done so.

    According to this provision, a lawful arrest or detention can only be occasioned on 'reasonable suspicion' that the accused has committed an offence. The standard of reasonableness may be subject to review by the European Court. For example, in *Fox, Campbell and Hartley* v *United Kingdom* (1990) 13 EHRR 157, the Court was asked to consider whether arrests effected under the Northern Ireland (Emergency Provisions) Act 1978, on the ground that officers 'genuinely and honestly' believed that the suspects had committed offences, was reasonable in the circumstances. The Court rejected the contention that this standard was sufficient to satisfy the test of reasonableness. The absence of sufficient material evidence to support the charges was pointed to as being fatal to the argument that the suspicions were reasonable.
4. The detention of a minor by a lawful order for the purpose of educational supervision; or his lawful detention for the purpose of bringing him before the competent legal authority: see *Nielsen* v *Denmark* (1988) 11 EHRR 175.
5. The lawful detention of persons for the prevention of the spreading of infectious diseases, and of persons of unsound mind, alcoholics or drug addicts or vagrants. But, detention of such classes of individual cannot be permitted without allowing a person so detained access to a court or tribunal to allow the legality of the detention to be assessed: see *Van der Leer* v *The Netherlands* (1990) 12 EHRR 567 and *E* v *Norway* (1994) 17 EHRR 30.
6. The lawful arrest or detention of a person to prevent his effecting an unauthorised entry into the country, or of a person against whom action is being taken with a view to deportation or extradition: see *Sanchez-Reisse* v *Switzerland* [1986] 9 EHRR 71.

In each of these instances of detention or arrest the state is obliged to ensure that the proper procedure, as prescribed by law, is ensured. In addition Article 5 also prescribes a number of safeguards to prevent abusive arrest or detention.

Thus, every person arrested is entitled to be informed promptly, and in a language which he or she understands, of the reasons for his or her arrest and of any charge against him or her: Article 5(2). So where a German national who could not speak Italian was notified of charges presented against him in an Italian court, and the notification was in Italian and without a translation, an infringement of this provision was upheld. The applicant had not been informed of the charges in a language which he understood: *Brozicek* v *Italy* (1990) 12 EHRR 371.

Any person arrested or detained in accordance with the exception stated above must be brought promptly before a judge or other officer authorised by law to exercise judicial power: Article 5(3). But no period is specified in the Convention for detention without charge or without being brought before a court, tribunal or magistrate for determination of the legality of the charges.

In *Brogan and Others* v *United Kingdom* (1989) 11 EHRR 117 the Court had occasion to consider this issue. Four suspected terrorists were detained under s12 of the Prevention of Terrorism Act for a period of four days without being either charged with any offence or brought before a magistrate. The applicants claimed that they had not been promptly brought before a competent authority to determine the lawfulness or otherwise of their detention.

In its decision the Court placed considerable emphasis on the term 'prompt' in Article 5. The promptness or otherwise of bring an accused before a magistrate had to be assessed in the light and purpose of Article 5. Since this provision constituted 'a fundamental human right', interference with the exercise of this had to be minimised in order to avoid arbitrariness. Hence, the scope for flexibility in interpreting and applying the notion of promptness was very limited.

Eventually, the Court held that a period of detention of four days and six hours was outside the strict constraints imposed under Article 5(3), despite the particular circumstances of the situation in Northern Ireland. The Court was unwilling to entertain this period as being within the meaning of 'prompt' in the provision, and hence the United Kingdom was found to have violated Article 5(3).

The evaluation of promptness is made in relation to the nature of the case against the accused and any special features raised by the facts forming the basis of the case. But the underlying principle behind the concept of promptness is that the element of minimum delay should never be impaired: see *Koster* v *The Netherlands* (1992) 14 EHRR 396.

The length of pre-trial detention may be extended beyond what would otherwise be consider reasonable where there is adequate continuous review of the case by an appropriate national court, as long as any unnecessary delay cannot be attributed to the fault of the national authorities: see *W* v *Switzerland* (1994) 17 EHRR 60.

An accused is also entitled to a trial within a reasonable time or to release pending trial. The right to trial within a reasonable time is also stated in Article 6(1). Release pending trial may lawfully be conditioned by guarantees to appear for trial.

As a related right, a person accused of a crime and deprived of his or her liberty by arrest or detention is entitled to take proceedings by which the lawfulness of this detention may be expeditiously decided by a court: Article 5(4). In the event that the arrest or detention is not lawful, the release of the individual must be ordered: *Bezicheri* v *Italy* (1989) 12 EHRR 210.

Finally, an individual who has been the victim of unlawful arrest or detention in contravention of the provisions of the Convention must have an enforceable right to compensation: Article 5(5).

15.5 The right to a fair trial

The Convention requirement for a fair trial are relatively strict. Article 6(1) provides in part:

> 'In the determination of his civil rights and obligations or of any criminal charge against him, everyone is entitled to a fair and public hearing within a reasonable time by an independent and impartial tribunal established by law.'

This provision imposes three separate safeguards. First, the hearing must be fair and in public. Second, it must be conducted within a reasonable time. Third, the court or tribunal hearing the case must be both independent and impartial.

The requirement that the hearing is fair implies that the proceedings must be objective and impartial. No unfair or inequitable advantage should be permitted to one side without a countervailing right to the other side. This obligation applies in both civil and criminal proceedings.

The need for a judicial hearing to be carried out in public is intended to eliminate the possibility of secret or clandestine trials of suspects. Further, in normal circumstances, a judgment must be pronounced publicly. The press or public can only excluded from all or part of the trial if such exclusion can be shown to be:

1. in the interest of morals, public order or national security in a democratic society;
2. where the interests of juveniles or the protection of the private lives of the parties so requires; or
3. when, in the opinion of the court, special circumstances exist in which publicity would prejudice the interests of justice.

The obligation imposed on national authorities to conduct the trial within a 'reasonable time' has generated a considerable volume of jurisprudence on the part of the Court, the denial of this right being a frequent ground of complaint.

The overriding principle is that states are obliged under the Convention to organise their legal systems in such a manner that unreasonable delays are avoided. Other than this general rule, the Court has set down a number of rules to assist to determine periods which are reasonable, depending on whether the proceedings have a civil or criminal nature.

In a civil action, the Court has held that a delay of almost seven years before judgment was rendered was excessive and unreasonable: *Sautilli* v *Italy* (1992) 14 EHRR 421. The assessment of 'reasonable' in the length of proceedings was made in the light of the particular circumstances of the case, its complexity, the behaviour of the litigants and the performance of the judicial system itself: see *Darnell* v *United Kingdom* (1994) 18 EHRR 205.

Stricter time limits have been imposed by the Court in relation to criminal proceedings. While the general principle has been that the Court will allow greater latitude for serious charges, its tolerance for unreasonable delays is extremely limited.

For minor charges of fraud, a period of eight years between charges being raised and trial has been found unreasonable: see *Motta* v *Italy* (1992) 14 EHRR 434. Similarly, charges for trespass, a relatively minor offence, were time-barred by the Court after five years: see *Pugliese* v *Italy (No 1)* (1992) 14 EHRR 413.

No maximum permissible pre-trial period for criminal charges has ever been set by the Court, but national authorities are responsible for ensuring that such detention does not exceed a reasonable period. The reasonableness or otherwise of a period is decided in accordance with a number of factors.

The Court has recently held that the continued existence of a reasonable suspicion that the accused committed the offences charged is the primary rationale behind permitting detention, which implies that once that suspicion has subsided the lawfulness of continued detention deteriorates in proportion: see *Letellier* v *France* (1992) 14 EHRR 83. But even continued suspicion does not justify detention after a certain period of time, although the Court has been reluctant to define the exact scope of such a period. In the same case the Court also considered other factors to be relevant, including any genuine risk to witnesses, the possibility that the suspect might leave the country and any threat posed to public order.

A person charged with serious offences and detained for a period of two years nine months prior to trial was considered by the Court to have had his rights under Article 5 infringed: *Kemmache* v *France* (1992) 14 EHRR 520. The Court found that this period was unreasonably lengthy in the light of the circumstances of the case but, interestingly, did not find the same for the initial period of detention for six weeks during which the investigating magistrate carried out his investigation. A similar finding was made in a case concerning a period of delay of 25 months prior to conviction: see *Toth* v *Austria* (1992) 14 EHRR 557.

In certain circumstances, national authorities may be under a positive obligation to expedite proceedings, both civil and criminal. Thus, where an Aids victim had applied for compensation from a government for injury caused after being infected by a blood transfusion, and an appeal was lodged against this refusal, a duty of 'exceptional diligence' was imposed on the national authorities to act promptly; *X* v *France* (1992) 14 EHRR 483. In this case the Court criticised the French government for failing to speed up proceedings even although the condition of the applicant was known to the authorities and the gravity of the situation was obvious.

The court or tribunal charged with adjudicating a case must also be impartial and independent. Impartiality is decided on the basis of the personal convictions of the particular judge in a given case – a subjective test – and whether a judge offers sufficient guarantees to exclude any legitimate doubt in this respect – an objective test: see *Hauschildt* v *Denmark* (1990) 12 EHRR 266. Naturally, a judge with a personal interest in a case would be an illustration of a situation where the requirement of impartiality would be possibly lacking.

The independence of a body is also a fundamental element in the constitution of a fair court or tribunal. In one case the European Court found that a finding of contempt by a parliamentary body, and the subsequent imposition of a fine against the person found in contempt, did not satisfy the requirement of independence. The parliamentary body imposing the sanctions was not sufficiently impartial or independent of the persons in whose interest the finding of contempt had been made: *Demicoli* v *Malta* (1992) 14 EHRR 47. It is likely that this finding may set certain limits on the UK Parliament's traditional right to find persons in contempt of Parliament for failing to act as instructed by parliamentary bodies.

The United Kingdom has been found guilty of infringing Article 6(1) in *Saunders* v *United Kingdom* (1996) 23 EHRR 313. In this case, the Court held that compelling a private individual to answer questions or face a penalty of a maximum of two years imprisonment constituted a breach of Article 6(2), and the subsequent use of the evidence thereby obtained constituted an additional breach of the rights of an individual under Article 6(1).

Article 6(1) has also been interpreted by the Court as including several rights, including the right not to incriminate oneself even though this right is not specifically stipulated in the provision itself. An attempt by national authorities to coerce an individual into providing incriminating document in a prosecution may also constitute a violation of Article 6(1): see *Funke* v *France* (1993) 16 EHRR 297.

After stating these rights, Articles 6(2) and 6(3) continue to elaborate a number of further safeguards..

Article 6(3) sets out the rule that anyone charged with a criminal offence shall be presumed innocent until proved guilty according to law. In addition, anyone charged with a criminal offence must be assured of the following minimum rights:

1. To be informed promptly, in a language which he or she understands and in detail, of the nature and cause of the accusations against him or her.
2. To have adequate time and facilities for the preparation of his defence. This right has been held to include the right to the privacy of client-lawyer communications: *S* v *Switzerland* (1992)14 EHRR 670.
3. To defend himself in person or through legal assistance of his own choosing or, if he has not sufficient means to pay for legal assistance, to be given it free when the interests of justice so require. The right to legal aid, where an individual has insufficient means to pay for legal representation, extends not only to trial but also to appeals.
4. To examine or to have examined witnesses against him, and to obtain the attendance and examination of witnesses on his behalf under the same conditions as witnesses against him. Thus, where a person was convicted on the basis of the evidence of an anonymous witness who was not heard at trial but submitted

evidence by way of affidavit, the right to examine and contradict this evidence was denied, resulting in a breach of the Convention: *Kostovski* v *The Netherlands* (1990) 12 EHRR 434.

5. To have the free assistance of an interpreter if he cannot understand or speak the language used in court.

Of these rights, denial of the right to examine witnesses has perhaps given rise to the greatest number of complaints. A court is under an obligation to ensure that all essential witnesses attend the hearing to give evidence. This obligation extends even to appeal proceedings: see *Delta* v *France* (1993) 16 EHRR 574.

It is interesting to note that none of these provisions prevents a state from trying a person in absentia. Trial of an individual in his or her absence will only involve an infringement of Article 6(2), as a denial of the right to a fair trial, if there are circumstances showing that the conduct of the trial is manifestly disproportionate to the aim to be achieved: *FCB* v *Italy* (1992) 14 EHRR 909.

Article 7(1) of the Convention also contains a related substantive right, namely that no one shall be held guilty of any criminal offence on account of any act or omission which did not constitute a criminal offence under national or international law at the time when it was committed. The same provision also prohibits the imposition of a heavier penalty than one that was applicable at the time a criminal offence was committed.

For the avoidance of doubt, Article 7(2) provides that the above does not prejudice the trial and punishment of any person for any act or omission which, at the time when it was committed, was criminal according to the general principles of law recognised by civilised nations.

15.6 The right to privacy

Article 8(1) of the Convention establishes the following right in connection with the privacy of the individual:

> 'Everyone has the right to respect for private and family life, his home and his correspondence.'

The purpose of this provision is to limit the unrestricted interference of the state in private affairs. But, as we shall see, the exceptions created to the general rule have substantially undermined the imperative nature of this obligation.

In fact the right to privacy can be broken down into four separate, but related, rights, namely respect for private life, respect for family relationships, protection of the home from unwarranted violations and respect for privacy in communications. The ambit of each of these rights has been drawn in broad terms by both the Court and the Commission in their decisions.

The right to respect for the private life of individuals has been the basis for a number of complaints of different natures. In particular, the provision has been relied on in the following circumstances:

1. Obtaining access to confidential personal records held on private individuals by public authorities: see *Gaskin* v *United Kingdom* (1989) 12 EHRR 36.
2. Challenging the rights of the secret service to compile and store information relating to the private lives of individuals in non-accessible police files without cause to believe that offences are being committed: *Hewitt and Harman* v *United Kingdom* (1992) 14 EHRR 657.
3. Challenging prohibitions on homosexuality: see *Dudgeon* v *United Kingdom* (1981) 4 EHRR 149 and *Norris* v *Ireland* (1988) 13 EHRR 186.
4. Attempting to amend public records to reflect changes in gender: *Rees* v *United Kingdom* (1986) 9 EHRR 56.

The right to protection from unwarranted interference in family life has also had wide applications. The relationship between parent and child has been closely examined at the European human rights level in decisions concerning the rights of illegitimate children *(Marckx Case* (1979) 2 EHRR 330), access rights to children in care of local authorities *(W* v *United Kingdom* (1987) 10 EHRR 29) and the expulsion of parents resulting in the inability to maintain regular contact with their children *(Berrehab* v *The Netherlands* (1988) 11 EHRR 322).

The relationship between husband and wife is also covered by the article; for example, the prohibition in Irish law against divorce was challenged in *Johnston* v *Ireland* (1986) 9 EHRR 203. In this case the applicant wished to divorce his spouse, a process not recognised in Irish law, and to marry another women. Since his first marriage could not be terminated, he was effectively prevented from re-marrying.

It was claimed that this was a violation of Article 8(1) since the right of the applicant to found a family was frustrated by the Irish authorities due to the enforcement of the prohibition. The main issue was therefore whether Ireland was under a positive obligation to introduce measures that would permit divorce. This was held by the Court as being too broad an interpretation of Article 8(1). There was consequently no failure to respect the family life of the applicants.

The integrity of the home from unwarranted search by police or security forces has not been challenged as often under this article as might be expected. In fact, there is a dearth of cases on the point. The most significant case is *Chappell* v *United Kingdom* (1989) 12 EHRR 1, which involved the search of the applicant's premise pursuant to an injunction issued in civil proceedings. An action was raised against the applicant for breach of copyright, and an Anton Piller order (search order) was issued by the court for the search of the applicant's premises by representatives of the plaintiffs. In carrying out this search an investigator noticed copies of obscene videos and notified the police of this fact.

Acting on this information, the police searched the premises after serving the appropriate warrant, and a substantial amount of material was seized. The applicant challenged the legality of the Anton Piller order in relation to its terms, the manner of service and the content of the order.

The European Court held that the actual granting of such orders was necessary to protect the rights of other individuals. Further, the order contained a number of safeguards in favour of the defendant. While the Court criticised certain aspects of the execution of the order, such as the failure to allow the applicant to refuse entry to the investigators, these procedural defects were insufficient to invalidate the order.

In conducting search and seizure operations, the European Court has also recently held that, where wide powers are conferred when conducting such operations, two principles must be observed: (a) in the absence of a judicial warrant, the restrictions and conditions for any search must be strictly proportionate to the legitimate aim being pursued; and (b) seizures which are wholesale and indiscriminate will not be permitted: see *Miailhe* v *France* (1993) 16 EHRR 332.

Another issue relating to the right to the sanctity of the home concerns the expropriation of land by national authorities for public purposes: see *Jacobsson* v *Sweden* (1989) 12 EHRR 56.

The right to privacy of communications has been the basis for a number of complaints concerning both the interception of correspondence and the tapping of telephone conversations.

The most common circumstances in which the authorities have interfered in the right of communication between private individuals is in connection with correspondence with prisoners. In one of the earliest cases brought before the Court, the rights of a prisoner to correspond with his solicitor without interference from the prison authorities was challenged. In *Golder* v *United Kingdom* (1975) 1 EHRR 524 a prisoner addressed a petition to the Home Secretary requesting the right to consult with a solicitor on the subject of a possible libel suit against a prison officer who had alleged that the applicant had participated in a serious disturbance at the prison.

This request was denied, and the matter was brought before the European Court which held that impeding an individual from even initiating correspondence constituted one of the most far-reaching forms of interference in the exercise of the right to respect correspondence. Such interference could not be tolerated in the circumstances of the case, and a violation of Article 8(1) was found.

In a more recent case, *McCallum* v *United Kingdom* (1990) 13 EHRR 597, the Court held that the prison authorities were not permitted to stop five letters written by the applicant, nor to withhold copies of two letters written on his behalf, without violating Article 8 of the Convention. See also *Campbell* v *United Kingdom* (1993) 15 EHRR 137.

The issue of tapping telephone conversations is one in which the conflict between the national laws of the United Kingdom and the Convention have come to dramatic confrontation. As evidence for a prosecution of an antique dealer charged with the dishonest handling of stolen goods, the Crown produced transcripts of telephone conversations intercepted by the police during their investigation. This evidence had been gathered on the authority of a warrant issued by the Secretary of State for the Home Department.

The accused subsequently instituted civil proceedings against the police seeking a declaration that, even if the interception and monitoring of the telephone conversations had been carried out on the authority of the Secretary of State, these actions were unlawful without his consent. This action was dismissed: see *Malone* v *Metropolitan Police Commissioner (No 2)* [1979] 1 All ER 620.

The applicant complained to the European Commission that the interception of the telephone conversations amounted to a violation of Article 8(1) of the Convention because such practices amounted to an arbitrary interference in the exercise of his right to private correspondence. The matter came before the European Court, which found that UK rules on the interception of telephone conversations were vague and uncertain. The minimum degree of legal protection to which individuals were entitled under the rule of law in a democratic society was not present. The interceptions were not in accordance with the law, as required by Article 8, and were consequently a violation of its terms.

In relation to telephone tapping, the Court has also held that unauthorised acts of police investigators still involve state responsibility for their actions even though the actions of the officers exceed the scope of their authority under the law: *A* v *France* (1994) 17 EHRR 462.

There have been numerous cases developing this right which may be referred to for a more comprehensive understanding of the operation of this freedom: see *Schenk* v *Switzerland* (1988) 13 EHRR 242 and *Kruslin* v *France* (1990) 12 EHRR 547.

All four of these individual rights are subject to the qualification that restrictions may be permitted for the following purposes:

1. In the interests of national security: see *Leander* v *Sweden* (1987) 9 EHRR 433.
2. For public safety or the economic well-being of the country.
3. To prevent disorder or crime.
4. For the protection of health or morals.
5. For the protection of the rights and freedoms of others.

The exception for the protection of public health and morals has frequently been employed by states in attempts to justify interferences with the exercise of the right to privacy. Thus, in *Dudgeon* v *United Kingdom*, above, this exception was invoked by the UK authorities to justify the prohibition in Northern Irish law in certain forms of homosexual conduct. In this particular case the Court felt that the extent of the prohibition was excessive in relation to the object pursued by the restriction and disproportionate to the aims sought to be achieved.

Any restrictions introduced or maintained on the basis of any one of the exceptions are permitted only in so far as they are 'in accordance with the law' and 'necessary in a democratic society'. Both these concepts have been developed in the jurisprudence of the Court in the interpretation of Article 8(2) of the Convention.

The requirement that the restriction must be in accordance with the law implies that the authority for the measure must lie in a formal source of law such as a statute, a statutory instrument or a decision of a competent court. Not only should the measure have a legitimate basis in domestic law, but it must also be accessible to the person to whom it applies, and the consequences of the application of the measure must be foreseeable to the behaviour in question.

The requirement of foreseeability was at the source of the Court's decision in *Kruslin* v *France*, above, which concerned the telephone tapping of conversations under a law that was not precise as to the circumstances in which interception would be authorised. In particular, the category of persons liable to have telephone conversations intercepted was not defined in the law. This uncertainty resulted in the Court finding a violation of Article 8 on the ground that the measures involved were not in accordance with law.

This is not to imply that telephone tapping is ipso facto contrary to the terms of the Convention. If the interceptions are conducted for the legitimate purpose of preventing crime and are accompanied by proper safeguards, such practices may be compatible with the Convention: see, eg, *Ludi* v *Switzerland* (1993) 15 EHRR 173.

The measure of the requirements which are necessary in a democratic society has led the Court to develop the notion of a 'margin of appreciation' on the part of the national authorities in deciding this issue. This concept was considered in *Klass* v *Germany* (1978) 2 EHRR 214. The question was raised whether the powers of the German police to engage in secret surveillance infringed Article 8(1). In making this assessment the Court recognised that states enjoyed a margin of appreciation in setting the conditions under which a system of surveillance was to operate, but this discretion was exceeded where there were no adequate and effective guarantees against abuse.

In another case the Court held that, while the margin of appreciation conferred on the national authorities in matters of morals was particularly broad, it was not unlimited: *Norris* v *Ireland* (above). Although primary responsibility for prescribing the moral limits of a country resided with the state authorities, this would not prevent the Court from conducting a review of moral standards in the light of the terms of the Convention.

15.7 The right to freedom of expression

The right to freedom of expression, contained in Article 10(1) of the Convention, has been characterised by the Court as 'one of the essential foundations of a society and one of the basic conditions for its progress and for the development of every man': see *Handyside* v *United Kingdom* (1976) 1 EHRR 737. In the opinion of the Court, this right forms one of the pillars of the democracy that characterise the societies of the contracting states. Restrictions on this freedom are narrowly construed.

The basic right is stated in Article 10(1) with sober simplicity as follows:

'Everyone has the right to freedom of expression. This right shall include freedom to hold opinions and to receive and impart information and ideas without interference by public authority and regardless of frontiers.'

There are two basic aspects of this: the right to hold opinions and views, and the related right to receive and impart these ideas and views to other individuals. Since in practice imparting views is the most likely cause for confrontation with national authorities it is hardly surprising that the exercise of this right has given rise to the most number of references to the Commission under Article 10(1).

The right to receive and impart ideas has been extended to:

1. The freedom of artistic expression: see *Muller* v *Switzerland* (1988) 13 EHRR 212.
2. The freedom of the press: see *Sunday Times* v *United Kingdom* (1979) 2 EHRR 245 and *The Observer and The Guardian* v *United Kingdom* (1992) 14 EHRR 153.
3. Public broadcasting by television and radio transmission: see *Groppera Radio AG* v *Switzerland* (1990) 12 EHRR 321.
4. The freedom to criticise public organisations and officials in relation to matters of legitimate public concern: see *Thorgierson* v *Iceland* (1992) 14 EHRR 843.

The right to freedom of expression cannot be impeded unless such interference can be justified under one of the exceptions listed below. Thus the right of a journalist who was convicted for defamation of a politician, such criminal charges being competent in Austria, to freedom of expression under Article 10 was violated when the statements were in the public interest: *Oberschlick* v *Austria* (1991) 19 EHRR 389. Criminal charges for such actions were considered to be disproportionate to the objectives sought to be achieved, namely to ensure respect for the reputations of other individuals. This strongly implies that the Court is willing to interpret the exceptions to the general rule strictly, in order to expand the scope of the right itself.

In the light of modern forms of communication, the fact that the right of freedom of expression applies notwithstanding the existence of international frontiers is an important extension. This right has important applications for radio, television and satellite transmissions as well as for forms of direct communication such as telecommunications.

In *Autronic AG* v *Switzerland* (1990) 12 EHRR 485 the Court was asked to consider whether restrictions placed by the Swiss authorities on the right to retransmit satellite broadcasts from Soviet satellites without the consent of the Soviet authorities were compatible with Article 10(1). While the Court held that regulations to control telecommunications fell within the competence of national authorities, in this particular case the nature of the restriction was excessive and fell outside the margin of appreciation reserved to them by the Convention in assessing the need for such restrictions.

But the right of freedom of expression is declared not to prevent states from requiring the licensing of broadcasting, television or cinema enterprises – presumably as long as these restrictions are not disproportionate to their objectives.

There are seven exceptions to the general right to freedom of expression. The exercise of this freedom may be subject to such formalities, conditions, restrictions or penalties as are prescribed by law, and are necessary in a democratic society, for the following purposes:

1. The preservation of national security. But the protection of the efficiency and reputation of the security services cannot justify publication of information which is a matter of legitimate public concern: see *The Observer and The Guardian* v *United Kingdom* (above).
2. To protect territorial integrity or public safety.
3. To prevent disorder or crime.
4. To protect health or morals: see *Gay News Ltd and Lemon* v *United Kingdom* (1982) 5 EHRR 123.
5. To ensure the reputation or rights of others, for example the laws of libel: see *Lingens* v *Austria* (1986) 8 EHRR 407.
6. To prevent the disclosure of information received in confidence. Information which could be considered confidential, but which has been published in another country, can no longer form the basis of a measure of repression: see *The Observer and the Guardian* v *UK*, above.
7. To maintain the authority and impartiality of the judiciary: see *Sunday Times* v *United Kingdom*, above.

Again, these exceptions may only be relied on if they are prescribed in law and necessary in a democratic society. At the same time, the measures which interfere with the right of freedom of expression must be proportionate to the aim sought to be achieved: see *Open Door Counselling and Dublin Well Woman Centre* v *Ireland* (1993) 15 EHRR 244.

15.8 The right of peaceful assembly

The right to assemble for peaceful purposes is contained in Article 11(1) which provides:

> 'Everyone has the right to freedom of peaceful assembly and to freedom of association with others, including the right to form and to join trade unions for the protection of his interests.'

In fact, this Article declares two separate freedoms – of peaceful assembly and of association with other individuals. The right to form and join a union is a sub-category of the latter right.

The exercise of the right to assemble for peaceful purposes has surprisingly not occupied much of the attention of either the Court or the Commission. The case law in relation to this right is negligible, despite the fact that it covers the conditions which peaceful assemblies or demonstrations must satisfy to be both lawful and peaceful. It also determines which assemblies and demonstrations are to be permitted, restricted or prohibited. (But see also *Platform Arzte für das Leben* v *Austria* (1991) 13 EHRR 204.)

The general rule is that freedom of peaceful assembly cannot be restricted as long as the persons exercising the right are not engaged in any reprehensible act or actions which have an unlawful effect: see *Ezelin* v *France* (1992) 14 EHRR 362.

The right to peaceful assembly does not confer a right to enter private premises or property without permission for the purposes of exercising that right: see *Hector* v *United Kingdom* (1990) The Guardian 20 April.

The vast majority of the complaints received concerning violations of Article 11(1) have related to the right of association and, in particular, to the relationships between individuals and trade unions. In this context the Court has been required to consider the right to strike, the legality of closed shop agreements, the freedom to refuse to join a union and the right of unions to be consulted during the process of enacting legislation.

The right to strike was considered in *Schmidt and Dalstrom* v *Sweden* (1976) 1 EHRR 637. The applicants averred that the right to strike was an organic right enshrined in the freedom of association embodied in Article 11(1). The Court rejected this argument by commenting that the right to strike was only one of many methods of protecting the interests of trade union measures. Further, the right of association does not imply the right to any particular or special treatment in pay and conditions negotiations from individuals not associated to a union. Hence there was no breach of Article 11 by the Swedish government.

While the Court has not yet had an opportunity to comment on the legality of closed shop agreements, it has considered applications concerning the refusal of employees to join in such agreements. In *Young, James and Webster* v *United Kingdom* (1981) 4 EHRR 38 the Court reviewed the consistency with the Convention of the failure of the UK government to establish the right not to be compelled to join a union.

The principal issue was whether the right to association also conferred the right on an individual to disassociate himself or herself from a union. In other words, did Article 11 imply a negative right as well as the positive one? In the end, the Court in fact held that the failure to protect individuals from being compelled to join a union did contravene the terms of Article 11.

The Court has also held that the right to form a union does not impose on a state an obligation to consult that body during the legislative process: see *Belgian Police Federation* v *Belgium* (1975) 1 EHRR 578.

There are four express exceptions to the freedoms of assembly and association:

1. in the interests of national security or public safety;
2. for the prevention of disorder or crime;

3. for the protection of health or morals; and
4. for the protection of the rights and freedoms of others.

However, no restrictions may be placed on the exercise of either of the two rights for any of these purposes unless such restrictions are prescribed by law and are necessary in a democratic society. Again, any interference with these rights must be proportionate to the aim to be achieved under one of the permitted exceptions: *Ezelin* v *France*, above.

15.9 The right to marriage

Article 12 of the Convention stipulates a right related to the right to privacy of family life, namely the right to marry and found a family. More precisely, Article 12 declares:

> 'Men and women of marriageable age have the right to marry and to found a family, according to the national laws governing the exercise of this right.'

Ironically, the right to marry has been invoked in numerous complaints relating to restrictions on divorce. Thus in *F* v *Switzerland* (1987) 10 EHRR 411 the applicant challenged the terms of the Swiss Civil Code which imposed a three-year prohibition on remarriage by a spouse deemed at fault after divorce proceedings on the ground of adultery.

Similarly, in *Johnston* v *Ireland* (1986) 9 EHRR 203 the right to marry was invoked in an attempt to challenge the prohibition in Irish law against divorce. This prohibition, so the applicant claimed, impeded his right to remarry. This argument was rejected by the Court since the article itself made no reference to the dissolution of marriage relationships and, in any event, such a restriction was not considered to be unduly restrictive.

The complex issue of whether persons who have undergone gender reassignment surgery can competently marry members of the same gender as they were prior to such operations has been brought before the Court in a number of cases: see *Rees* v *United Kingdom* (1986) 9 EHRR 56. The issue arose most recently in *Cossey* v *United Kingdom* (1991) 13 EHRR 337. In its judgment the Court declined to interfere with the laws of the contracting parties declaring such marriages to be ipso facto void.

The concept of marriage in Article 12 has been restricted to the traditional notion of marriage between persons of the opposite biological sex. This interpretation stems from the overall context of the provision which links the concept of marriage to that of the family.

Recent Cases

16

Recent Cases

16.1 The institutions of the European Union

16.2 Direct actions against European Community institutions

16.3 Free movement of persons

16.1 The institutions of the European Union

Eurotunnel SA and Others v *SeaFrance* Case C–408/95 [1998] 2 CMLR
293 European Court of Justice

Powers of the Council to change Commission's proposals – extent of such powers –
powers measured relative to legal basis for measure – amendments not ultra vires

Facts
Eurotunnel brought proceedings in the French courts against SeaFrance, a company
operating cross-channel ferries. The basis of the claim was that SeaFrance was cross-
subsidising its ferry fares with revenues from the sale of goods free of tax and excise
duty. SeaFrance had been authorised to provide duty-free sales on the basis of
authorisations given by the French Government based on the provisions of the Sixth
VAT Directive and Council Directive 92/12 on excise duties. However, the
applicants alleged that these authorisations gave SeaFrance an unfair competitive
advantage.

As part of its case, Eurotunnel claimed that the two directives had been
unlawfully adopted by the Council because, when the Council adopted these
measures, it had departed from the terms of the Commission's original proposal to
such an extent that the final text could not be said to have been adopted on the
basis of the Commission's proposal. In addition, the terms of the final measures
were sufficiently different from the text given to the European Parliament in the
consultation process that the Council should have engaged in re-consultations with
the Parliament.

Held
The Council had power under art 250(1) of the EC Treaty to amend the proposal from
the Commission provided that the voting requirements on which the measure was

based had been fulfilled. In this particular case, unanimity was required under art 93 of the EC Treaty, and this requirement had been met by the Council when adopting the measures. Furthermore, the Council's amendments made to the proposals remained within the scope of those directives as defined in the original proposals. Hence, the Council had not exceeded its powers to make amendments to the proposal and, consequently, the regulations in question could not be annulled on this ground.

As regards the requirement for the European Parliament to be re-consulted, the Court reiterated the principle that re-consultations are required whenever the text finally adopted, taken as a whole, differs in essence from the text given to the Parliament in the consultation process. This is, of course, unless the amendments substantially correspond to those proposed by the Parliament. The amendments made by the Council were consistent with both the approach and proposed amendments made by the Parliament and therefore it was unnecessary for the latter to be re-consulted.

The Court therefore upheld the legal validity of the two directives and rejected the claim that the Council had breached any essential procedural requirements when adopting them.

16.2 Direct actions against European Community institutions

Germany v *European Commission (Re Construction Products)* Case C–263/95 [1998] 2 CMLR 1235 European Court of Justice

Deviation from the specified procedures for the adoption of Community measures – German language version not circulated to German representatives – English language version not adequate – breach of an essential procedural requirement – measure annulled

Facts
Council Directive 89/106 sets down procedures for the attestation of the conformity of certain construction products to mandatory technical specifications. This is carried out by a standing committee of representatives of each member states acting in conjunction with Commission. Under the terms of the Directive, the Commission submitted proposals for approvals to the permanent representation offices of the member states as well as the committee representatives.

Germany sought the annulment of an approval decision on the grounds that the German version of the draft measure had not been sent to its permanent representative nor the German member of the Commission within the time period specified. The Commission had acknowledged the delay in sending the German version but had circulated the English version of the draft decision in time to the German delegation. On this basis, it proceeded to adopt the approval decision, exercising its powers to do so under delegated powers.

The German government brought an action in the ECJ challenging the validity of the approval decision on the grounds that the Commission had infringed an essential procedural requirement by not circulating the German version of the proposal to the German delegation within the specified time period.

Held
The failure to send the German version to the German delegation, within the appropriate time limits, constituted an infringement of an essential procedural requirement justifying the annulment of the Commission's approval decision. The English version of the proposed measure could not be considered as an adequate substitute for the German language version. The Commission was bound to strictly adhere to the letter of the procedural requirements specified in the directive granting it delegated powers.

16.3 Free movement of persons

Clean Car Auto Service GmbH and Landeshauptmann von Wien Case C–350/96 [1998] 2 CMLR 637 European Court of Justice

Austrian requirements imposing nationality restrictions on company managers – discrimination on the grounds of nationality – infringement of art 48 EC Treaty – Austrian law declared to be incompatible with Community law

Facts
The European Court of Justice has given its ruling on Austrian laws which require that a manager of certain businesses must reside in Austria. The case involved an Austrian company which applied for registration to trade as required by Austrian law, but was rejected on the grounds that the company had appointed as manager a person not resident in Austria. The Austrian government had claimed that this requirement was necessary to ensure the effective management of a company.

Held
The Court held that the rule of equal treatment in the context of the free movement of workers enshrined in art 48 of the EC Treaty could be relied upon by an employer wishing to employ in the member state in which he is established workers who are nationals of another state, as well as being relied upon by the workers themselves, as is usually the case.

Further, the Court found that the residence requirement contained in the Austrian laws constitute unjustified indirect discrimination contrary to the EC Treaty rules on freedom of movement. The ECJ observed that, whilst it is true that the Austrian rules apply without regard to the nationality of the person to be appointed as manager, national rules under which a distinction is drawn on the basis of residence are likely to operate mainly to the detriment of nationals of other member states, as non-residents are in the majority of cases foreigners.

Index

Old Bailey Press

The Old Bailey Press integrated student library is planned and written to help you at every stage of your studies. Each of our range of Textbooks, Casebooks, Revision WorkBooks and Statutes are all designed to work together and are regularly revised and updated.

We are also able to offer you Suggested Solutions which provide you with past examination questions and solutions for most of the subject areas listed below.

You can buy Old Bailey Press books from your University Bookshop or your local Bookshop, or in case of difficulty, order direct using this form.

Here is the selection of modules covered by our series:

Administrative Law; Commercial Law; Company Law (no Single Paper 1997); Conflict of Laws (no Suggested Solutions Pack); Constitutional Law: The Machinery of Government; Obligations: Contract Law; Conveyancing (no Revision Workbook); Criminology (Sourcebook in place of a Casebook or Revision WorkBook); Criminal Law; English Legal System; Equity and Trusts; Law of The European Union; Evidence; Family Law; Jurisprudence: The Philosophy of Law (Sourcebook in place of a Casebook); Land: The Law of Real Property; Law of International Trade; Legal Skills and System (Textbook only); Public International Law; Revenue Law (no Casebook); Succession: The Law of Wills and Estates; Obligations: The Law of Tort.

Mail order prices:

Textbook £11.95

Casebook £9.95

Revision WorkBook £7.95

Statutes £9.95

Suggested Solutions Pack (1991–1995) £6.95

Single Paper 1996 £3.00

Single Paper 1997 £3.00

To complete your order, please fill in the form below:

Module	Books required	Quantity	Price	Cost
		Postage		
		TOTAL		

For Europe, add 15% postage and packing (£20 maximum).
For the rest of the world, add 40% for airmail.

ORDERING

By telephone to Mail Order at 020 7385 3377, with your credit card to hand.

By fax to 020 7381 3377 (giving your credit card details).

By post to:

Old Bailey Press, 200 Greyhound Road, London W14 9RY.

When ordering by post, please enclose full payment by cheque or banker's draft, or complete the credit card details below.

We aim to despatch your books within 3 working days of receiving your order.

Name

Address

Postcode   Telephone

Total value of order, including postage: £

I enclose a cheque/banker's draft for the above sum, or

charge my   ☐ Access/Mastercard   ☐ Visa   ☐ American Express
Card number

☐☐☐☐ ☐☐☐☐ ☐☐☐☐ ☐☐☐☐

Expiry date   ☐☐☐☐

Signature: ....Date: ....